CLOWN MAGIC

By David Ginn

 PICCADILLY BOOKS
COLORADO SPRINGS, COLORADO

ACKNOWLEDGEMENTS

Special thanks in preparing and inspiring this book go to Leon McBryde; Bruce "Sparkles" Johnson; Richard Snowberg; Jim Howle; Earl Chaney; Karrell Fox; Don Burda; Bev Bergeron; Holly Thomas; Roger Grant; Harold Taylor; Olsen and Johnson; Dorny; Abb Dickson; John B. Hall; Mary Beth Martin; Charlie Sable; Vickie Miller; Joyce Quisenberry; Jean and Bill Rath; J.C. Doty; Bruce Fife; Jack Chanin; Stan and Olli;, Larry, Moe, Curly, and Shemp; Bud and Lou; my dad Frank Ginn; and my grandfater, Fred Hill Ginn. I appreciate all your feedback and humor. I also thank Cathy and Bob Gibbons of *Laugh-Makers* magazine and David Goodsell of *M-U-M* magazine for allowing me to reprint several items which originally appeared in their pages. Thanks to my wife Lynne and my daughter Autumn for their relative patience while I finished the book.

Line Drawings by Jim Kleefeld
Cover Photo by Tony Jagnesak
Cover Design by Michael Donahue
Edited by Bruce Fife

Piccadilly Books
P.O. Box 25203
Colorado Springs, CO 80936
U.S.A.

Library of Congress Cataloging-in-Publication Data

Ginn, David.
    Clown magic / by David Ginn.
        p.   cm.
    Includes bibliographical references and index.
    ISBN 0-941599-21-3
      1. Conjuring.   2. Clowning.   I. Title.
GV1547.G536 1993
793.8--dc20
                                      92-46228
                                        CIP

DEDICATION

To Leon "Buttons" McBryde who started me on this road to clowning 13 years ago, applied my first makeup, and assured me that there is some kind of clown inside of me too. His very name defines clowning to me, and his friendship I value highly.

TABLE OF CONTENTS

David Ginn and Leon McBryde.

FOREWORD

In May of 1980 I came home for three days in the middle of a month-long lecture tour across the United States. My wife Lynne was holding down the fort—processing the mail, dealing with phone calls about shows, and handling a hundred other responsibilities, business and personal.

One telephone call, she said, came from a country-sounding man from Buchanan, Virginia. He wanted me to lecture at some kind of "clown seminars in July in Chicago, Washington D.C., and Los Angeles." Probably nothing worth pursuing, we thought. You see, we get these crank calls from time to time, and this was probably one of them. Anyway, the one time I had lectured at a clown convention was a disappointment and a disaster.

Next thing I knew, the man from Buchanan, Virginia, called me. "When could we meet and talk?" he wanted to know.

"Well, I don't know," I told him. "I'm in the middle of a 29-city lecture tour. Day after tomorrow I leave for Oshkosh, Wisconsin."

He asked for details of the lecture, what flights I'd take from Atlanta to Chicago, then to Oshkosh. I told him.

"All right," he said. "I'll meet you in the Chicago airport with my photographer friend, and we'll go see you in Oshkosh."

What else could I say? All right, I told him, like I really believed he'd show up. Which means I DIDN'T believe he'd show up.

Two days later I arrived at O'Hare Airport and proceeded to the Oshkosh gate. And there was this huge man who reminded me a little of Hoss Cartwright from Bonanza, wearing a cowboy hat and standing about seven feet tall. He shook my hand and nearly broke it, but I liked him instantly. I liked his photographer friend, Dallas Kinney, too.

We went to Oshkosh. I lectured to three dozen magicians on magic and comedy, with my emphasis on working with children and family audiences. I had fun, the lecture went well, the magicians bought books and tapes and props so they could have fun too. And the big guy from Buchanan told me I was the man for the job to teach comedy magic to 150 clowns at three seminars that summer.

"Earl Chaney said you were good," he told me. "He showed me your book *Professional Magic for Children*. But I just had to come see for myself. And you're exactly what we need for this job."

That's how I met Leon "Buttons" McBryde, former advance clown with Ringling Brothers Barnum & Bailey Circus, "the Greatest Show on Earth," student of Lou Jacobs, Coco, and Mark Anthony, and a man with sawdust in his veins and a heart of gold. For all these years, he has been my clown mentor and friend.

We worked together that summer of 1980, did the seminars again two years later in 1982, and kept in touch.

In 1983 Richard Snowberg invited me to lecture at Clown Camp in LaCrosse, Wisconsin, which turned out to be a wonderful experience for both the students and me. A year later I had talked Leon into coming to Clown Camp with me, to teach and share and have fun and to help me become a clown for one night.

You see, I told the nice folks in 1983 that if I returned, I'd agree to get in makeup, so I needed help. As you'll find out later in this book, I needed lots of help, especially from Leon McBryde and Earl Chaney.

About 300 times a year, I drive out of my home with rabbit in cage and perform comedy magic shows at schools, churches, and family functions all over my state of Georgia. I love my job, love being with the kids because, you see, I'm a kid at heart. I make the kids laugh, and I clown around a lot, but I'm not a clown.

Leon McBryde is a clown. Big wig, big red nose, big shoes—the classic definition of a clown. Exaggerated makeup, a walking cartoon character. That's Leon's clown character "Buttons." That's a clown.

A clown in me? Yes, I'd certainly agree to that. There is a clown in me, and he comes out in many ways, even when I'm not in makeup.

But understand that David Ginn is *not* a clown authority. I've been in makeup only a dozen times in ten years. I have clown friends who do makeup 350 days a year! So don't ask me about makeup.

A costumer? Not me. My clown costume for my first dozen times out belonged to Leon McBryde. I do have my own red nose (Leon poured it) and my own shoes (Leon's pro shoes) and even my own Georgia clown socks. But the rest is borrowed.

So I don't have all the answers to clowning, makeup, or costuming. What I do have is a sense of fun and comedy, a bag of tricks and magical theory learned from reading, studying, and trying all the magic tricks I could from age eleven up—and a powerful, creative imagination.

And that's how, inspired by Leon, Earl, Richard, and a hundred other clown friends, I have created this book of clown magic—something old, something new, something borrowed (with permission), nothing blue (because I believe in a clean show). I have filled it with comedy and fun and laughter, with silly stuff and corny jokes, with advice from Leon and other friends, with some original never-published tricks, routines, and skits, and with some thoughts on being *entertainingly funny* to children and family groups.

I've tried to offer you both finished routines and suggestions for developing your own creativity. Why? Because I want you to have a basis for performing clown magic, yet at the same time I want you to think: How would my clown character do this?

Clowning is fun. Magic is fun. Most people enjoy both clowns and magic. Therefore, the two together makes a very logical combination that can double the entertainment. That, of course, is up to you and how you mix magic and clowning. By the time you finish reading these pages, you'll have a better idea of how to effectively combine the two.

This book is for beginners and professionals. The principles, skits, and routines discussed are easy enough for the unexperienced, yet stimulating and creative enough to be of benefit to experienced entertainers.

Whatever you do—have fun reading this and *make fun* performing some of it. Make some people smile and laugh and love you. Find the clown in you and enjoy *yourself* while you entertain *them*.

—DAVID GINN

CHAPTER 1

MAGIC AND CLOWNING

In a conversation years ago following one of my lectures, a lady told me that her husband, who loved clowning, had been taking "magic lessons" from an established magician. His teacher insisted that magic and clowning did not mix, saying that "clowns should not do magic" because "magic should be taken seriously."

Her husband, she said, was quite confused. He liked magic, and he liked clowning. Yet with his instructor's remarks, he didn't know which way to turn. She wanted to know what I thought?

First, I told her, the idea that clowns shouldn't do magic is ridiculous. If that were true, then should magicians not use clowning or comedy? Personally, I use clowning techniques all the time—without makeup—and my school show audiences love it.

Second, I do take my magic seriously, and I seriously try to entertain with it. With my 300 school programs a year, I perform my magic with plenty of humor. The kids enjoy themselves and the show while learning something along the way.

Can you imagine how I would go over if my entire show were void of comedy and clowning? With school kids, *I would die!*

David Ginn and his rabbit Elmo, getting set for a jungle magic show.

BEING FUNNY

One year, when I was on the staff of Clown Camp at the University of Wisconsin in LaCrosse, I sat in on a session when this question camp up: Aside from makeup and costuming, what is the difference between clowning and comedy?

Different answers were offered by the audience. The answer that struck me most was this: A comedian says or does funny things. A clown, on the other hand, does or says things in funny ways.

Certainly, there is a distinction there. A comedy magician, for example, might pick up an object from a table and use it in a funny routine. A clown, on the other hand, might create humor simply by picking up the same object *in a funny manner,* something that might be "normal" within the realm of his clown character.

Either way, the object gets picked up. It's the attitude that makes the real difference—not even the makeup or costuming. Neither way is wrong or right. Each is correct in its own realm.

Years ago, a clown taught me a circus stunt that I subsequently put into my show and used for an entire year. I used it to close my show *as a magician.* Did I worry that it came from a clown? On the contrary, I continue to be thankful for that clown's willingness to share with me.

Let's go back to the "serious" side of things for a moment. I said that I am serious about my magic—about entertaining people, about booking shows, about producing a good new theme show each year. Yet at the same time, I see fellow magicians who take their magic, as well as themselves, too seriously.

Example: In 1976 I released a mass market paperback called *Starting in Magic,* a beginner's magic book. One customer on my mail order list wrote me a letter stating, "If you intend to expose magic secrets to the general public, I want to be taken off your list and will have nothing to do with you!"

How ridiculous, I thought. My book was a rehash of tricks I had learned as a kid from reading books in the local public library, adding stories and touches from my own kid-like imagination. Probably the same kind of things my customer critic had read when he was a budding magician. And where are young magicians supposed to start learning anyway? If we left it to the guy I quoted, there would be no new magicians.

When I first worked on TV, I was very guarded about letting TV personnel and studio audiences see anything secret. "Keep it a secret" was my motto. But there were times, I *finally* learned, when I needed to tell the TV people how the tricks worked so they wouldn't accidentally spoil the trick with a bad camera angle and expose it to thousands of people watching at home.

My problem at the time was taking myself and the magic too seriously. Since that time, I have definitely loosened up. Specifically, I have changed my priority from "fooling them" with the magic to "entertaining them" with the magic. And I'm still quite serious about it.

When I first worked at Clown Camp in 1983, I arrived with skeptical feelings about clowns. Years before, I had dealt with a group of convention clowns who gave me a bad impression—they were smoking, drinking, chewing tobacco, sometimes in costume and makeup, even telling inappropriate jokes.

But Clown Camp was different. Within days I met lots of men and women who, unlike the first group, were very serious about clowning and entertaining people. Some were magicians as well. Some even used the same tricks, whether performing as clowns or as magicians—only they changed their stage characters depending on which mode they were working. In clowning, I observed, they "hammed" it up more. I knew, from working with my school show kids, that their shows were lots of fun for young audiences.

And don't we comedy magicians do the same thing? We work one way—loose, funny, slapstick—for little kids; and another way, more grown-up but still funny, for bigger kids; and still another way, more "sophisticated," for teens and adult audiences.

If you're a magician, don't be afraid of clowning. And clowns, don't be afraid of magic. The two can easily go hand in hand, especially if you stick to magic that is mechanically easy, allowing you to pour your effort into presentation.

For me, those distinctions I mentioned earlier—doing or saying funny things versus doing or saying things in funny ways—are divided by a very fine line, a line I am constantly crossing over.

In my entire life, I've been in full clown makeup only a dozen or so times. The experience is always fun, but I wouldn't want to get made up every day to work my schools that way.

Yet, because of my experience and the fact that I have worked with clown pros, I have great respect for real clowning as an art and as an *attitude.* And I seriously believe that the majority of clowns have their sights set on the most important part of showbiz—*entertaining the audience,* whether it be one child in a hospital bed, hundreds of people at a picnic or grand opening, or a thousand kids in a school gymnasium.

JUNE 1986: Clown Camp staff photo, as follows: Back Row (left to right): Betty "Pee-Wee" Cash, Dorothy "Blab-A-Gail" Miller, Leon "Buttons" McBryde, David Ginn, Don "Homer" Burda, Richard "Snowflake" Snowberg. Middle Row (left to right): Barry "Bonzo" DeChant, Kim "Kimbo" McRae, Mark Anthony, Earl "Mr. Clown" Chaney, Steve Rancatore, Al "Whistles" Fast. Front Row (left to right): Janet "Jellybean" Tucker, Leslie "Flower" Homann, O. J. Anderson. Lying down: Jeff "Billy Bob" McMullen.

Frederick the Great with Leon "Buttons" McBryde. This photo shows Frederick's first attempt at putting his makeup on without help. Buttons was probably thinking: It's good enough for stage, but for walk-arounds, well...

One year at Clown Camp in LaCrosse, I showed a videotape of the comedy musical ending to my imagination magic show, "Through the Magic Window." There was no "real magic" in the ending, yet the children thoroughly enjoyed it.

At the end of the videotape, I said to the class: *"Now—was that NOT clowning?"* They roared their approval with a hearty round of applause.

Yet, in the show I was not wearing clown makeup or a wig or funny shoes or a big red nose. Granted, I had on red suspenders, a striped shirt, and rather wild purple tennis shoes.

Was this comedy or clowning? Why must we fiddle around with labels? Personally, I've given up on that. I say do what you enjoy and do what your audience likes. Enjoy yourself, and entertain your audiences. If you're both having fun—everybody wins.

CLOWN CHARACTER

According to Bruce Fife, author of *Creative Clowning* and other popular books on clowning and related arts, in order to combine magic with clowning effectivley, you first need to understand what clowns are, how they think, and how they act. Much of the following material in this chapter comes from Bruce.

There is more to the art of clowning than just telling jokes or acting silly. Clowns are actors playing the roles of exaggerated comic characters. As a clown you are creating an illusion, a fantasy, by bringing a cartoon-like figure to life. In order to make this illusion effective, you must develop a unique clown character or personality with likes and dislikes, strengths and weaknesses.

Developing a stage character is one of the basic principles of good acting. When a performer, whether he be a clown, magician, stand-up comic, actor, or whatever, comes onto the stage, the audience immediately begins to make assumptions about his character. They want to know if he is smart, clever, funny, brave, cowardly, good-natured, serious, and so forth. This is a subconscious process we all do in order to identify the players and fit them properly in their roles. Being able to identify the performer's personality allows the audience to focus on the show and gain greater enjoyment.

Most people have some preconceived notions about how clowns are supposed to act. General character traits such as being funny, silly, and friendly are almost universal. All clowns have those traits to some degree, but each clown should have and should develop more specific personality traits. Are you skilled or clumsy? Are you intelligent, but absent minded or eccentric, or are you just plain stupid? Are you bold or shy, timid or daring, a show-off or passive? There are many traits that can fit the general personality of the clown.

Your performing style and your own natural personality, sense of humor, speech patterns and abilities, physical appearance, as well as your talents, will determine your clown character. If you like to talk, your character may be an energetic chatterbox. A naturally quiet person may have a more mellow or easygoing clown character. Your clown's appearance, way of moving, and actions are all influenced by your character's personality.

Comedian Jack Benny was recognized as a tightwad. All he had to do to get a laugh was to allude to his stinginess. In one skit Benny was confronted by a mugger who demanded, "Your money or your life!" Benny just looked at him, so the mugger snarled, "Well?...Which is it, your money or your life?" Benny replied, "I'm thinking, I'm thinking!" Everybody caught the punch line and laughed. This joke would not have worked if Benny had not clearly established his stage character.

Physical characteristics can also be used to advantage. Jackie Gleason because of his large size, was successful doing fat jokes. He made fun of himself, not of anyone else. Likewise, Jimmy Durante, Danny Thomas, and Bob Hope have had fun with nose jokes. Jokes of this type are funny because they relate directly to the character of the person telling them.

All of the jokes, tricks, and stunts you use must fit your clown personality. At times you may be tempted to use a gag or a trick you think is amusing, but doesn't quite fit your character. Don't do it! It may be very funny performed by someone else, but not when you do it because it is out of place. You might be lucky and even get a few laughs with it, but if it is not you, then you are only creating confusion for the audience, and your entire show will suffer.

If you begin your show as a clumsy oaf in one trick, for example, don't become a skilled performer for the next. It is confusing and distracting to the audience and is unprofessional. In the first few moments of your show the audience is mentally sizing you up, trying to figure out who you are and what you are like. Once they get a general impression of your personality and character they will recognize your humor more easily and will gain more enjoyment from the show. If you suddenly change characters, such as from being clumsy to being skilled, it confuses the audience and they must rationalize the change in their minds or readjust their perception of you, which distracts them from your show. They have to redefine who you are.

Once your character is established, if you contradict the audience's perception of that character, you give people the impression that you are not really a clown, but just somebody who is dressed up. When your character's actions and appearance are consistent with your personality, the audience is more willing to accept you, which heightens the fun and fantasy you create.

Make all of your actions and humor reflect the same personality. If you do step out of character for a given trick or routine, give a reason for it so the audience is not confused. If you establish your clown character as being shy and clumsy, but want to perform a routine depicting a boastful overly-confident clown, make a logical transition. For example, after defining the clown's character as being clumsy and unskilled, accidently, and to his surprise, perform a trick correctly, building his confidence. He then gets cocky with his newfound skill and attempts tricks which would be out of place for his original personality and character. Build up to more difficult tricks or stunts which in the end backfire to expose his incompetence and place him back into his original situation and character. He could perform the tricks purely by accident, or he may be the object of a trick by another clown who has set him up or even by an audience member who appears to have played a trick on him.

Once you have defined your character, you will become more comfortable and successful in your performances. Choosing gags, props, and tricks will be simpler because you will know what will complement your character. You will know how to react to situations, tricks, and stunts, especially if they backfire or something goes wrong. You will also know which tricks or type of magic fits your character and how to approach it for best results.

Creating your clown character will not be done overnight. In fact, it may take several years before your clown personality is clearly defined. But you should find and develop some general attributes about your clown personality from the start. As you work with your character, you will gradually learn more about how that character thinks and reacts in various situations.

CLOWN HUMOR

There are two general types of humor—verbal and nonverbal. Verbal comedy is relayed through words, jokes, and stories. Nonverbal, or physical, comedy is expressed by body movement and facial expression. Although most clowns use a combination of these, they rely heavily on physical comedy to express themselves and create laughter. In fact, exaggerated physical actions and slapstick comedy are characteristic of clowning.

A trademark of clown humor is exaggeration. Exaggerated expressions, actions, and personality traits are the primary characteristics which separate clowns from other types of comedians. Clothes, makeup, props, jokes, and actions are stretched to the point of being ridiculous. A comedian might wear mismatched clothes that don't quite fit, but a clown will wear clothes that are grossly oversize or undersize and that display bizarre color combinations. A comedian might hit his companion with a hammer; a clown, on the other hand, would use a giant sledgehammer or perhaps a big fish or even a cream pie.

Many of the early slapstick comedians such as Charlie Chaplin, Laurel and Hardy, and the Three Stooges were clownish in their actions and humor. Even though they did not wear clown costumes or makeup, many considered them to be clowns.

Clowns are easily identified by their distinctive costumes and makeup, but if they don't have the character of a clown then they are regarded as imposters, people who are just dressed up. Character, not clothes, is what makes the real clown.

CLOWN MAGIC VERSUS COMEDY MAGIC

Many modern magicians use comedy in their acts, and many clowns use magic. What is the difference, if any, between the comedy magic of magicians and the funny magic performed by clowns?

To answer that question let's make a comparison. Magicians and clowns are entertainers, each portraying a specific type of character. In order to understand the type of magic they use and how they use it, we need to understand the general personality traits of the characters they portray.

The traditional magician can be defined as someone who is majestic, highly skilled, mysterious, somber, clever, serious, intelligent, and powerful. The magician wears a black tuxedo, which symbolizes mystery, power, and prestige, which supports these character traits. This is the image most people have of a magician.

A clown, on the other hand, is completely the opposite. Clowns are silly, friendly, outlandish, clumsy, funny, foolish, and weak. They typically wear brightly colored costumes which are usually either too big or too small. Makeup enhances their facial features and projects a friendly, funny character.

Because the basic character of clowns and magicians is different, their approach to magic and comedy will be different. The magician approaches comedy from a serious side, usually with more emphasis on verbal humor. Clowns attempt magic with more physical fanfare, as dictated by their outlandish characters.

The magician who does comedy magic is still a magician. He can and does perform magic tricks that work. Although he is skilled, he may slip up once in awhile or have an accident now and then or encounter situations, people, and assistants, that give him a hard time, which creates humor.

Clowns take comedy magic a step further. They are not magicians, but are clowns pretending to be magicians or attempting to perform magic. By their very nature, the magic they try to create backfires. They cannot perform real magic like a magician, because they are clowns. It is out of character for them to be successful magicians. When a trick does work, it is usually by "accident," not by design.

When a clown performs a magic trick, it never works as it is supposed to. In reality, the clown may be a skilled magician and may perform some incredible feats of magic, but he does it in such a way as to appear completely out of control—just the opposite of a real magician, who is always in complete control. However, comic magicians will occasionally make mistakes, but even then, they use verbal humor, funny stories and stunts, combined with magic that works, rather than giving the appearance of incompetence, as is the case with a clown.

The clown also incorporates a heavy dose of silliness, physical comedy, and exaggerated actions and movements into his tricks. Indeed, these are characteristic traits of clown humor. Magicians are usually more dignified even when they are being funny.

ARE YOU A REAL CLOWN?

Mary Beth Martin

How many times have you been asked that? A million times? A jillion times? What does make a real clown?

Although it is very important to look the best you can, this alone doesn't make you a real clown. How many times have you seen great-looking clowns in competition, but when it comes to actual clowning, they are missing something?

As the Skin Horse said in *The Velveteen Rabbit*, "Real isn't how you are made. It's a thing that happens to you." For you to become real, it takes a long time.

One of the first things necessary to become real is *the desire*. You have to *want* to be a real clown. You also have to *believe* you are a real clown. People will believe in you if you believe in yourself.

The second thing necessary to become real is *a strong character*. This is important in convincing people you are not an ordinary person. You look, act, and think like a clown. The way a clown thinks or acts is not always logical. A clown may think what he is doing is perfectly normal, but in reality, it is not. Your own clown personality sets you apart from other clowns and people.

The third thing necessary to become a real clown comes from within you. You must have *the heart of a clown*. You must love children and love being a clown. You must enjoy what you are doing, and it will show.

I believe kids can sense how you are feeling and how you feel about them. Even when I am not in makeup, kids see me and I have a strong feeling they "know" I am a clown. Out of a whole room of adults, a child I don't know, will pick me out to smile at, to play a peeping game with, or to talk to. I think they know I have the heart of a clown. It is like mental telepathy. I have seen it happen with other clowns too.

The last thing is the most important. *Becoming a real clown takes time.* As quoted in *The Velveteen Rabbit*, "When a child loves you for a long, long time, not just to play with, but REALLY loves you, then you become real." I believe this is true with clowns.

Mary Beth Martin as "Dr. Pokum."

I was clowning at a birthday party once, and a little girl came up to me and said, "You're not a real clown!" I told her that I was. She repeated her statement, then sat down.

So I started my show, and we all had a great time. When I finished, this same little girl came back up to me, gave me a hug, and said, "You *are* a real clown, and I love you!"

This is what it's all about.

Reprinted with permission from *Clowning Around*, the official publication of the World Clown Association.

Although I have presented a distinction between the magician and the clown, some comedy magicians incorporate heavy doses of fun and silliness that can appear almost clownish. Likewise, some clowns may be more skilled than others and may actually be able to, occasionally, perform magic tricks correctly.

As you will see in later chapters, many of the routines described in this book can be performed by either magicians or clowns. The primary difference being how the tricks and gags are approached by the performer. Rather than performing the routines in this book exactly as written, you should adapt them to your own personal character and embellish them with your own performing style.

TYPES OF CLOWN MAGIC

Clown magic isn't a matter of just haphazardly stumbling through a bunch of tricks; it's a well organized series of events, sometimes requiring all the skills of an experienced magician.

There are basically three types of magic that complement the clown character. The first is to accomplish magical effects by accident. The second is to accomplish magic by trickery. The third is to perform the trick correctly, but with a surprise comedy finish.

The clown magician is primarily a clown, and by his very nature he is considered incapable of performing real magic. For this reason, when magic happens it is by mistake, or the magic performed is totally different from that which was expected, or the trick may not even work at all. The clown may try to turn a coin into a rabbit, but ends up with a bouquet of flowers instead. Magic was performed, but it was not what the clown wanted. He appears to be out of control and incompetent, all to the delight of the audience.

He may also try to perform a trick that backfires. He borrows a hat from a friend and dumps milk, eggs, sugar, and flour into it and attempts to magically produce a cake. He says the magic words, reaches in to pull out a fully baked cake, but ends up with a handfull of gooey dough.

The clown can also use trickery. He knows he can't really do magic, so he tries to fake it. He uses a gimmick to perform his tricks. At some point during the routine, his trick is revealed, exposing him as a fake. An example is the "electric deck," a deck of cards that are attached together. The clown can attempt to perform some difficult shuffling movements which appears impressive at first, then accidentally drop the deck, revealing the secret. The audience laughs at his attempt to be something he's not.

Not all clowns are totally inept. Some clowns do possess certain skills such as being able to juggle, make balloon animals, play musical instruments, and even do magic. But to combine these skills with your clown character, you must use your imagination and be creative. As with magic, a clown who can perform difficult juggling moves or play beautiful music is out of place. This does not mean that a skilled clown cannot juggle, play music, or do magic correctly, but that the skills should appear to be basic and should be combined with a story that will produce a comic ending. A clown who can juggle six balls is impressive, not funny and not clownish. The same is true of the clown magician who can saw a girl in half or do other incredible feats of magic which are out of character. All magic tricks performed by clowns should be done with a comic flair—never serious magic. A serious trick, such as would be performed by a magician, however, can become funny when combined with the exaggerated actions and smile of a clown.

The magic tricks, of course, are always accompanied by the clown's distinctive personality and character, including silly jokes, zany movements, and funny facial expressions and reactions. *This is clown magic!*

CHAPTER 2

ENTERTAINING WITH CLOWN MAGIC

There is much more to magic and particularly clown magic than just performing a bunch of tricks and telling jokes. In this chapter you will learn the basic concepts of magic and how they relate to comedy and clowning. You will also pick up some ideas on how to make magic funny and entertaining.

CREATING MAGIC

To start off this chapter I want to introduce you to some of the basic concepts of magic. In order to be a good magician or clown magician, you need to have an understanding of magic.

An important concept to keep in mind when performing magic is the principle of *cause and effect*. The effect is the magic that is created. The effects are *caused* by something the magician or clown does. The clown does not have the power to produce the magic himself. He must wave a magic wand, say magic words, sprinkle pixie dust, clap his hands to produce a magic sound, or perform some other act to create the magic. Magic doesn't just happen; the effect is caused by something the clown does.

You can use this concept to your advantage to create comedy and get the audience involved. Saying silly magic words, for example, can bring both a laugh and cause the magic to happen. Some other actions you might do would be to stomp your foot in a particular rhythm, wiggle your ears or your nose, recite a tongue twister or silly rhyme, wave a magic shoe, spray an invisible magic solution, and so forth. You can also involve the audience in the production of the magic by having them perform a silly action or say something funny.

Effects can be classified into at least 12 general categories.

1. Vanish—making something disappear
2. Production—making something from nothing
3. Transformation—changing an object into something else
4. Transposition—making something go from one place to another
5. Restoration—restoring something that was destroyed
6. Identification—identifying something that otherwise should not be known
7. Psychic Phenomena—mind reading, ESP, X-ray vision, and communication with spirits
8. Penetration—passing one solid object into or through another
9. Levitation—making something float in the air
10. Attraction—causing something to attract or stick to something else

11. Animation—bringing an inanimate object to life
12. Escapes—removing handcuffs, escaping from a strait jacket or a locked cell, etc.

When you are putting a magic show together you should use a variety of these effects. A show which uses only vanishing and production effects, for example, would soon become boring. Even in clowning, where humor is most important, you can keep excitement alive and increase the fun by mixing the effects you use.

Stringing the tricks you use together into a logical sequence will make your show flow more smoothly and be more enjoyable. Make a connection from one trick to another. If you develop a good story to tell or skit to act out, each trick should lead smoothly to the next. This will help eliminate slow spots and distracting breaks in your routine.

THE SECRETS OF MISDIRECTION

Hundreds of books have been written on magic, and from them, you can find an endless number of tricks to perform. But few sources reveal the secrets of misdirection. Al-

Magician Clint Hope in clown makeup getting assistance from Mona Clary. Clint's comedy magic served as inspiration for some of David Ginn's successful kidshow routines.

though many books on magic allude to misdirection, few address the topic directly. The use of misdirection is very important to magic. In fact, it is a vital element of any magic trick and is the secret to performing magic successfully—even clown magic. A very simple magic trick can be totally baffling to an audience with the proper use of misdirection.

Misdirection techniques lead the audience to look at, think, and believe what the magician wants them to. With misdirection the magician diverts or draws the spectators' attention away from something they are not supposed to see. He can lead the audience to look at one of his hands while secretly performing the magic with the other. He can make the audience believe his hand is holding a coin when it is really empty. Performed properly, misdirection is so subtle that the audience is unaware that they are being controlled. It also gives the audience a strong psychological impression that they see everything the magician does, which makes the magic that much better.

Every magic trick should incorporate misdirection. I will describe some the most useful techniques.

Personality and Character

The personality of the performer plays an important part in misdirection. The audience's attitude toward the magician dictates how critically they observe his actions. A magician who presents himself as being superior to the audience and speaks down to them trying to impress them with his wonderful skills or even embarrass audience members in order to get a laugh may likely alienate them. They in turn, will watch his moves very closely and listen critically to his words in order to catch him in his deception and knock him off the pedestal he has placed himself.

On the other hand, a performer who focuses on entertaining the audience, rather than fooling them, and presents himself in a friendly manner will be better received. The audience will relax and pay more attention to the performance and less attention to trying to figure out how the tricks are done. The audience will relax to the extent dictated by the personality of the performer.

For this reason comic magicians and clowns should, by the nature of their stage characters, set the audience at ease. You, however, do not want to be a show-off or play tricks on audience members that might humiliate them. All sucker gags that may be embarrassing should be played on the clown or someone with the show, never the spectators or helpers. This will build trust and friendship with the audience.

By being cheerful, foolish, or clumsy, and by appearing to have troubles performing the magic, the audience will be led not to expect a dazzling display of magic. The audience will not watch the clown as closely as they would the serious magician. Silly actions or illogical movements, which may work a sleight, are not questioned because they can be considered all part of the clown's personality. The clown can make movements that otherwise may appear to be suspicious. So when the climax is reached and the magic is suddenly revealed, it is received with more surprise, enjoyment, and applause.

A clown who is a show-off and performs serious magic is out of character. Clowns play the roll of fools and so should not be superior to the audience. If he does step out of character, the spectators will sense this inconsistency and watch him critically.

The Eyes

Your eyes play a very important roll in misdirection. You will learn that if you look in a certain direction the audience's eyes will look there also. This is important because you can look toward your right hand while casually doing something sneaky in with the other.

You should never let your eyes rest on the hand that is performing the sleight, but always on the other hand or on some object away from that hand. The audience will always look to where the magician looks. For this reason you should train your hands to operate independently and without the need of looking at either of them.

Movement

Movement is another important misdirection technique. The eyes of the audience will always follow movement, particularly when it first begins. Removing your hat, turning your head, and waving a wand, are a few examples. Any sudden or unexpected motion will quickly draw attention. The motion, however, must be natural or innocent to avoid suspicion. Even moving your lips as you speak will attract the audience's attention toward your face. This fact is used by ventriloquists and puppeteers to draw attention to the figure supposedly doing the speaking.

Pointing your finger or gesturing toward something will lead the audience's eyes in that direction. The eye will always follow the hand that moves, particularly if the magician is also looking at it. You move one hand as a decoy as the other inconspicuously works the sleight. Be careful, if you have too much visible motion in your sleight-of-hand operation it will act as a magnet and attract everyone's eyes.

Surprise

One of the strongest forms of misdirection is the element of surprise. The best time to do a sleight-of-hand maneuver is at the same moment the result of a magic trick is revealed to the audience. At this time, the entire audience's attention is focused on the trick. The thought that something sneaky is occurring at the same time is beyond comprehension. Surprise will always cover a simultaneous sleight.

As an example, when the magician magically produces a bouquet of flowers, he may at the same time pull another prop from his pocket and palm it in his hand. This prop may be magically produced a few moments later.

Distraction

A distraction, such as "accidently" dropping something, tripping, or falling down is a surprise which attracts the audience's attention. Any unexpected action can serve as a distraction whereby you can work your sleight. Again, the sleight must be performed simultaneously with the distraction to be effective.

The distraction can be caused by the magician who clumsily drops or spills something. It could be caused by an assistant who accidentally trips while walking across the stage, talks out of turn, or causes some problem. The magician may ask a member of the audience to answer a question or perform an action. As the helper responds, the audience's attention is distracted from the magician, allowing him to work his sleight.

Accidents, although effective, normally can not be used too often during a single show. As a clown you would be able to get away with this device more often than a magician could. Clowns are expected to be clumsy so mishaps are not unusual. However, a magician would look incompentent if he had too many accidents.

Patter

The words you speak, called *patter*, can help deceive the audience. As you talk, the audience's minds are occupied with what you are saying and are therefore less likely to concentrate on analyzing your movements. Comic patter is an excellent tool for keeping their minds off guard and occupied. Patter can also serve to distract the attention of the audience at the critical moment, away from the object or hand performing the sleight. You can direct the audience to "look at my hand" or to "look closely at the water in this vase." The eye cannot look two places at once. So as they look where you have directed, you secretly work the trick.

You may also lead the audience to false conclusions. Seemingly innocent words such as "the coin is in this hand" when in reality it is not; or "the coin will drop into the box," combined with a clinking sound, will make it appear as if a coin was dropped into the box.

Talking and giving instructions to volunteers can be used as misdirection. As the volunteers follow your instructions to put the scarf in the box, open the lid of the container, or stand behind the chair, for example, the audience's eyes will follow their actions, allowing you to perform the sleight.

Laughter and Applause

When the audience is laughing or applauding can be an excellent time to work a sleight. It is at these times that the audience is least expecting anything sneaky to be happening and their attention is completely diverted.

The clown, for example, may "accidently" step into a bucket and get his foot stuck. As the audience laughs at his attempts to free himself he can work the sleight undetected. In this instance his silly actions could completely cover a secret movement.

Timing

People tend to think that the secret to the magic is worked just prior to revealing the trick. Therefore, the magician can perform the secret move long before the conclusion of the trick with greater effectiveness. The longer you can allow the better. In a routine where two or more tricks are performed, you may work one while doing another. Or by taking the time to do or say something seemingly unrelated to the trick, the sleight can be worked. Allowing some time to elapse after the sleight will erase all memory of any questionable behavior on your part.

You may enhance the effectiveness of the trick if you perform an action just prior to finishing it. This added action works as a ploy to make the audience believe that this was the time the secret to the magic was performed and makes figuring out the trick more difficult.

You may also bring a trick to its apparent conclusion, only to reveal one final effect. The audience, believing the trick to be over, will relax their attention enabling the magician to set up the last effect. They may be laughing or applauding at this time as well, making your sleight even more undetectable.

Acting

Misdirection can also create impressions which are not true. An empty box can be made to look full and heavy by the way the magician lifts or moves it. If you pretend to place a coin into your left hand, you must grab and hold the imaginary coin as if you are really holding it.

You must be a good actor in order to deceive your audience. If you are secretly holding something in your hand, it can be very obvious to everyone if your hand is not in a natural position. The fingers may be curled too much or the wrist twisted slightly too far. These signs will give you away, and you may not be aware of it. Look at yourself in the mirror and examine the position of your wrist and hands when you are not holding anything. Try to imitate this position *exactly* when you are palming an article. All your actions must be natural in order to deceive and thus misdirect the audience. Analyze all of the movements that are involved in your magic and make them all look natural.

Frequently, you will want to hide something in your pocket. This must be done naturally and without raising suspicion. You must have a reason for reaching into your pocket, perhaps to pull out a handful of pixie dust to sprinkle around or to remove a handkerchief or some other item. As you reach into your pocket, deposit the article and continue. You may also position your body during the course of the trick so that you can easily drop the item into a pocket that is out of view of the audience.

Your face must never betray your actions. Sometimes when trying to do something sneaky, we clench our teeth, poke out the tip of our tongues, blink, or do things that signal something is happening. When you practice, ask someone to look at your face, and work on making it look natural.

Using Misdirection

Most of the tricks described in this book require little or no sleight-of-hand skill. However, they all require the use of various misdirection techniques in order to achieve the best results. I am going to describe to you one sleight known as "the pass," which will enable you to make a coin disappear from one hand and reappear in the other. With this move you will be able to delight people with a variety of tricks, including the classic stunt of pulling a coin out from behind a child's ear. The mechanics behind this sleight are very easy. The secret to making it work is misdirection.

Using your right hand, hold a coin between your thumb and your middle and ring fingers. Hold the coin near its edge so the audience can easily see it (Figure 1). You will pretend to pass the coin to your other hand. To do this, place the coin into the palm of your left hand (Figure 2), but do not let go of it with the right hand. Simply push the coin behind the fingers of your right hand as you pretend to place it into the palm of your left hand (Figure 3). The left hand immediately closes around the

fingers of the right hand as if grabbing the coin. With the coin now concealed behind the fingers of the right hand, move the left hand away, and let the right hand casually drop to your side. As you perform this movement, always keep you eyes looking to where the coin is supposed to be. So, when you move your left hand away make sure you are looking at it and pay no attention to your right hand. As the right hand drops to your side, relax your hand and thumb, letting the coin rest in your slightly curled fingers. Practice to make this movement feel and look natural.

Focus your attention on your left hand. This would be an excellent time to take a moment to make a few comic remarks. Now, walk up to a child and have him perform some act to make the magic work. For example, have him grab some pixie dust from his pocket and sprinkle it on your closed fist. Open your left hand to show that the coin has now disappeared.

To make the coin reappear, reach behind the child's ear with your right hand, which is palming the coin, and pretend to pull the coin out.

This is a very simple trick and highly amusing to children. As you can see, very little sleight-of-hand skill was required. You could master the movements with just a few minutes practice. There are several ways of doing the pass with a coin, some of them more difficult, but none more deceptive than this. What makes this trick so effective is the misdirection techniques that were incorporated with it.

In this description of the pass, how many misdirection methods were used? The first one you would use would be your *personality*. Being friendly puts the audience off guard. Another one of the major devices used were the *eyes*. You should always look at where the coin is supposed to be thus creating an illusion with the audience. *Movement* was also used. The right hand, while holding the coin, visibly transferred the coin to the left hand. The left hand then moved away from the right, drawing all eyes with it. This was reinforced by the *patter* used. You tell the audience you are transferring the coin from your right to your left hand. *Timing* was also involved. The sleight was performed before the magic was caused to happen by the pixie dust and long before pulling the coin from the ear. Finally, *acting* like you really did have the coin in your left hand and that the right hand was empty, helped convince the audience this was true.

As you see, more than one method of misdirection was used. Your magic will become stronger if you incorporate as many misdirection devices as possible. Friendly personality, good acting, focusing your eyes, timing, and carefully selecting your patter should be used

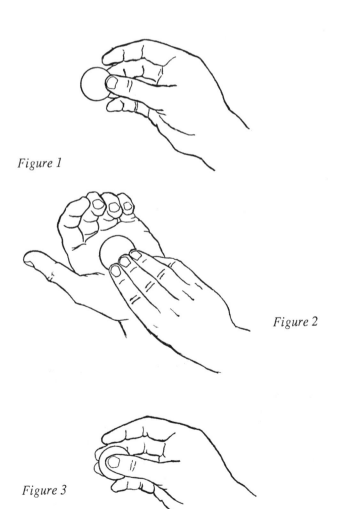

Figure 1

Figure 2

Figure 3

with most all magic tricks. By using misdirection techniques a good magician can direct the audience to look at and believe almost anything that he wants them to. Keep these ideas in mind as you read and perform the tricks and routines contained in this book. In many cases, specific misdirection techniques are indicated and explained. Whether they are specifically outlined or not, always incorporate misdirection with your magic.

TRICKS AND PROPS

Tricks Versus Routines

In these pages you will read the words *trick* and *routine* many times. Let me take just a moment to explain the two, from a professional's point of view.

When I say *trick,* I normally mean the prop or props used in a performance. The trick is what you buy at the magic shop, convention, lecture, or from a mail order catalog or even construct at home yourself. There's nothing wrong with the word trick, but keep in mind that it indicates merely the *physical properties* you use for performing.

The word *routine,* however, goes beyond the trick. The routine is what you do with the trick, how you present the tricks or gags or props to your audiences. The routine is what you do and say and how you act and, ultimately, how you *entertain* with the tricks and props. Routines involve more than props; they involve showmanship and presentation, your character, your message, and the fun you offer.

Please bear in mind the difference between the trick and the routine. The material in this book will make a lot more sense that way.

Magic Props

Props are the objects clowns use to create comedy and magic effects. The most obvious type of props used in clown magic are the magic tricks. Some of the popular props which clowns use and that you will read about in this book are the thumb tip, breakaway wand, and magic coloring book. Each of these and many other articles commonly used in magic are described in greater detail in Appendix A. Many of these props are specially made to create a magic effect. Some look like ordinary objects such

Frederick the Great surrounded by an assortment of props.

as keys, cups, and cards, while others, like the change bag and dove pan, are unique to magic. These tricks contain some type of gimmick to make the magic work.

In order to discover the secret behind the trick you either must have someone teach it to you, or you must purchase the trick from a store or magic dealer. Instructions come with the tricks. Actually, when you buy a magic prop you are not just buying the trick, you are also buying the knowledge of how the trick works. For this reason, you should refrain from telling others the secret to the tricks. Many tricks also come with sample routines to show how they are used. Although some of these routines can be effective, it is best to create your own routines using your own personality and style of humor.

Some magic tricks are very easy to operate and require very little skill or training; others, like multiplying billiard balls or linking rings, require many hours of practice and sleight-of-hand skill to learn how to effectively use.

Some magic props get their magic totally from the skill of the magician. Playing cards, for example, can be manipulated in hundreds of ways, but card manipulation requires hours of dedicated practice to perfect. Many coin tricks also rely on the manipulative skills of the magician.

In many of the routines described in this book, a silk scarf or handkerchief is used. Magicians refer to these as *silks,* and that is the term most often used in this book. However, it is better to call them scarves or handkerchiefs in front of an audience. Silk is very thin and can be compressed, without excess wrinkling, into a much smaller space than other types of cloth. Ordinary scarves and hanks are relatively thick in comparison to silk, making the tricks more difficult to figure out.

Expensive props are not necessary in order to perform an entertaining clown magic show. In fact, you could create a good show without using any specially prepared magic props. Even everyday objects can be used effectively. What's important is how you present yourself, not the props you use.

Try to choose tricks that employ materials and situations familiar to the children. Specially made props, which are only used by magicians, are looked upon with some degree of skepticism because the audience suspects they might contain a gimmick which allows the magic to work. Magic performed with ordinary-looking props are regarded with less suspicion so the magic effects seem more miraculous. Many magicians, for example, love to do card tricks; however, young children generally do not care for these types of tricks. Most small children do not use these types of cards and are generally unfamiliar with them. That does not mean you cannot do card tricks. What it means is that you should adapt the cards you use to your audience. For young children, rather than using ordinary playing cards, consider using a deck of cards children are familiar with or cards with pictures of animals or toys on them.

With children you should use tricks that are highly visible, colorful, and fun. You may make a prop more identifiable to the children by giving it a name, or even have the children choose a name. One clown magician I know turned his dove pan into a clown assistant by giving it a name and adding on to it a clown face with a red nose and wig. His use of the clown face dove pan makes his tricks more interesting to the children.

It is also a good idea to vary the types of props you use in a single act. If you have two rope routines, for example, substitute silks for the rope in one of them. Using a variety of colorful or interesting props will help build visual interest.

With the many props that are available, you may try to use more than you need or buy the largest or fanciest items. You, however, don't want to load yourself down with too many props. Remember you're going to have to carry them in and out of your show area. In some cases you will be able to carry everything you need in your pockets. If you have props or equipment that will not fit easily into your pocket you will need some type of carrying case. This could be a sturdy bag, a suitcase, a trunk on wheels, or a specially built cabinet that can also serve as a table on which to perform your magic. There are many commercial cases available in various sizes that could use or you can custom make your own. Having wheels, particularly if the case is large or heavy, is a definite advantage.

Roll-on table serves as both a table and a suitcase for carrying props.

Comedy Props

A careful selection of comedy props can add variety and novelty to your show. There are many gimmicked props that are built especially for comic effects. Spring snakes, chattering teeth, breakaway wands, squeakers, and wilting flowers are just a few of the comedy props you could use. I describe how to use many of them is the routines contained in this book. One particular novelty item, the spring snake, is so useful and funny that an entire chapter is devoted to it. The fact is, with a little imagination, you can create a lot of good clown magic from most any comedy prop.

A type of prop that is very popular with clowns is the jumbo, or oversized, prop. Oversized props are excellent for circus and stage use because they are easy for the audience to see.

Just the fact that a prop is large isn't necessarily funny. What is funny is how you use it. Make use of the size contrast with smaller objects or tasks. For example, use a jumbo tool to accomplish a small task: a huge pair of scissors to cut someone's hair or a foam sledgehammer to hammer a tiny tack or swat a pesky little fly. A small magic wand can be used to perform a trick, but if the trick doesn't work use a larger wand and then a larger one until

A breakaway wand falling appart in the volunteer's hand.

you end up with a giant wand. Used in such ways, oversized props can be hilarious.

A common comedy item used by clowns and magicians is the breakaway prop. This type of prop is designed to come apart or collapse. Breakaway magic wands and fans appear to be rigid when the clown uses them, but when he hands them to a helper they fall apart or go limp. The wilting flower is another item of this type. It looks straight and healthy, but when the clown hands it to a child it falls over as if dead. Articles of clothing can also serve as breakaway props. Buttons, pom poms, sleeves, and other items can be attached with Velcro and easily ripped off for comedy effects.

Squirting props are another type of novelty item that can be fun to use. Catsup containers, hot water bottles, flowers, fruit, and cameras are some props that are built to squirt a stream of water. When using a squirting prop, never shoot it into the audience. Many people do not like to get wet. Squirt yourself or another clown.

Magic tricks and clown props are available at your local magic or novelty shop. Many mail order dealers also carry these items. See Appendix B for some resources.

Cream Pies

Although there are only a few skits in this book which include pie throwing, because it is a common clown prop, I felt it was important to include a few comments about it.

The rabbit wand with roll down banner.

Leon McBryde whipping up a batch of soap bubbles to make cream pies.

Pie throwing can be very funny if done properly. A pie in the face is often used as a humorous ending, or *blow-off*, to a clown skit. The following advice from Leon McBryde about pies is more or less in Leon's own words.

First, understand that you never use a real coconut cream pie or any other type of real food pie for these stunts. It's a waste of good food and too expensive.

If you're doing pies in a big arena, like the circus, using real whipped cream is also too expensive. Soap is the way to go. At Ringling Brothers we used to mix dishwasher liquid with water and whip it up, anywhere from five to 55 gallons before a show. It's cheap, and you can even color the stuff to look like paint for a gag, if needed. You have to be careful with this, however, because if you make it up too long before showtime, the foam settles and it loses its fluffy quality. From a distance, like you have in circus areas, this whipped-up soap looks fine as a cream pie.

For stage shows and picnics, when you don't need so much "cream," either instant shaving cream or whipping cream will do. I'm talking about the type which comes in a pressurized can. Both will wash out of your clothing, so that's not a problem. One can will make five to ten pies.

If the weather is warm, you can keep a can of whipped cream on ice in a cooler. Then prepare your pie offstage about five minutes before you need it. Like soap, preparing either whipped cream or shaving cream too long before showtime is not good because it will settle and lose its foam.

Pie pans can range from paper or cardboard plates to an aluminum pan. It's simply a matter of squirting the foam cream into the pie pan to make it look like a cream pie.

Whatever you do, do not use a heavy metal pie pan. Such a pan could break your partner's nose, knock out a tooth, or even stun your partner with a blow to the head, ruining your performance.

You've all seen those old Three Stooges pie throwing scenes in the movies. Remember, those were shot in many "takes," carefully performed for film purposes. You cannot do that on a stage or even at a picnic if you're trying to entertain people. So, move your mind away from "throwing" pies; instead, think in terms of "placing" pies in faces.

"Would you like to have some pie?"

Learn how to "take a pie." Put on your bathing suits, go out in the back yard on a warm day, and practice "giving a pie" to someone's face and "taking a pie" in your own face.

When getting a pie in the face, remember to close your eyes just before the pie makes contact. If you close your eyes several seconds before you get hit, it kills the gag.

If you use whipped cream, your mouth can be open; if you choose shaving cream, you may want to close your mouth. Just remember to work on your timing.

The audience basically knows you're going to get hit with a pie, but at the same time, they want the person hit to be surprised. So, depending on your skit, act either surprised, or surprised and upset. Mug!

Don't wait until showtime to practice. You'll look amateurish, and something could go wrong.

A clown class practice throwing and receiving pies.

SUCCESSFUL CLOWN MAGIC

Entertainment Comes First

You can have all of the comedy props and magic tricks in the world and still not be entertaining. It doesn't matter what types of props or tricks you use, what really matters is how you use them. Props by themselves are rarely funny or entertaining. It is what you do with them that makes them funny.

Watching someone perform a magic trick is mildly interesting, but not particularly entertaining. Watching a magician or a clown perform trick after trick without much character or patter, quickly becomes boring. To truly entertain, you must incorporate with your tricks a story and comic patter that reflect your personality and clown character.

Whether you work as a clown or a magician or any other type of entertainer, this rule still holds true—and I want you to fix it in your mind and heart early in the game: *Entertaining your audience comes first!*

This means that entertaining the audience is more important than the trick itself. And it's how you deliver the trick that counts, not the trick itself. *Presentation is the key.* Your personality on the stage is most important. The tricks are merely vehicles with which you entertain.

Read that paragraph again and again. Fix its truth in your conscious and subconscious mind. I was 20 years old before someone hammered it into my head, and it changed my entire outlook on magic. In fact, it gave my performances and my career a new direction.

Entertainment comes first, not fooling the audience with a trick, not impressing them with some great stunt, but letting them have a good time through what you do and, more important, how you do it.

As you plan your clowning, as you think through and rehearse your tricks and routines, keep the entertainment angle heavily in mind.

Easy Mechanics, Strong Presentation

If you're new to clowning and performing, here is an idea that may save you countless hours and headaches. In fact, even if you've been performing for some time already, this way of working may still help you out.

I'll give you the basic premise in one sentence, then we'll talk about it: *If the trick is easy mechanically, you can (and should) put your energy and effort elsewhere— into the showmanship, presentation, character, message, and entertainment aspects of the routine.*

Go ahead. Read that again, slowly.

This means that if you choose easy mechanical tricks to perform, especially as a beginner, you can spend more time perfecting the presentation because they are easy to work. If the trick takes you 20 hours of practice to perfect, that's time lost that you could have used to work on your routine.

This is not to say that you shouldn't try difficult tricks from time to time. Several years ago I spent three weeks of daily practice learning Mike Caveney's "Linking Coathangers" routine. I worked harder on that than on any trick or routine I've done in my adult life. Yet, I have used it in two school seasons of some 350 shows each, plus in over 100 miscellaneous performances at theaters, churches, and conventions. Yes, the practice paid off. But I still promote the concept: *easy mechanics, strong presentation.*

Think of it this way: If you are at ease with the working of the trick or prop, you can more easily entertain with that trick. If you're worried about whether the trick will work, or whether you'll perform it properly due to its degree of difficulty, such worrying can inhibit your ability to entertain with it properly.

So, consider this point for yourself, as well as for your audience. After all, your audience doesn't care how many hours you spent in rehearsal. They just want to laugh, smile, and be filled with fun.

Mixing Clowning with Magic

Since I met Leon "Buttons" McBryde in 1980, he has been my friend and clown mentor of sorts. When I think of clowning, I think in terms of how Buttons would do something. That helps me think clowning. It gives me a point of reference.

Buttons is a cartoon character brought to life. Bigger than life, to be exact. Just look at him on the cover of this book!

Buttons approaches everything as if it were in a fantasy-like world. Everything has its own kind of magic, as far as he can see. But to find out what makes Buttons tick, we must remove several layers of makeup and talk to the man who created Buttons—Leon McBryde, currently a resident of Buchanan, Virginia, and formerly an advance clown for Ringling Brothers Barnum and Bailey Circus, the Greatest Show on Earth, with a half dozen years experience on the road and lots more years experience elsewhere.

Can clowns perform magic? "Of course they can!" says Leon. "Only, it's important that a clown approach each magic trick and routine *as a clown*. Remember, clowns live in a fantasy world.

"If a magician makes a rabbit vanish, it may not come back during that performance. On the other hand, if a clown makes a rabbit vanish, he HAS to bring it back. It cannot stay gone!"

So, Leon, how do you differentiate between comedy magic and clowning?

"Just because it's a comedy magic trick, from a magic shop or mail order catalog," says Leon, "that doesn't mean it's a clown magic trick. To perform that trick as a clown, you must involve your clown character in the trick or routine.

"When I look at magic tricks, I try to see them with my clown eyes. *Will it complement my clown character?* That's what I ask. When I get a new trick or prop, I may study and think about it for weeks, even months. I consider what patter I'll use to add humor to its presentation. How will my character, Buttons, use this trick or prop? There has to be an answer to that question, not just for me, but for every performing clown.

Richard "Snowflake" Snowberg the director of Clown Camp.

"And there are other questions to consider: How will Buttons pick it up? How will he operate it? Will it work at all? Will it fail and work later? Will he play dumb and not understand the trick? Maybe it will work in spite of his stupidity? This is how I tackle mixing magic and clowning."

This book contains many examples of stories or skits you can use. Read them, analyze them, and adapt them to your own clown character. Don't rely on material created by others. In order to achieve the greatest degree of success in clown magic, you need to adapt existing routines and create your own routines to fit your clown character and comic personality.

BASIC RULES OF MAGIC

I feel compelled to state in black and white some basic rules of magic, at least for the sake of any beginners reading this book. Even if you're performing magic as a clown, for the most part these rules still apply.

Rule One: Never tell how you do a trick.

This is magic's most important rule—to keep it a secret. People are fascinated by magic as long as they cannot figure out how it's done. In terms of clowning, sometimes we will reveal what might be termed "stupid secrets" for the sake of comedy, but in most cases we never reveal the "real magic secrets."

Rule Two: Never repeat a trick for the same audience.

When friends ask you to do it again, don't! They'll be watching you more closely the next time, and they might catch your method.   Instead, go on to another trick. Sometimes you can repeat a trick if you switch methods or if the repetition is a natural part of the trick. Just beware of spectators wanting you to perform the entire routine again—they'll be watching to catch you!

Rule Three: Never tell your audience what you are going to do ahead of time.

Remember that *surprise* is very important in magic. Always keep your audiences guessing. Often, however, in magic and clowning, you can announce ahead of time that you are going to do something, which then turns into a gag or joke, or has a completely different ending, all for comedy's sake.

Rule Four: Work on your character when performing magic.

In clowning, this may be the "real you," an extension of your personality, or even a completely different character from your normal self. Any of these possibilities can be fine as long as you work on "who you are" while you are on the stage. In other words, develop your character as you develop your magic and comedy. Your performance of magic and comedy will come easier this way—when you understand who you are—and your audience will enjoy you much more.

Rule Five: Practice, practice, practice!

Practice not only how to do the tricks, stunts, and gags themselves, but also how to present your routines for maximum entertainment value. Practice your magic in front of a mirror so you can see how it looks from the audience's viewpoint. Practice how you will walk onto the stage, how you will pick up the props, what you'll say, and what you'll do with props when you've finished using them. Practice your closing and your bows and your exit. Practice individual parts of your act, then the entire thing together. Consider every little show a rehearsal for the bigger ones.

CHAPTER 3

MOST CLOWNS TALK

Out loud, in spoken words, most clowns talk. Yes, I know, there are clowns who work without talking, pantomime clowns who communicate through actions, motions, and noise from other sources. But most clowns talk. Spoken language, after all, is our primary means of communication. Furthermore, speaking is easier than working silent.

Some clowns say funny things. Other clowns say serious things. Some clowns say funny things in serious ways. Other clowns say serious things in funny ways. Some clowns rehearse their lines and gags; other clowns are great at ad-libbing.

The fact is, clowning includes both kinds—talkers and nontalkers—but often just getting into a clown character transforms a nontalker into a talker. Why? Because most clowns talk. In a way, I think people expect it.

When I first put on the greasepaint, I wasn't sure who I would be as a clown. But I knew for sure I would be a talker. Why is that? Well, I'm a writer and talker in real life, and Frederick the Great (my clown character) would have to be an extension of me. Therefore, he would have to be a talker. Here was my chance to get away with all my cornball jokes. Frederick the Great, a pompous whiteface, would be the perfect fool to use such material. It never crossed my mind, or Frederick's, to be a nontalking clown. It just wasn't natural for me—or him.

Talking, therefore, is the theme of this chapter: *words you can use to bring your clown character to life, or to give him or her even more vitality.* In these next few pages, and indeed throughout the book, I'll do my best to share with you ways to communicate funny things.

In magic, we call the words used in a trick routine patter. In clowning you might call the same thing gab, blab, or just talk. How you deliver that talk depends on your clown character. After all, you may be a s-l-o-w w-o-r-k-i-n-g clown, or a *FAST-TALKING CLOWN.* Either way, you can adapt the words and advice in this chapter to suit yourself.

GREETING YOUR AUDIENCE

The best way to get any performance off to a good start is to greet your audience with warmth and happiness, then get them laughing and applauding right away. Comedy magician Bob Jepson says, "If you don't have the audience laughing and applauding in your first 30 seconds on stage, you're doing something wrong!" Here are some lines to get your audiences and you off on the right foot.

- How do you like the show so far? (You've done nothing yet.)

- What a great-looking bunch you are. I don't know how long you've been hanging on the tree, but you're a great-looking bunch!

- Let me tell you folks—you're in for a DULL time tonight! I'm only kidding. You're going to have more fun than I can imagine.

- Just look around you. You're in a room full of real, live people. What a thrill!

- And we have gone to absolutely NO EXPENSE to bring you the finest show PASSABLE.

- Personally, I'm SO HAPPY to be here! (Look offstage and ask toward the wings.) By the way, where are we?

- I'd like to announce that tonight's show is made possible by a grant from Hefty Garbage Bags.

- And for the next 45 minutes, we're going to spend AN HOUR together.

- It's so much fun clowning around like this . . . making people laugh . . . lifting the spirits of mankind . . . earning $1.35 an hour!

- SMALL CROWD: Say, did all of you get here in the same taxi?

- Boy, if all of you had been with me today, there would be absolutely no use in our being together tonight!

- By the way, during the show I'd like for all of you to keep your seat belts fastened and tray tables in their upright and locked position—and REMEMBER, your seat cushion can be used for floatation in case of a water landing.

- I just flew in to do this show, and right after the show I have to fly back to Decatur. (Name a small town just a few miles away.)

- The best part of the show is that all of YOU are here. Why, without you, I'd have to install a big mirror on the front row and watch this stuff by myself!

- So get ready for the best show you're going to see in the next 30 minutes. It's also the ONLY show you're going to see in the next 30 minutes!

Leon "Buttons" McBryde and Don "Homer" Burda.

- Boy, is this show going to be good! That's exactly what I want to know—IS THIS SHOW GOING TO BE GOOD?

Which of these lines fits you? Pick a few. Rehearse them to establish your own delivery and wording, then try them in a live show situation. See how they fit with your character. If they work, great. If not, try others and other ways of delivering them.

COVERING MISTAKES

Clowns are always making mistakes for laughs, and comedy magicians are not far behind. In fact, I discussed this topic under the title "Magician-in-Trouble Syndrome" in my textbook, *Kidbiz*. The idea is simple: Kids love to see a magician or clown goof up, make mistakes, even get hurt in a slapstick sort of way. The question for this section is: What are you going to say when you do make an unexpected mistake?

Try these for answers:

- Did you hear the one about the clown that goofed?

- Now, wait a minute. I didn't really mess up, did I?

- Oh, boy! I've just figured out a stupid new way to do this!

- Sorry! I forgot to rig the whammy-jam to the thing-a-ma-jig, and that's why the velcron overlapped the zerosinator. Come to think of it, next time I'll samstall the birdwell control to coordinate with the fastilado. I hope you understand that too.

- Hey, any clown can make a mistake. It just proves I'm subhuman!

- Bet you'd like to try that too!

- I didn't mean to do that. You would cry too if it happened to you!

- How could I do that? How could I do that? How in the world could I possibly do that? It's a good question for which I have no intelligent answer!

- Did you hear the one about the goofed up clown? No? Well, neither did I!

- Remember, the best laid plans of mice and men . . . sometimes spoil the cheese.

- I goofed, messed up, made a mistake. I don't want anybody talking about it. I apologize. I won't do it again. Never. Ever. In my entire life. Even if I live to be 99 years old. I'll never do that again. I'm sorry. So, so, sorry. I mean, after all, *I goofed* . . . (Here you start repeating the entire speech over, as though heavily rehearsed. Then you catch yourself and stop.) Hey! I've already said that!

NEW MAGIC WORDS

Please don't fall into the stereotyped trap of using the same old tried, hackneyed, and commonplace magic words that every clown and magician in the English-speaking world is using. Write the words "abracadabra," "hocus pocus," "presto," and "allakazam" in bold letters on a piece of paper, stare at them intently, then rip the paper to shreds and *never* use those words again.

Instead, tailor some magic words to suit yourself and your stage character, whether you're a clown or a magician. Many places I perform remember me for my favorite magic words, "purple puppy chow."

"That's what my dog eats! (Pause for the laugh.) After all, what would YOU feed a purple puppy? He won't eat red or pink or green puppy chow. It has to be purple!"

As you see, the magic words have a ring to them, plus a built-in bit of automatic humor. But by adding a few comments following the initial pronunciation of the magic words, you not only make them funnier and get more laughs, but you also reinforce the special words in the minds of the audience members.

With this in mind, I'll share with you a smattering of funny magic words to get you thinking. I've stolen these from my books *Comedy Warm-ups for Children's Shows, Bringing Home the Laughs,* and *Children Laugh Louder,* plus added a few brand new lines. Feel free to use some of these yourself or, better yet, use them to help you think up your own!

- COLD COLLARD GREENS! With marshmallow sauce!

- LICORICE ICE CREAM! Yummy, I love it!

- KALAMAZOO ORANGE JUICE! Green off the tree!

- BWANA IGUANA. That's what the native guide said to the hunter just before the hunter stepped into the big lizard's mouth: "Bwana! Iguana!"

- LONG LOVELY LIZARD GIZZARDS. A frightful delight to bite!

- ARFUS NOCHES. That's Spanish for "the dog barks through his nose!"

- BIG BALONEY SANDWICHES. With hot fudge!

- PINK PANTHER PICKLES. Those are the kind of pickles the Pink Panther eats. You know what color they are? What? PINK? No, they're green! Pickles are green! The Pink Panther is PINK!

- MINNIE HENRY HA-HA! (Say these words dramatically to evoke laughs.)

- BRUNHILDA ES LARGA. That's Spanish for "the girl needs caffeine-free Diet Coke!"

- OSHKOSH! WABASH! FIDDLESTICKS! I can't think up anything better than that!

- LIVER, SAUSAGE, CHICKEN, STEAK! MAKE THIS WORK—GIMME A BREAK!

- GAMMA-GAMMA RAMMA LAMMA DING DONG! That was a hit record back in the 1950s!

- SIR BUBBA DOE DOE! In Swahili, that means "Mr. Throckmorton ain't got no smarts!"

- And the magic words are—YOU'VE JUST WON 40 MILLION DOLLARS FROM PUBLISHER'S CLEAR-INGHOUSE! And if you believe that, then I'm Ed McMahon!

OUTDOOR SHOWS

A lot of clowning takes place outdoors during warmer months at picnics and parties. With the heat and flying insects to contend with, a working clown needs to have something intelligent, or at least funny, to say. Try some of these:

- It's a pleasure to be working here in the great outdoors . . . among the trees and below the sky . . . where birds fly overhead and greet us with calls of the wild—and little deposits.

- I was going to use a big, colorful scarf for this trick, but the wind blew it away!

- Ah, to work outdoors with the babbling of a little brook in the background. Brook? Where are you? I'd like that little girl named Brook to stand up and babble for us!

- How do you like this outdoor carpeting? (Indicate the grass.) I bet it didn't cost $25 a yard!

- Hey—there are ANTS on my stage!

- How do you like this natural air-conditioning?

- I love trees. I know all about them. That's a pine tree. It's full of sap. And that one's a dogwood. I can tell by its bark.

- Since we're outdoors, you can laugh and applaud as loud as you desire—it won't bother me!

- SWAT BEE OR FLY. Say, who opened the door and let that bee in my theater?

- Ah, the great outdoors! So this is where FRESH AIR comes from!

- Aren't you glad they mowed the stage before the show? I am!

BIRTHDAY PARTY LAUGHS

My magic career started with home birthday parties for small groups. These shows allowed me to make lots of mistakes before I tackled larger crowds at schools, churches, and theaters.

Since I do few birthday parties these days, I've asked two of my California clown friends, Vickie Miller (Ruffles) and Joyce Quisenberry (Bubbles) to share some of their favorite birthday gags and lines for your audience's amusement, because Ruffles and Bubbles do lots of birthday parties!

So now, more or less in their own words, I give you advice from Ruffles and Bubbles.

- Here's a fun opening gag: Upon arrival at the birthday party, start looking for the birthday child under the couch cushions, behind the TV set, under the tables and so on until finally the birthday child identifies himself or herself. This often takes away the "scary" nature of a clown for little kids because they get caught up in you (the clown) trying to find them.

- Try to guess a child's name by using silly names. Some that we use are Freddy Fudge, Charlie Choo Choo, Willamina Hamburger, and Sally Swingdinger.

- Ask a child helper, "Are you married? Did you bring your wife or husband with you? What about your children? Are they here too?" This makes kids laugh as they try to explain to you that they are *not* married.

The California Girls, Joyce "Bubbles" Quisenberry and Vickie "Ruffles" Miller.

- If the birthday child is a boy, be sure to ask all the *girls* if they are the birthday boy. Reverse this procedure for a birthday girl.

- "How old are you?" you ask the birthday child. "SIX," comes the answer. "Oh," you say, "I'm sorry you're SICK! Can I take your temperature? Should I call the doctor?"

- If you see a child with no teeth, try these lines: "Oh, no, you forgot to put your teeth in!" The child will usually reply, "No, I lost them." So you come back with, "You lost them! Well, we'd better call the POLICE and report this. We'll need to give them a description of your teeth!" Or, if you like, you can start looking for the "missing teeth" all over the floor, perhaps pulling out a magnifying glass or some crazy gadget you've made up, calling it a "Tooth Detector."

- "What's your real name, Bubbles?" kids will often ask. My reply is, "My real name is Willimina Bag and Sack . . . so it's just easier to say BUBBLES!"

- "I see your skin!" is another typical child remark upon a close encounter with a clown. Sometimes it's the first time little kids realize that a clown is also a human person. Our favorite comeback is this: "Of course I have skin—otherwise, my bones would fall onto the floor!"

- "You're not really a clown!" is another often-heard remark. We find it best not to argue with this child mentality. So we say, "I know. I'm really a Ninja Turtle!" Just name any popular TV character. "But whatever you do, don't tell anyone!"

- "Do you have a card?" Or, "Can I have your card?" Naturally, we hear this a lot, and we use it for laughs. We pull out a deck of playing cards and say, "Sure, I have a card—I have 52 of them! Which one do you want? The queen of hearts? The seven of spades? The ace of clubs? They're all here!"

- "Can I get a picture?" people often ask, camera in hand. "Sure," you tell them, whipping out your wallet of family photos to show them. "Here's one of our vacation to Disneyland and one to Florida and one to New York City. Which one do you want?" Of course, you finally do let them photograph you, but you have fun with this bit of business first.

- "Look at your big feet!" some kids will remark. Reply: "I don't have big feet. I just have LONG TOES! Personally, I don't know how your puney little feet hold you up!"

- If there's a child wearing sandals, point to the sandals and act surprised. Say, "Oh, you poor thing! You need new shoes! You've worn holes in those shoes! You'd better tell your mother about that."

- Another question kids often ask clowns is "Where do you live?" Our answer: "I live in CLOWN TOWN in a CLOWN-DOMENIUM. It's right next to Hoboville and Cartoonland."

- When leaving a birthday party, tell the kids, "Well, it's getting late, and I gotta go home. It's my turn to feed the elephants. See ya later!"

- A good remark, when they're taking your picture is "Hey, just be sure it doesn't end up in the *National Enquirer*." Or name some other tabloid that has a dubious reputation.

- In doing coloring tricks at parties—tricks like the *magic coloring book, instant art,* or *vanishing crayons*—we make up silly color poems like this:
    PINK, PINK, my brother's feet STINK!
    or GREEN, GREEN, don't be mean!
    or YELLOW, YELLOW, I love cute fellows!

- The hand squeaker has a thousand uses, and it's perfect for clowns interacting with children at birthday parties. Examples: Touch kids' tummies or toes, squeaking the squeaker hidden in your hand or glove each time. "How do you like that!" you remark. "You're really SQUEAKY CLEAN for this party!"

- If you pop a balloon, say, "Oh, no! That's where I hid that popcorn! I was looking all over for it." Or, have one of those large plastic ears of corn hidden nearby. When the balloon pops, quickly pull out the ear of corn and say, "Ouch! That noise hurts my ear!" (GINN-NOTE: That gag is worth popping a balloon!)

- If you see that a child is afraid of you as a clown, hide behind another person (kid or grown-up). Then tell the child who is afraid of you, "Please don't scare me . . . because I don't like being scared!"

- Ask the child with a cold, "Hey, are you one of those backward kids . . . where your NOSE RUNS and your FEET SMELL?" At least it gets them laughing!

- "Ruffles and Bubbles, do you do your own makeup?" Bubbles answers, "Of course, we do! Some people call this a Maybelline Miracle Beauty Make-Over!" Then Ruffles kicks in, "Actually, we used to be beauty consultants for K-Mart! Or was it beauty desultants? Or beauty destructors? I can't remember. Anyway, that's where we met David Ginn. He was riding the mechanical horse in front of K-Mart, and he was sliding off under the saddle! We had to unplug that horse to save David's life!"

All right, girls! That's enough. No use telling the readers everything! I do appreciate you sharing these birthday party and kidbiz bits with my readers. Some of these sound pretty crazy on paper, but when you're doing them with kids at a party or picnic, I know they're very funny and right in line with good, clean clowning. Thanks, a-Ginn, and keep making those kids laugh!

CHAPTER 4

WORKING WITH CHILDREN

Knowing what children like, how to get them excited and enjoying themselves without letting them get out of hand, how to avoid problems that may disrupt or slow down the show, and how to gently ease fears and apprehensions, is all a part of knowing how to work with children. In this chapter I will discuss techniques that have proven successful in working with children that will help to make you a successful children's entertainer.

WARMING UP YOUR AUDIENCE

Twenty years ago I tried to start my children's shows with a segment of musical magic. Often I would get 10 minutes into the show with no applause, no laughter, no reaction whatsoever.

That's when my friend Harold Taylor suggested I start the children's shows by going out in front of the curtain or equipment and "warming up my audience" before I started doing the "real magic." The first time I tried his suggestion it worked wonders. By warming up the kids at the beginning of the show, I garnered more applause and laughter throughout the program.

Over the years, I developed and polished this comedy warm-up technique to make it work for me as well as my audience. These days the comedy warm-up is a vital part of every performance I do for children, teens, adults, and family groups.

Let's look at it this way: Most of us do a one-man or one-woman show, or perhaps work with a partner or a small troupe. We are the show. There is no professional master of ceremonies to prepare the crowd. Therefore, we have to do that job and warm up the audience ourselves.

The only time I do not present a comedy warm-up now is when I work a convention show which has a professional MC. Sometimes, even in that case, I work the personality parts of my warm-up into my opening remarks.

Why is the comedy warm-up so important? That's easy to answer, especially when it comes to kids. Live performers these days, like clowns and magicians, are automatically competing with television, that mile-a-second medium which affects the civilized world on a daily, hourly, minute-by-minute basis. Children sit and watch TV for hours, glued to their sets. They may laugh a little, but never like they should in a live performance, and they never applaud.

Therefore, you must warm them up to the truth that "this is not TV folks, it's a real live show!" And my personal comedy warm-up technique does that in three easy steps.

Step One: Get Them to Applaud

When I come onto the stage, I want to come on with applause. Getting someone else to lead that applause is important, whether you're working for ten children at a birthday party or a thousand students in a school gymnasium. For that reason, I ask the school principal or whoever is in charge, to get the audience quiet at the beginning of the show and bring me on with a round of applause. That gets the applause rolling from a source other than me. Even a birthday mom can do this.

Once I'm on the stage (meaning wherever I am performing), I greet the audience cheerfully and begin talking. Here is a typical opening remark:

"Good afternoon, boys and girls. I'm David Ginn, and this is the show I call 'Jungle Tales of Magic.' We're going to have some fun today and learn a few things about the jungle you never knew. But before we get started, I want you to know *two things* about the show."

"First, if you see or hear anything during the performance that you like or enjoy, I want you to feel free to clap your hands and applaud whenever you like. In fact, let me see how good you can clap your hands again right now!"

Following my suggestion, the children clap their hands and this gets my second round of applause less than 10 seconds into the show!

Notice above I used the phrase, "Let me see *how good* you can clap your hands." If the audience is already up, active, and cheerful, that's exactly what I say. In some shows, however, I walk on to a very reserved, quiet audience. Maybe they are just extremely well behaved, or maybe their teachers or the principal has threatened them with their lives if they make any noise. Either way, I've got to "shake them up" and make them into my kind of audience, an audience which will have fun in a controlled way. In that case, I change my phrase, saying, "Let me see *how loud* you can clap your hands!" That gets them started and lets them be kids.

Step Two: Get Them to Laugh

As soon as I elicit that round of applause, I hurry on to the next step.

"Second, if you see or hear anything during the show that *looks funny* or *sounds funny,* I want you to go right ahead and laugh. Go ahead! Laugh right now!" And they do. "Don't wait until the show is over because I'll be gone, and you'll be gone. In fact, some of you already look gone!"

In just a few sentences, I've mechanically made them laugh once (by telling them to laugh) and automatically made them laugh a second time (by saying something amusing). Notice that I am less than 15 seconds into my performance, and we've had two rounds of applause and two audience laughter episodes.

This is what the warm-up is all about: loosening up your audience, getting them accustomed to the performing, priming the pump to get applause and laughter started early in the show. And if you start this applause and laughter snowballing early in the performance—in the first 30 seconds you're in front of the group—it will continue to roll (with help) throughout your act.

Step Three:
Do Something Magical, Skillful, or Funny

The third part of the warm-up completes the bonding between performer and audience. It impresses the audience with the fact that you can do magic or juggling or comedy or whatever your specialty happens to be. In essence, it says "that clown knows his stuff."

As a comedy magician most of the time, I get my school show audiences to applaud and laugh, then impress them with one quick comedy magic trick. Among my favorites are the "Color Changing Shoelaces," "Vanishing Liter Coke Bottle," "Axtell's Magic Drawing Board," "Flaming Hot Book," "Computer Baby," and the "Comedy Blooming Bouquet" (inspired by Welch magician Trevor Lewis). Each of these tricks allows for ample comedy in two or three minutes, and four of them have a "magical" finish, making the kids wonder how I did it. And they are all fine for clowns.

However, your preference may be to do something skillful at this point, juggling perhaps. That's fine too. Or maybe you'd prefer simply to go for comedy.

Let me share four very workable comedy routines I have used in my comedy warm-up, borrowed from my booklet *Comedy Warm-Ups for Children's Shows.*

DON'T LAUGH ROUTINE. If I feel the audience is already in a good, playful mood, I might use this: "If you see anything funny during the show, whatever you do— DON'T LAUGH." Even as I say this seriously, the kids either giggle or laugh out loud. "Not even one GIGGLE or SNICKER or GRIN." That brings more laughs.

"In fact, I don't want even one smile. Not even one!" Saying this makes kids automatically smile. "This is a very serious show, VERY SERIOUS! There is NOTHING FUNNY about this show!"

A typical school show audience seated on the gymnasium floor.

You can try this several times, then change to clapping hands or other activities. The idea is simply to get them participating, to create a better and more active audience.

RAISING HANDS GAG. Begin by asking the audience several standard questions to which they should always answer "yes" by a show of hands.

"How many of you like ice cream? Hands up! Hands down! How many like pizza? Hands up! Hands down! How many like chocolate candy? Hands up! Hands down!"

After asking five or six questions along these lines, with hands going up and down rapidly, ask this: "How many of you are BAD BOYS AND GIRLS? Hands up!" Their hands will be up before they realize what you've said, and then they'll burst into laughter.

By this time the kids are busting out and laughing openly. If you're working as a clown in makeup and deliver this dramatically, though tongue in cheek, I guarantee you'll get laughs.

Suddenly, I turn to one side of the audience and shout, "NOW, WHAT'S SO FUNNY ABOUT THAT?"

This statement makes them howl with laughter, if it's the right crowd, and I compound it by turning to the other side of the group, pointing, and shouting, "I SEE YOU LAUGHING OVER THERE—GIGGLING AND SMILING TOO!"

Then I relax.

"You know what? I was only kidding. You really can laugh all you want. After all, laughter is good for you. It makes you feel good. And you can giggle too. In fact, I see some BOYS giggling in the front row right now! Go ahead and smile too, because we're here to have a good time together, so let's get on with the show!"

SHOUTING CONTEST. Divide the audience into two groups. They could be left and right, girls and boys, younger and older grades, whatever you like.

"When I raise my hand, I want group one to shout as loud as you can. When I drop my hand, stop shouting as quickly as you can and cut it right off. Here we go." Let group one shout, then stop it.

"Well, that was pretty good. Let's try group two. Ready, go!" Group two shouts.

TOTAL RECALL. "Before we start today's show, I'd like to find out who's here. After all, you all know my name, David Ginn, so I'd like to find out your names. And I've come up with an easy way to do that in about two seconds.

"You see, I have a total recall memory. And if I can hear all of your names at once, I'll know who you are. So here's how we'll do it. I'll count to three, and all of you shout your *first names* only, just one time. I'll listen very carefully, and I will actually hear and comprehend every single name. All right, this is it. One! Two! Three!"

The kids scream their names. The moment they shout, I cup my hands to my ears as though trying to catch every name. Then I remove my hands and hold them up to restore order if needed.

Once they are quiet, I announce: "I heard every one of them. *Every one!* For instance, I heard girls by the name of Mary, Holly, Wendy, Betty, Lynne, Autumn, Susan, Sandra, Margaret, Jean, Angela, Carmen, Martha, Tina, Allison, Adrienne, Karen . . ." and I name a dozen more. "And I heard boys with names like Larry, Charlie, Steve, Bobby, Jimmy, George, Phil, six Johns, two Joes, a Gregory, Harry, Clyde . . . and one boy by the name of LEE-E-E-E-ROY!"

Instant laughter. I always end the list with a name I think will be funny at that show location, names like Archibald, Brockhurst, Elroy, or Chinkio Kinkanelli. Wherever you live, pick a funny name to call out last.

The moment the kids start laughing at the mention of Leroy, I look around and point toward the back of the audience. "There he is!" I shout, pointing, then waving my hand at the imaginary boy, "Hello, Leroy, how are you doing?"

Immediately the crowd turns to look for Leroy, but I shout, "DON'T LOOK! Don't turn around! Oh, see there, you scared him and he ran out the door!"

Yes, they often laugh at that remark too.

"Well, anyway, at least I know who's here, so we can get on with the show and have some fun."

Do you see what is happening in each of these examples? The comedy warm-up is drawing the audience and me together, making us friends. It has worked for me for 20 years, and it will also work for you.

Within weeks after I started using this technique, I found myself getting 100 percent audience reaction to the entire show. The warm-up helped both the audience and me to have a better time, building better rapport between us.

Audiences Love to Participate

Remember, every time kids raise their hands, shout out things you've asked for, clap their hands for you and so on, *they are participating.* And they love to participate. In every children's audience, virtually every child would like to get onto the stage with the clown or magician to help do something. That, of course, is usually not possible, except for small birthday parties. So, in warming them up, you are allowing them to immediately feel a part of the show because they are helping you. And that makes children feel good, which equals entertainment.

I have continued to talk in terms of children here, but let me assure you that adult and family shows need a comedy warm-up too. It's a time to share your personality with the audience. Let them get to know you a little and to understand your character. That will make even adult shows go better.

Harold Taylor pointed out to me years ago that a three to four minute warm-up subtracts that much time from your overall show, allowing you to perform fewer tricks, perhaps even do less work! But the comedy warm-up can be the best three minutes you'll spend in your show because it can make or break your performance.

So don't be afraid to try this. Play with it and develop the concept within your clown character. After all, the comedy warm-up is not only functional within a performance, it is fun. And I mean fun for both the audience and you, the entertainer.

My comedy warm-ups usually last from two to three minutes, and never more than five. After that I plunge into my musical magic, other comedy, or audience participation. You should do the same. After all, once you have the engine cranked, drive it!

So, get out there and start that applause and laughter snowball rolling. Then reinforce it throughout your performance with good comedy, magic, skills, and fun, so the snowball rolls bigger and bigger until the end of the show. That's when you get the big applause—the big applause which would not have been the same if you had not warmed up your audience in the first place.

AUDIENCE PARTICIPATION

The heart of my kidshow is audience participation. Children are full of energy and excitement. They love to be involved in anything fun. When you interact with audience members and use the audience in your routines, the children become a part of the act and the show becomes more entertaining to them. I've discussed how to use audience participation in your warm-ups. Now let me suggest at least three ways of involving the audience during the show.

The most used audience participation technique is to bring helpers up onto the stage. Virtually every child watching a magic or clown show would love to come on stage and help the performer, thus becoming part of the show. That, of course, is impossible unless you're doing a home birthday party for nine kids and you use nine helpers during the show. So, by using a variety of helpers from different parts of the audience, those who didn't come up at least to feel they are a part of the show.

Another way to involve audience members is by having individuals help from their seats. Instead of physically bringing helpers up onto the stage, you can have them assist you from anyplace in the audience. In some of my routines *I point to children in the audience, have them stand,* and let them make decisions about the trick being performed on the stage. In this way I can use a child from the back of the gymnasium without taking the time for him to walk all the way to the stage. In the same manner, I can also use a handicapped child on crutches or in a wheelchair who otherwise might have difficulty coming up onto the stage.

A third method for participation is to have the entire audience help. They can do this by shouting magic words, raising hands, singing songs, reciting poems, and responding to you through words and motions. This version of audience participation is especially good in the opening warm-up moments, when you have the audience working together as a unit. A great example of this is "The Split-Up," as performed by Leon McBryde and Jim Howle, described later in this book. Many of the routines described throughout this book use audience participation techniques.

Selecting Helpers

In selecting audience helpers, I always look for children who are sitting quietly, raising their hands, and have their mouths closed. I usually explain this to the children during my performances, which helps settle the crowd. After all, they all want to be picked to help. Selecting children who are noisy and jumping up and down will simply give you trouble. It is a reward for a child to help a clown or magician on stage; it is best to reward nice children.

Sometimes I watch the children ahead of time, like when I am setting up at a party, picnic, or church banquet

Getting the volunteer's name.

where the group is in sight. I observe various children and consider which ones might be good helpers for this or that routine. In some routines I use a girl, in some a boy, and in some two children. For some routines I need a tall boy or girl; for others, a four to five year old will do.

At schools I almost never preplan who I will select. I simply pick children at random, according to the types I need for various routines. However, I make it a point always to pick (1) from all over the audience, (2) from every ethnic group represented, (3) from various school grades, and (4) from various hair colors and shapes and sizes of bodies. Therefore, if I use ten children during a show, I will have one from each grade (say K-6 at an elementary school) some blacks, whites, and Hispanics, some with blonde, brown, or black hair, some kids who are tall, short, thin, and (yes) fat.

I do this in all fairness, and I also select kids this way so that virtually every child in the audience can identify with some child helper on the stage during my performance. For me, it works.

Once I indicate which children I want to help me— "The boy there (pointing) in the green striped shirt and the girl in the second row in the red T-shirt with 'Georgia Bulldogs' on it"— I always do two things that I consider extremely important: create applause for the helpers, and get their names.

I bring audience helpers up and send them back with a round of applause. This applause keeps the audience clapping their hands during the show, which makes everyone feel good, including the performer.

Also, I always ask for their names. Learning a child's name, especially in front of a crowd, makes him or her feel like somebody. If you can't understand a child's name, ask the child to spell it for you, or ask his teacher . . . or even give him or her a special name for the show, like "Tarzan" or "Jane." The point is: be able to address the child by a name during your routine instead of just "you do this or that." This makes the relationship more personal.

COMEDY FOR CHILDREN

Children love to laugh, but not at long, drawn out jokes or sophisticated one-liners. Corny situation comedy works much better. Jokes and planned ad-libs told along with your tricks, skits, and routines fill the bill. You'll find plenty of this in these pages.

Children also love physical comedy and slapstick. For example, one of the funniest kidshow bits I've ever done was hitting my hand against a metal microphone stand. The first time I did it by accident, and it really hurt me, but the kids thought it was funny when I yelled "OUCH!" and laughed their heads off. Since then, I've "accidentally" hit my hand many times, just to create a laugh.

Another thing children love is seeing grown-ups, especially performers like clowns and comedy magicians, goof up. Indeed, I often make mistakes on purpose just to create laughter. In *Kidbiz,* I called this idea the "Magician-in-Trouble Syndrome," but perhaps here we could call it the "Clown-in-Trouble Syndrome." We could chart it like this:

Clown Goofs Up = Children Laugh
Clown Makes a Mistake = Children Laugh
Clown Compounds Mistake = Children Laugh Louder

Yet through all of this clown-in-trouble comedy, the children will still love you for being the clown, for being funny, and for being you.

About ten years ago, Earl Chaney was working a show as "Mr. Clown," and I was in the audience watching. Let me share how Earl used this clown-in-trouble business.

Mr. Clown was trying to restore a rope he had cut and tied back together. When he unwrapped the rope from his hand, the knot was still there. Surprised and upset, Mr. Clown threw a child-like temper tantrum, stamping his feet up and down, waving his arms, and crying out loud because the trick didn't work. He turned his back on the crowd, threw the rope down on his table, and a moment later turned back to the audience. The tantrum was gone, and with a perfectly straight face he said, "So we WON'T do that trick!"

What a laugh it got, not only from the children, but especially from the adults present!

In these pages I'll share a lot of other ways to make children laugh. Just remember, it takes more than "looking funny."

SEATING THE AUDIENCE

In my schools, most of the audiences are in fixed seats, folding chairs, gym bleachers or stands, or even on the floor. Even then, I must be careful how far away from me the teachers place the students. Why? Because if they are too far away, it *hurts* my show.

Yes, you read right. Hurts. For me to build the type of kidshow rapport I wish between the children and me, I need to be relatively close to them. That means my front row should be only five to eight feet from where I am performing, if at all possible. This makes the show go better. If the front row is 20 feet away, and I perform a good show, it would have gone even better had the kids been seated closer.

Therefore, when teachers march in that first group, I personally make sure they are seated at the right distance. If the kids are sitting on the floor, this often involves setting down plastic cones or laying out a rope or a piece of masking tape to indicate the front row.

The same idea can be applied to birthday parties, small church shows, or other functions with no real seating. Lay a rope or tape across the floor, call it your magic line and tell the kids to sit right behind it "and if anyone crosses that line, I will have to stop the show because the magic will be broken."

A library audience seated on a carpeted floor about six feet from the stage area.

SUPERVISING CHILDREN

At schools, I have teachers and principals to help supervise the kids, and very seldom do I have problems. In private party work, in fact, in all out-of-school work I insist on adult supervision.

"Remember," I often tell those booking me, "I am the entertainer, not the disciplinarian. My job is to make the kids happy. Your job is to keep them in a reasonable order. If we have any young hecklers who think they know it all and want to mouth off during the show, please HELP ME by getting those kids to calm down so that I can continue the show. If I have to stop and deal with them, it hurts the show, and sometimes I have to cut things short. And since I enjoy PERFORMING the show for THEM, please do your part in supervising the children."

A little talk in your own words along those lines goes a long way to help, both when you book the show and on the scene. Many adults think you're just going to walk in and take over the party, and the kids will automatically click into adult-like courtesy. If only it were so!

Since it is not so, *ask for help*. A good rule of thumb is to have one adult for every 50 children in a family night program. At a birthday party with 20 children, two or three grown-ups would be fine. Just give them that polite talk ahead of time.

Personally, I warm up my audiences by telling them they can clap their hands (and we practice that) and laugh (and we practice that) *at the proper times*. Magician Brian Flora adds something like this: "And when I am talking and explaining the magic, it is your job to LISTEN so you will understand what is happening. I CANNOT talk if you are talking, and since we only have a certain amount of time for the show, if you are talking I will have to cut out some of the best tricks and fun." I think including a statement such as this is a good idea.

CLOWNS UP CLOSE

Picture this scene: You are a well-dressed clown with brand new size 22 shoes, a big red nose, a giant head of hair, and a funny hat a foot taller than your head. Wearing your motley clown garb you stand over seven feet tall.

Now, you walk into little four-year old Billy's birthday party, and little Billy spots you for the first time. He has never seen a live clown. Maybe he has seen one on TV, but those clowns are only inches tall. Now, here you are at his front door. He looks up at you like the children did at Arnold Schwarzenegger in the movie *Kindergarten Cop*. Then he slaps both hands to his face and screams, like Macaulay Culkin did after applying aftershave in *Home Alone,* before he goes running away crying.

If you haven't had this experience as a clown, look out—it's coming! The point is that many small children are afraid of clowns, just as they are afraid of Santa Claus and the mall Easter Bunny. Clowns, you must realize, do not look like mom or dad or the nice lady Sunday School teacher who smells good, not even like grandma or grandpa. To very small children, clowns look like something from outer space, and that's scary!

Understanding this fact is your first step in overcoming this natural obstacle. Let me share some of Richard Snowberg's thoughts on the size difference and how to handle it:

"In working with young children, an obvious difference exists between the size of a performer and that of the child. A short performer like Earl Chaney probably has the advantage of being able to more easily relate to the younger child.

"In my clown costume as Snowflake, I stand six feet five inches tall. For a moment, place yourself in the shoes of a first grader, all three feet five inches of him. Better yet, think about preschoolers. Now, what would YOUR FEELINGS be when this red-haired, brightly dressed performer dwarfs you by a full thirty-six inches?

"Some children just stand there with their mouths open, looking up. (Come to think of it, when you look way *up*, it's hard to keep your mouth closed! Just try it right now. See what I mean?) How do you handle this situation, particularly if you notice the child is uncomfortable?

"First, I acknowledge our size difference and suggest that my helper stand up straighter. That not helping much, I suggest that he needs something to stand on. Playing the situation for one quick laugh, I lay a newspaper down at his feet and have him stand on it. He doesn't get much taller, but it does get a laugh. Just watch his expression!

"After the laughter dies down, I recognize my stupidity in not having given the child something thicker. Thereby, the laugh was really at MY expense and not the child's.

"Then I get down on my knees and just smile at the child. The absurdity of the performer on his knees never fails to tickle your helper and cause the audience to go into fits of laughter. (Take a look at me doing this in the photo on the next page.) When you try this, don't get up until you're done with the child, whether performing or greeting. By staying down and knee-walking to your table to get a prop, then knee-walking back to the child, you'll get even more laughs. In this way you will be working at your assistant's level and garnering fantastic audience response.

"And let me stress this point: Although I get down on the child's level as a clown, it will work equally well for a magician, juggler, or other entertainer in regular dress."

Wonderful advice, Richard. That sure helps in the size difference department. But what are we going to do about chasing away the fear some children have of clowns? Having sat in on dozens of classes and sessions at various clown camps, let me share with you three key points in this area:

• Don't approach young children too quickly, especially if you detect that they are frightened. Drop to one knee to diminish your size, and wait for them to approach you.

• Never force little kids into close proximity with the clown, and don't allow well-meaning parents to do this either. Many parents do not realize that this may scare a child even more and destroy his or her good feelings for clowns for life.

• If the child is using mom, dad, or an older child for protection, interact or play with that person, seeming to ignore the frightened child. Often, the timid child will join in the play after he or she sees that mom or dad or brother is playing with you and realizes you're okay.

Richard Snowberg shares a little more advice at this point:

"Once you get into the kneeling down position, your young friend may get very familiar or bold—enough, in fact, to want to squeeze your nose or test your hair. This is something that requires you to be careful, since you don't want the child to pull off your nose or wig.

"For this reason, I often take the initiative and grasp both hands of my helper and press our noses together. Once more, this is a funny situation and one that birthday mothers love for picture taking, so don't forget to forewarn them of this occurrence."

This is a great photo opportunity, plus a way to let the timid child get accustomed to a real clown, and yet another way to provoke smiles and laughter, goodwill and love.

Remember, what you do as a clown and the way you deal with children goes much further than just you. It affects children and clowns around the world. So, watch out for young, timid children who you might inadvertently frighten. Treat them with care and gentle love.

Richard "Snowflake" Snowberg in 1978.

SHAKE HANDS FOR LAUGHS

One way to put children at ease is with a funny handshake. Shaking hands, of course, is a common greeting children see adults doing all the time, so it is accepted as normal. The act of shaking hands, therefore, puts the performer and helper on friendly ground. Furthermore, if you put humor into the handshake, the ground becomes even more friendly.

From the pages of my book *Children Laugh Louder*, let me share with you a dozen ways to shake hands and have fun. What others can you add to my list?

Snake-Turn

With two children, one standing on each side of you, extend your hand to shake hands with one child. As the child reaches for your hand, turn and shake the other child's hand. Repeat as desired.

Shake-Miss

Extend your hand to shake a child's, but purposely miss the child's hand by going to the right or left of the child's hand. Repeat this several times until you finally do shake the kid's hand.

Rubber Arm

Take the child's hand, and shake it up and down in snake-like fashion, giving the shake a rubbery effect.

Repeat Shake

With a child on your left, shake the child's right hand with your right hand. As you do so, place your left hand under the child's right elbow. When you finish the handshake, let go of the child's hand with your hand. Then, as the child starts to drop his hand back to his side, use your left hand at his elbow to pivot his forearm back up into the handshake position. Immediately take his right hand with yours, and shake it again. Repeat as desired to milk the gag for laughs. Even though this is a very old gag—I think it was invented by veteran school show magician Gene Gordon back in the 1920s—it still is immensely effective with children.

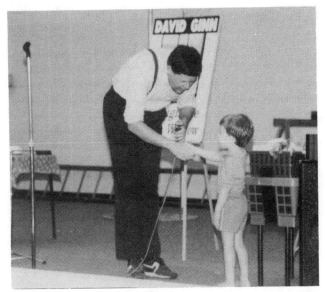

Shaking hands for a laugh on a gym stage.

Handshake Mix-Up

Extend your right hand toward a child to shake. Just as the child reaches out to take your hand, withdraw that hand and extend your left hand. This will at first confuse the child, but usually she will extend her left hand then. The moment she does, withdraw your left hand before she can grasp it, and again extend your right hand. Repeat this until you feel you've done it enough. Finally, grab the child's right hand in your right and the left hand in your left, crisscrossed, and shake both her hands at once. This usually gets a nice laugh.

The Missing Shake

Walk toward the child as he comes onto the stage and extend your hand to shake his, saying something like, "Here, let me shake your hand." As you get near the boy and he reaches out his hand, sidestep him and walk right past him. Stop a few feet past him, and look around as though you are confused. Finally, turn around and spot him. "Oh," you say, "there you are! I thought I lost you!" Then shake his hand, learn his name, and begin your routine.

Cow Hand

Reach for a child's hand to shake and say, "Here—let me shake your old cow hand!" It usually gets a laugh, especially if you happen to have a youngster wearing a cowboy suit or cowboy hat. (See Instant Costumes in Chapter 6.)

Rubber Hand

"Would you like to shake my hand?" you ask your audience volunteer. If he answers "yes," quickly pull out a rubber hand (novelty prop) and give it to him or her, saying, "Well, here it is—shake it all you want." If the child answers "no," pull out the rubber hand anyway and reply, "In that case, I'll just shake it myself!" Then take the rubber hand and either shake it like a handshake or hold it by one finger and shake it back and forth in front of you.

Strong Arm

Shake hands with an audience volunteer. As you do, act as though the child has superhuman strength in his hand, a super strong grip. Fall down on one knee, acting as if you are in pain and yell, "OUCH!" Let go of the child's hand, stand up, and rub your hand as though it is hurt. Remark, "Who do you think you are? Superman?" The idea of a child physically hurting a grown-up is very funny.

The Boxers

With two children, one on each side of you, first shake hands with each child. Then, have the two kids shake hands. After they shake, say to them, "And now, into your corners and COME OUT FIGHTING!"

Glue Hand

Shake hands with the child and act as though you cannot let go. Finally, pull your hand away and look at it. Ask the child, "What have you been eating—*glue?*"

Static Electricity

Go to shake hands with a child, and the moment you touch her hand, jump back as though you have received an electrical shock. Yell, "WOW! STATIC ELECTRIC-ITY!"

WHAT CHILDREN LIKE

The best way to entertain children is to offer them what they like. What things do children like in a show? Let's look at a short list, then you can add to it as you gain experience working with children.

Action and Pace

A slow, um-pah-pah show does not work for children these days. Remember, your live show must compete with everything they see on television, whether you like it or not. This is not to say you cannot have a quiet moment or two in your act. But generally, your program for children must move along with a steady pace. You must keep ahead of them like an engineer driving a train, making it their job to pay attention and keep up with you, the performer.

Animals

No doubt you understand how Walt Disney made his millions, starting with Mickey Mouse and Donald Duck. There's something basic in kids, in fact, in most adults, that makes us warm up to animals, especially dogs and cats and bunnies, even live doves and hamsters and goldfish. Here you have two choices: live animals, or imitation. For me, there's nothing better than a real live rabbit to make a hit with children. Your situation may not allow that. But there are imitation rabbits as well as stuffed animals of other types: Rocky Raccoon, the fur-covered spring animal puppet that many performers make appear alive in their hands, and other animal puppets of all types. Some little children actually believe those animal puppets are real when manipulated properly.

Clowns

Yes, most children love clowns. They are fascinated by the colorful clothing, the big shoes, the big red nose, and the strange variety of hair colors of our wigs. Remember, some little kids have strange ideas about clowns, thinking clowns are "born that way." To children, clowns are cartoon characters. Boston clown/magician Joe Howard told me a little boy met him up close one day and ran screaming back to his mother, "Mommy, Mommy! CLOWNS HAVE TEETH!"

Color

Children love colorful props—boxes, scarves, pictures, flowers, tubes, clothing. That's one reason children love clowns! This is not to say that everything you do must be gaudy. But remember the color factor when cooking up children's magic; instead of using a black and a white set of scarves, go for red and yellow.

Costumes

Yes, children love dressing up in mom and dad's clothing. You can have lots of fun using a bit of dress up in your program, plus it can help turn a simple trick into a full fledged routine. See examples of this in Chapter 6.

Finding You Out

Children love to think they've figured out your tricks, and this is okay. Often, I use "sucker tricks" where I let the children think they know how I did it; then I turn the tables on them at the end, with some surprise climax. We must be careful at this point not to finish such a trick as a smart aleck; instead, end the trick with being surprised yourself, or have some silly pseudoscientific explanation for why the trick worked.

Laughter

Yes, if I haven't said it by now, children love to laugh. And the best part for children's entertainers is that children open up more than teens or adults, let their inhibitions loose, and laugh louder! Why do you think I enjoy entertaining them so much? So, let's give them things to laugh about!

Magic

Understand that I am talking here about colorful, kid-oriented tricks with lots of kidbiz like you'll find in this book and in the books recommended in Appendix B. I am not talking about long, drawn-out card tricks which involve counting, or mentalism, or anything vulgar, naughty, or risque.

Music

These days children hear all kinds of music on a regular basis—rock, pop, soul, jazz, rap, classical—on radio, on TV, at school, at home, in the car. Using clean music that kids enjoy puts you, the performer, on their side, making you one of them in a way. Use the music as a friendly tool.

Playing and Having Fun

To children clowns and magicians are automatic symbols of fun and play. Even in my educational school programs, the kids intrinsically know that we're going to have fun. And I give them the fun they expect, using all of the above elements and more.

Stories

We all love stories, especially children. Often in magic and clowning we bring stories to life, using props and tricks and costuming to help with the visual side. If, as a clown, you choose simply to tell a story, you must do so as a clown, animating it every step of the way, acting it out with your face and hands and feet and body.

Scary Funny Stuff

A quick scare, such as a spring snake popping out of a can, will entertain children if you handle it right. How? Well, don't let the scare be too close to little children, for one thing. In other words, don't pop that spring snake out into a five-year old's face; instead, let it pop you in the face, or at least go over your head. Next, when the scare happens, you act frightened and ham it up to take any fright away from the children. The kids will laugh at you instead of being afraid of it. Believe me, it works! Remember the Clown-in-Trouble Syndrome? Yes, I'm sure you do! Final point: Let the scare be over quickly and turn it into laughter.

Remember, your clown show or magic show doesn't have to be all one thing. Children enjoy a mixture of things, a variety program using many different arts. Indeed, the real magic is in the fun and laughter and good feelings developed between the audience and the performer. And if that audience likes YOU, they'll like anything you do.

SHOWMANSHIP

A single chapter cannot cover everything you need to know about working with children, especially when you consider the gamut of venues in which clowns work: from school shows to birthday parties to walk-arounds and picnics. There's a mountain of good material in the books listed in Appendix B, and to tell you the truth, even though I've written lots about working with kids, I am still learning. Although I have discussed many aspects of showmanship so far, I'll wrap up this chapter with a trio of valuable hints on this matter for you to consider, then we'll jump back into the comedy, magic, and clowning.

Know Your Show

Before you ever step onto a stage in front of people, children or otherwise, know what you're going to do. The same thing applies to meet and greet situations on a close-up level. Know each trick, each gag, each joke. In an actual show, know the sequence of the tricks in the program. If you have to look at a piece of paper to know which trick comes next, you should have rehearsed more! To succeed as an entertainer, you must get past the mechanics of the tricks and the show before you can entertain with that show.

Be Organized

Know what comes next. Plan where your props will be, how you'll pick them up, where they'll go when finished. Have places on the stage—receptacles, I call them—where you put things away and take things out. Try to dispose of props during a performance in a neat, logical manner. Don't work on a junky, garbage-like stage. Keep it clean and neat, a better reflection on you.

Anticipate Audience Response

Be ready to receive applause or laughter when you think or know it might come. If you don't get the anticipated response, move right ahead. Audiences are much the same from place to place, but they can have differences too. If you don't get a certain response from a trick or gag, such as the demand from an audience member to "turn it around" (in a sucker trick), just pretend that someone in the audience said it. Then yell, "What? Who said that? Who said 'TURN IT AROUND?'" Then continue the trick as you usually do. Believe me, it works!

Frederick the Great anticipating audience response. If he flips those dishes onto the cement floor and breaks them, he'll get a big laugh and play up the result for comedy. On the other hand, if he successfully pulls the cloth from under the dishes without breaking a dish, he'll reap big applause for such a fantastic feat. Either way, Frederick wins—and so does the audience. What's your guess—did he succeed in pulling out the cloth without breaking a dish?

CHAPTER 5

SNAKY MAGIC FOR LAUGHS

A prop known as the *spring snake* can create fun in any show for children. Kids love the reaction caused by spring snakes. The snaky surprise sometimes causes a momentary scare, followed almost immediately by laughter. If the clown or magician plays up the sudden appearance of the snake for comedy, it produces even more laughter.

THE SPRING SNAKE

A spring snake is simply a metal spring covered with cloth or thin plastic. By collapsing or compressing this covered spring and securing it inside a container, it will stay small until the container is opened. A five-foot cloth-covered snake, for instance, collapses down to about two inches, yet springs open to 60 inches.

Some of the first spring snakes were covered with cloth in a snakeskin print, and thus came the idea of spring "snakes." As a kid, I first encountered these creatures in novelty cans of peanuts, peanut brittle, and supposed gift boxes. These containers would be eagerly opened, only to discover a spring snake popping out on you. The snake sprang out, scared you a bit, then made you laugh after you saw the silly thing that scared you.

Several years ago, one of the major producers of spring snakes stopped making them with cloth and began using plastic, which was less expensive. These are okay for novelty shop peanut cans, but not for clowns or magicians. The problem lies in the plastic covering: It is simply not porous enough to let the snakes open rapidly. There are holes punched here and there in the plastic, but there aren't enough. In addition, the plastic is thicker than cloth and slows down the popping out of the snake considerably.

In a nutshell, for clowning and magic shows, cloth-covered snakes are best.

Covering Your Snakes

The fact that thin cloth is more porous than plastic makes cloth-covered spring snakes zoom out of cans, boxes, and other hiding places—and that's what we kidshow performers want!

So what do clowns and magicians do?

Two answers: We either purchase cloth-covered snakes (which are more expensive now), or we re-cover the plastic-covered snakes with cloth ourselves, using the plastic cover as a pattern before throwing it away. Don't do like one clown I know, who sewed new cloth covers over the snakes, leaving the plastic covering on them. They'll never open up!

David Ginn with a spring snake coming out of his jumbo surprise wand.

Your next question is probably one I've heard at lectures and seminars across the United States: Where do I get snakeskin cloth material? My answer is always the same: *You don't need snakeskin material!* In fact, I'll go a step further and suggest that you may be better off without using a snake-like cloth. Why? Because I suspect that younger children, say under age five, are less frightened by colorful spring snakes that don't look like real snakes.

I've had snakes covered in a dozen different patterns and colors. I have orange snakes with black stripes and spots. Pink snakes with yellow and green flowers on them. Brown, blue, purple snakes. Red snakes with white dots all over them (they look like the measles!). Even spring snakes dressed up like magic wands.

My point is that the children don't care if the spring snakes look like real snakes. What excites them to laughter is the action of the snakes popping out. And children prefer bright colors anyway.

So cover your snakes colorfully!

Care, Loading, Hiding

If you're popping your spring snakes out on a daily or even weekly basis, there's no great problem with leaving them collapsed most of the time. However, I've found that leaving them collapsed for months at a time diminishes the strength of their spring. Therefore, if you're not going to use your spring snakes for a month or more, let them out of their containers so they can relax in their open position. That way they'll last longer.

It amuses me to see performers who are unfamiliar with spring snakes try to load them for the first time. Indeed, several of my magic show assistants have attempted to collapse the snakes in their hands first and *then* insert them into a can or box. That doesn't work. The snakes will end up popping out in your face.

The proper way to load spring snakes is to feed them into the container bit by bit, letting them collapse themselves as you push more snake down on top of what is already inside. If you are loading more than one snake into a container, then hold down the first snake with one hand while you start feeding the next snake. As the last snake goes inside, you apply a lid or cap to keep the snakes secured.

The lid or cap must be one that locks down, such as a screw-on, snap-on, or latch-down top. A slide-on cap will not work because the snakes will eventually pop it off.

Keep in mind, that the container into which you load the snakes must be just slightly larger than the snake's diameter. The five-foot snakes I use primarily are approximately $2^3/_4$-inches in diameter and fit nicely into a three-inch can or tube. However, if I were to load them into an eight-inch tube, they would turn sideways and possibly jam instead of popping out. On the other hand, these snakes loaded into a three-inch diameter space will pop out easily and in the direction you want.

One way to load snakes into a larger container is to mount loading cans for the snakes into the larger compartment. Figure 4 shows you the idea, based on my use of MAK Magic's drawer box. Placing a loose snake in the box simply did not work when I first used it in my "Computerized Magic Show." So I used duct tape to secure a small can inside the front of the loading drawer as

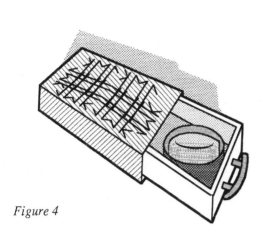

Figure 4

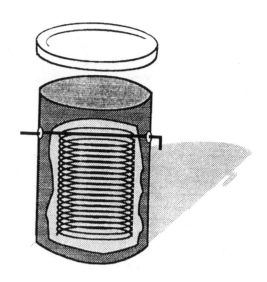

shown. Then I compressed one five-foot snake into the can and slid the drawer shut. When I opened the front part of the drawer during the show, the snake jumped right out.

The Pin Method

Figure 5 illustrates a relatively sure way of holding spring snakes down inside a can or box, even when there is no lid to do the job. Drill a hole in each side of the can or box as shown. Then make a pin from a coat hanger wire, being sure to bend or curl a handle so you can pull it out. To load, push the snake down into the can below the hole level. Slide the pin in one side, over the top of the snake and out the hole on the other side of the can. With a wooden box, one side can have a hole drilled only partway through so the pin doesn't show from the front.

The pin method can also be used to create a second or double load of snakes. For example, you load one or more snakes into a potato chip can, holding them in place with a pin. On top of this, place several potato chips, then snap on the lid (see Figure 6). When you open the potato chip can in a show, take out the chips and eat them. Snap the lid back on, and slide out the pin as you do. The next time you open the lid, perhaps to offer chips to someone, the snakes will fly out.

Some performers I've met like to have several snakes pop out at once, but object to having to pick up and reload five or six snakes. A clever way to get around this, if you desire, is to sew your snake load together into one long snake. Thus, six five-foot snakes become one long 30 foot snake. Reloading is merely a matter of feeding one long snake back into its hiding place. Though I have not yet

Figure 5

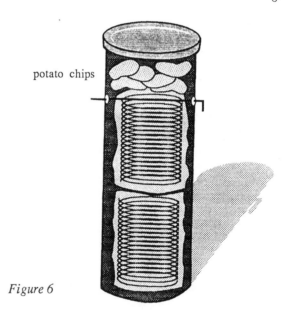

potato chips

Figure 6

personally used this method, I know several people who have done so successfully and I may employ it myself in the future. For now, I prefer having the snakes pop out separately.

Spring Snake Safety

Where do we let these spring snakes pop out? An excellent question. First, I will tell you where *not* to let spring snakes pop out—*into the audience.*

You should never throw or toss anything out into a crowd. Doing so courts danger for both the audience members and the performer. Audience members trying to catch whatever is thrown may get hurt in the scuffle, and the performer could end up in a lawsuit for causing such injuries.

Never, never, never throw anything into the audience, especially a kidshow audience. And never shoot spring snakes into your audience because (1) someone could get hurt grabbing at the snakes, and (2) kids will pull, tear, stretch, and basically ruin your spring snakes.

Let your spring snakes pop out *onto yourself or a fellow performer in the act.* Yes, having the snakes pop out on *you* is absolutely the safest and best bet, almost always creating more laughs if you handle the situation correctly. There is no danger to the kids in the audience, and any danger to you is created purely by the way you act when the snakes attack.

I'll talk about how you act a bit later in the chapter.

CAN ON THE TABLE

Have a metal can sitting on your table. The can should be a solid color so that no one knows what is inside it. Use office supply stick-on letters to attach the words "DO NOT OPEN" onto the front of the can. Of course, inside the can are three or four compressed spring snakes.

At some point in your performance, tell the kids, "Whatever you do, don't let me open that can!" Use this as a running gag. Keep saying things like, "I wonder what's in there? Well, never mind . . . because it says DO NOT OPEN." This whets the kids' appetites for the big finish.

Very late in the show, if not at the actual end, pick up the can and pretend you have decided to open it. Egg the kids on by having them vote. "How many want me to open it? Raise your hands! How many do not? Raise your hands! Oh, I can't decide."

Finally, you decide to take a little peek. You open the can just a little, look inside, tell the kids how dark it looks inside the can, how you can't see anything—then suddenly you let the snakes pop out, straight up over your head, yelling "SNAKES!" and jumping around, letting the snakes come down right on top of you.

And the children love it!

Why? Because kids enjoy seeing a performer goof up, get in trouble, even get *playfully hurt* in a slapstick sort of way. I call it the Performer-in-Trouble Syndrome, and it's a great way to get laughs.

BACK IN THE CAN

One way to create that performer-in-trouble image is to have trouble putting the snakes back in the can during the show. Bev Bergeron, magician and formerly Rebo the Clown on "The Magic Land of Allakazam" TV show, is a master of this.

With the snakes out of the can, he picks them off the floor one at a time. Carefully he loads them back into the can. As he holds a snake in place and reaches for the next snake, he lets go of the one in the can and it zooms back out. He repeats this several times, loading the snakes faster and faster, each time letting them jump out.

Finally, he gets all the snakes in the can, but he can't find the lid. It's on his table. When he reaches for the lid, all the snakes come charging out, and the audience is in stitches of laughter.

How would this fit you?

Bev Bergeron as Rebo.

Snake attack.

THE SNAKE ATTACK

One of my favorite ways to combine spring snakes with the Performer-in-Trouble Syndrome is to have the snakes attack me. The trick itself doesn't matter, just as long as the snakes pop out on the performer.

When they do, I go momentarily crazy. I yell and scream, "SNAKES! SNAKES!" The snakes jump out of whatever I'm holding and shoot into the air directly over me and come down directly on top of my head and shoulders. I treat them as though they are alive, grabbing them and wrestling with them, wrapping them around my neck and arms, hitting at them—*fighting for my life!*

Believe me, the effect on children is absolutely electric. They just love seeing a clown, magician, or other performer have something like this happen.

I continue to fight with the snakes for ten to thirty seconds, depending on audience reaction and staging, and the children laugh their heads off during the entire episode.

Finally, I toss the snakes out of sight, either offstage or behind my portable backdrop curtains. Often partially exhausted from this "snake fight," I lean down on my table

to rest for a moment and get a good breath of air. This action also lets the children calm down from all the laughter before I continue my performance.

FAKE SNAKE ATTACK

In my "Computerized Magic Show," I employed what I called a "fake" snake attack. Basically, I told the kids there was something in the empty drawer box when I peeked into it.

"It's something long . . . and brown . . . and green . . . and slimy . . . with two black eyes . . . and it's . . . a . . . S-N-A-K-E!"

As I stretched out my words dramatically, building them up, I then jerked the drawer open when I yelled "SNAKE!" and rushed toward the edge of the stage. But I also pulled open the *empty* drawer, immediately showing it empty to the kids. Then I started laughing.

"Ha! Ha! Ha! I can't believe you fell for that! I was just joking . . . it was just a trick . . . there was no snake at all."

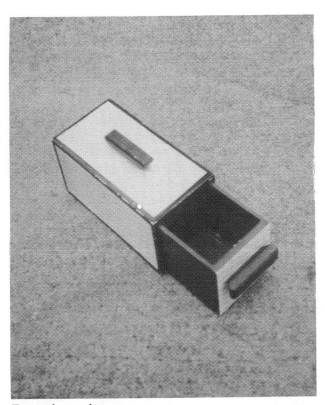

Empty drawer box.

As I said those words, I closed the drawer and kept laughing.

"That's right. There was no snake. And you thought there really was a snake in there. Well, there couldn't be a snake in there because I'm afraid of snakes, and I won't have a S-N-A-K-E!"

At this point I opened the drawer, this time releasing the spring snake and letting it jump out right in front of my face. I respond by going into my snake fight. I watched a videotape of this last year, and boy, did the kids howl with laughter. Yes, folks, it really works!

REPEAT SNAKE ATTACK

Sometimes the snakes come back for a repeat attack. Let me give you three examples from my experience.

At several shows my daughter Autumn was behind my backdrop curtain when I tossed the snakes over it. Playfully, she picked up a snake and threw it over the curtain back onto the stage after the kids and I thought everything was over. The kids started laughing again as I had a second snake fight. If you have an assistant, you could work something like this in every show.

In many performances I work under the basketball goal on a school gym floor. If the snakes shoot high enough, occasionally one may lodge and hang on the basketball goal above my head. Sometimes i don't even realize it; even if I do, I don't let on to the children that I see the hanging snake.

When I've tossed all the snakes aside, the children start yelling about the hanging snake, but I ignore it and play ignorant. No matter how loud they shout or where they point, I look everywhere except above my head. Finally, I get the idea and look up. I jump back, start yelling again, jump up and pull the snake down, fight with it a bit and toss it offstage. This second fight is always shorter than the first, something like an encore.

My third example involves the jumbo surprise wand, which shoots out five snakes or more. I always release these straight up, and all but the last snake leaves the wand tube. Due to the length of the wand, the last snake stays inside and hangs half way out. I purposely lay the wand over my shoulder after the snakes are out, pretending not to see the last snake which is dangling out of the wand behind by back. Sometimes I even kick the snakes off the stage. Naturally, the children tell me about the one in the wand. I pretend not to see it, but finally do, have a fight with it, and toss it off.

JUMBO SURPRISE WAND

Invented by California magician Steve Schreiner in 1980 and manufactured by me since that time, the jumbo surprise wand is a hard-shell plastic wand about three inches in diameter and four feet long. It has the advantage of a screw-on cap, which holds spring snakes inside perfectly. I supply these with five five-foot spring snakes, though the wand tube will hold more—a whole lot more, as you will soon see.

Joe White (Clif the Balloon Clown) brought his own jumbo wand to my lecture at the Clowns of America convention in Indianapolis. "Use this in your lecture," he offered, "and show them how many snakes it will hold."

Joe had re-covered his plastic snakes with thin lycra (a synthetic fabric) in a half dozen bright colors, each snake terminating in a different eight-inch color band so that they looked like colorful wobbly magic wands. When I uncapped the wand at my lecture, it took about 15 seconds for all the snakes to come out. Why? Joe had collapsed 18 five-foot snakes into the four-foot wand—90 feet of spring snakes!

Believe me, it was quite a sight. The most I'd ever used was five snakes, but 18 snakes made a great showing! Now Joe is planning on adding two more snakes to make it an even 100 feet!

In my book *Kidbiz* and on my videotape *Live Kidbiz*, you can see how I put the jumbo surprise wand to good use in a routine involving a group of children up on the stage. Also, in the instructions for the wand, I offer about two dozen ways to employ it for clown show or magic show comedy.

My basic concept has been to try a magic trick using many different wands to make it work. Whether the wands or the trick works is not important. What is important is that you finally resort to your "great big, giant-jumbo, super-duper colossal, A-number-1, customized, monster-size magic wand . . . and I mean THE BIG ONE!"

At the end of the routine, after trying to make the trick work, I have the helpers return to their seats. I then release the snakes under the pretense of checking the battery in the wand, followed by a snake fight as I have already shared.

MY FAVORITE SNAKE ROUTINES

In a handful of my books I have shared children's show routines involving the playful use of spring snakes.

Professional Magic for Children, my first major textbook, still houses my updated "Snake Can" routine employing potato chip cans with snap-on lids, which will hold three to five large snakes without popping off prematurely. My long-time friend Bruce "Sparkles" Johnson told me, "I get so many laughs from my embellished version of it that I often use it to close my show!"

In *Magic and Monsters for Kids I Love,* a book of spooky magic I wrote in 1984, I shared my "Dracula's Coffin" routine, a combination of Texas magician Van Cleve's "Comedy Jumping Coffin" and my own "Comedy Lunch Box." Two child helpers wear monster masks, a blood-stained handkerchief disappears, the 12-inch tall coffin dances around on my table, and finally, spring snakes pop out of the coffin with the missing handkerchief attached.

Later I developed a routine called "Which Movie," involving movie posters, snack food cans, and a large six-foot spring snake I call my "dragon." I used this in my imagination show called "Through the Magic Window" in the 1987-88 school year and published it in *Nearly Unpublished.* You can also see it performed live at a school on my fourth video, *Live Kidbiz II.*

Which brings us to the close of this chapter—almost.

Back in the 1970s I developed a school show routine with a pet show theme, adapted from Bill Larsen, Sr.'s book, *Conjuring for Children.* It involved four audience helpers, signs and sounds, and a child's school lunch box. After a year of performing it in some 300 school, church, and party situations, I published it as a little booklet describing the entire routine. I called it the "Comedy Lunch Box."

Ten years later, since the booklet was out of print, I condensed it for inclusion in the book and audio tape set, *School Show Presentation.* Since that set of books will be out of print in the next few years, and since I plan no reprint of that project, it seems only fitting for me to share my "Comedy Lunch Box" routine in these pages for a third time, though for most of you it will be the first time.

I hope you not only enjoy it, but adopt it, adapt it, and use it.

COMEDY LUNCH BOX

Brief Description

With four children on the stage, you hand out signs they hang around their necks, listing four animals from a school pet show. In telling the story, you produce rubber food from a school lunch box. A first place blue ribbon that is awarded to you visibly changes into a spring snake and escapes. More snakes pop out of the lunch box, bringing the missing blue ribbon with them to conclude the fun.

For this routine you will need four cardboard signs with the words "DOG," "CAT," "BIRD," and "RABBIT" printed on them. Mine have strings for hanging them around the helpers' necks.

In addition, you'll need three 12-inch blue ribbons, each one two inches wide. One ribbon is loose; a second ribbon is attached to the ribbon that changes into a snake; and the third ribbon is sewn to one of the two spring snakes that will pop out of the gimmicked lunch box.

Add to this as many rubber production food items as you can afford or can fit into the lunch box, and you're ready to perform.

Before getting into the full explanation, I'll let you read the patter and performance, transcribed from an audio tape of a live performance.

The Performance

I want to tell you what happened to me when I was in the third grade at my school. Oh, I tell you, something unusual happened. When I was in the third grade, we had a big pet show at my elementary school, and they let all the kids bring animals to school. I mean, dogs and cats, birds and fish, turtles and lizards, and snakes.

You know what I brought? I brought my rabbit, "Leroy the First." I've had many rabbits that I named Leroy, but I brought him. And they were having the radio station come out to give a live broadcast at our pet show. In fact, the radio DJ was going to award a blue ribbon to the best pet right on the air during the live broadcast. I want to show you what happened, but in order to show you, I need to get some very quiet people to come and help me recite the pet show.

Now, let me see who I can get. I want to get this girl right here in the pink. Come on up and help. There's one. I need to get another girl and a boy too. Let's see. I think, over here, I see a boy over there in a light blue jacket. Light blue. A little, short gentleman there. Let's have him come up. I think I need another girl and another boy. Here's a girl in a blue jacket right here. You come up and help me. And I need one more boy to help me. One more boy. Way at the back, the boy in the brown jacket. Right there. And he's got on a burgundy shirt. Come on up. Let's give them all a great big round of applause. (Kids come up.)

Okay, you come right on over here and stand right there. And let's have the other girl come stand right here. (Have fun moving the kids around.) Okay, tell you what, you two switch about so I can see her. You come here, and you come here. Now, I want you to come here on this side, and you come around here on this side. Here, you can stand right along there, and you stand along on his other side, and let us find out the names.

We'll start right here. What's your name? Carrie? Your name? Deshonda with a D? Lashonda. Okay, Carrie and Lashonda. What's your name? Carlos! Your name? Stevie! Hey, hey—are you Stevie Wonder, the famous singer? You're not? Oh, I guess not.

Okay. Well, we've got Carlos, Stevie, Lashonda, and Carrie. And let me get the signs. (Pick up animal signs.) Today, as we re-create the pet show, I brought some signs so these people can play the parts of some of the ANIMALS at the pet show. Now first, I don't know if you all know how to read these signs. Tell me if you can read them. What does that sign say? (Dog.) Dog, that's right. I'm going to let Carlos play the part of the dog. Carlos, we'll hang this around your neck. And Carlos, I want you to make the sound of a dog. Let me hear you. (Roof roof.) That's right.

Next, Stevie is going to play—the cat. Hang this around your neck like that, Stevie. Stevie, let me hear you make the sound of a cat. (Me-ow.) I think that was a cat with somebody stepping on his tail!

What does this next sign say? (Bird.) Bird. The bird is the word. And you, Carrie, are going to be our bird. Put that around your neck right there. Carrie, let me hear the sound of a bird.

(Tweet-tweet.) Right.

And last, Lashonda, you're going to play the part of the rabbit. Here we go. Now, I want you to give us the sound of a rabbit. (Pause.) Lashonda, give everybody the sound of a rabbit. What? Don't you know what a rabbit sounds like? You don't? Haven't you all ever heard this one? "Smack! Smack! Eh, what's up, doc?" That's a rabbit sound.

Now, let me tell you what happened when the DJ started to award the blue ribbon. Wait a minute. I'm getting a little hungry. Let me just check and see what my wife packed me for lunch. Hold on. (Bring out box.) Let me get my lunch box.

Ah! Here's my Snoopy lunch box. Let me see what we've got here. I'm not going to eat in front of everybody; I'm just kind of hungry, and I'm going to see what I'm going to eat. I'll eat it after the show. Oh man, look at this. (Production begins.) I've got corn on the cob! I love that! And a nice big cucumber. Look at that. I can eat that, slice

it up. And for Vitamin C, a nice juicy orange. Yeah. And look at this, I've got some juice. Ha-ha! Well, it's Coca-Cola juice. I'll put that right over there. And here's a nice, sweet, juicy pear. And some cherry pie. And some fish! (Skeleton fish.) Oh, I think the cat got to it! Get that out of the way. Well, that's about the size of it for lunch today. (Close the empty box and operate the mechanism as shown in Figure 7.) We can just close that up, put it over here, and I'll eat this stuff later. (Place the lunch box aside, but in sight.)

Figure 7

Let me tell you what happened in my pet show. They selected my rabbit to win the blue ribbon as the best pet. And the radio DJ went and got the blue ribbon, and he was about to announce it right there on the air, LIVE. Hold on, I'll get a blue ribbon and show you. (Get ribbon with spring snake attached. See Figure 8.) Here we go. Just as

Figure 8

the DJ started to award the blue ribbon, a terrible thing happened. When he started to pin that blue ribbon on the cage, a great big, long, mean, ugly—SNAKE GOT LOOSE! (Release snake, which pops into view.) And ate up the blue ribbon and took off out the door, and nobody could catch him. Oh, it was terrible. Everybody was sad. My rabbit started crying in his rabbit cage. (Retrieve signs as animals are mentioned.) And the bird started weeping in his bird food, and the cat started meowing in his meow cat mix. And the dog was going err-err-err! Oh, it was terrible. (Put signs aside.)

But, you know what? Back in the third grade I knew a little magic. Even back then. And I thought and I thought, and I looked to the side, and there was my lunch box. It was empty, but I thought maybe I could use it. So I picked up my lunch box, and I waved my hand, and I thought some special magic words, and I snapped my fingers, and do you know what happened? When I opened that lunch box, do you know what was inside? A blue ribbon? Yeah! And a couple of SNAKES! Wait a minute. But they were friendly snakes and they brought back the blue ribbon and saved the pet show. (Wave end of the snake to show blue ribbon.) And I want to thank all of these nice people for coming up here and helping me. And as they sit down, give them a big round of applause. Thank you.

Mechanics of It All

Now we'll dissect this whole routine briefly, describing the lunch box, loading the snakes, ribbon to snake, the performance, and a final note.

Using a standard kid's school lunch box, metal or plastic, rivet two clean tin cans into one side. One pop rivet in the bottom of each has held mine in place for 10 years.

Prepare two metal tracks and rivet them in place as shown in Figure 9.

Prepare a metal door. This door is the size that will slide into the pair of metal tracks in the lunch box and cover the open cans.

To the center of the door, rivet a swivel arm as shown in Figure 10. Use a washer between the arm and door for easy movement. Note that the arm is curved, which makes the mechanism work easily in performance.

Spray paint the entire inside of the lunch box black, including the arm, door, and cans. Glue black felt into the open side of the lunch box.

Attach one blue ribbon about 14 inches long to a five-foot spring snake (mine is sewn). Compress the snakes and the ribbon into the two cans, one snake per can.

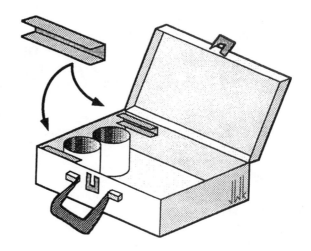

Figure 9

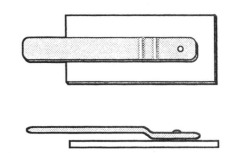

Figure 10

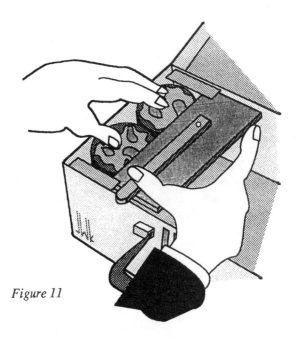

Figure 11

While holding the snakes down, slide the metal door into the tracks and over the snakes in the cans. The door will hold the snakes down until release time. The metal arm should be pointing to the back as in Figure 11.

Cut a piece of wooden dowel or broomstick to a length of about 2½ inches (1¼ inches in diameter). Paint it black.

Attach a screw eye to one end, and drill a ¼-inch hole through that end as in Figure 12. Get a large, long nail that will slide through the hole and stick out about one to two inches on each side.

Cut a disc out of wood or masonite slightly larger than the wooden core. Attach it to the core end as in Figure 13, using a long screw, not nails. Do not tighten it yet.

Remove the cover from a five-foot spring snake. If your snakes are plastic covered, use cheap thin cloth to make new covers and discard the plastic. Insert the wooden core into one end of the uncovered snake spring as in Figure 13.

Tuck part of the spring wire between the disc and the core. Then screw the disc on tight.

At the other end of the snake, tape the spring wires together to give a smoother opening. See Figure 14.

Slide the cloth cover over the snake starting at the core end. Using needle and thread, stitch the cloth cover around the end of the spring as shown in Figure 15.

Now slide the snake spring all the way back to the core, insert the nail, and the snake is kept compressed. Allow the blue ribbon to stick out as was illustrated in Figure 8.

Get four kids on the stage and do the comedy bit with the signs.

Introduce the lunch box. Make the food production.

As you close the box, swivel the metal arm out to the left as in Figure 7, and *shove* the arm to your right. This slides the metal door to the right and releases the snakes. At the same time you do this, hold the lid down. The moment you complete this action, completely close and latch the lid. Place the lunch box aside.

As you talk about the blue ribbon, reach into your bag or table and pick up the ribbon to snake. Pull the nail out and leave it. Bring it out, wave the ribbon around, and release to let the snake engulf the ribbon. Wave the snake around then toss it aside.

Pick up the lunch box, patter as described, then open the box to let snakes appear. I always let the snakes jump out on *me*, never on the children. Be sure and hold up the snake with the blue ribbon to show it has returned and emphasize that these are *friendly snakes*.

Your ribbon to snake can be made smaller if your hand is small. You could cut down the spring from five to

Figure 12

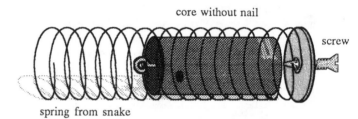

Figure 13

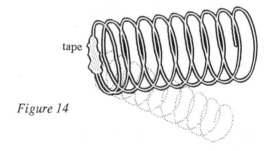

Figure 14

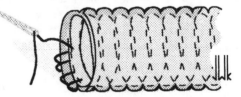

Figure 15

two or three feet, or you could use one of the smaller 18-24 inch springs found in those trick peanut cans. Because I have big hands, I've always preferred the largest snake possible for stage use. For yourself, adapt and enjoy.

By now I have just one thing left to say: If I haven't convinced you to use spring snakes in your act in some way, I've missed my mark. They are SO-O-O funny—if properly used.

CHAPTER 6

MAGICAL FUN WITH KIDS

In this chapter I will share with you several ways to have fun with children, using comedy magic as a base. The routines discussed here and in following chapters outline various tricks and gags that can be adapted by the clown magician. Use them as a basis for developing your own routines, incorporating your own unique style and personality. These routines will serve as guides for developing your own creativity. When adapting any of these routines to your clown character, remember to embellish them with your own brand of silly talk, facial and physical expressions, exaggeration, and enthusiasm. Be silly, be fun, and be entertaining!

FOLLOW INSTRUCTIONS

Begin by inviting a boy to come up on stage with you. Before you start the magic, tell him he must be able to follow instructions. Just to make sure, you'll give him a simple test.

Have him stand with both feet flat on the floor and hands by his sides. Tell him to do what you say as quickly as possible, starting with: "Right hand up!" Pause to make sure he follows. "Right hand down! Left hand up! Left hand down! Very good, Chip. Now, let's try it again: Right hand up! Right hand down! Left hand up! Left hand down!

"Right FOOT up! Right foot down! Left foot up! Left foot down!"

Give the boy a moment to rest, then resume.

"Now, let's try it one more time: Right hand up! Left hand up! Right hand down! Left hand down! Right hand up! Left hand up! Right FOOT up! Left FOOT UP!"

By this time the boy is trying to do everything so right that it gets a big laugh when you tell him to have both feet up at the same time. After getting this laugh, tell the boy, "That's a good try. You passed the test, so let's try some magic!"

Move into a clown magic routine.

CHICKEN FROM THE COAT

This is not a stand-alone trick in itself. But it's a funny and often amazing bit of kidshow business if you present it correctly.

In performance, you invite a boy who is wearing a jacket or coat onto the stage. You remark about how nice his coat is, pull it open, and immediately pull out a rubber chicken, fish, or other comedy production item.

I'll describe this routine using a rubber chicken, since nearly every clown and magician has one. If you don't, you should! It's an automatic, visual laugh.

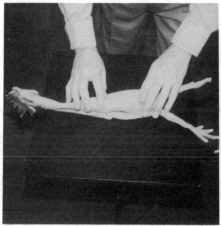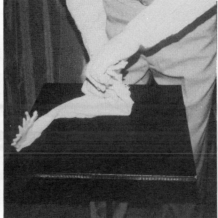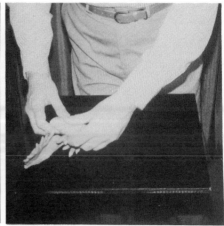

Folding a rubber chicken.

Fold and roll the rubber chicken as shown above. Then hide it in one of two places: (1) your back pocket, as shown in Figure 16, or (2) in a secure place in the top of your bag, case, or table. (See Figure 17.) You could even hide it in your left side pocket as long as no bulges show. If necessary, use a strong rubber band around the chicken to hold it compressed. I prefer not to do this if possible, since it is something else to deal with during the production.

Bring the boy on stage (with a round of applause) and stand him to your left. If the chicken is hidden in the table, bag, or case, stand the boy right in front of it.

Learn the young fellow's name and shake his hand. Then remark about his "nice coat" and pull his jacket open as in Figure 18. As you do this with your right hand, use the jacket's cover to sneak the rubber chicken from out of

your pocket or the table with your left hand. (See Figure 19.) Audience attention will be on the jacket. Remember, they don't know what you're going to do!

With your left hand, bring the collapsed chicken to the boy's back. Then reach inside his coat with your right hand as you simultaneously shove the chicken up under his coat with your left hand. Grab the chicken's feet with your right hand and pull it into view. (See Figure 20.)

The chicken immediately opens, and for all the kids can see, it looks as if the chicken came right out of the boy's coat.

"Well, George, do you always carry a CHICKEN in your coat? You're really prepared! Got a Coca-Cola and a peach pie on you too?"

It's quick, fairly simple . . . and it gets a laugh. But move now into a more solid, complete routine.

Figure 16

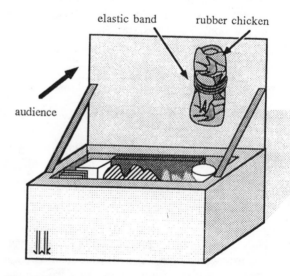

elastic band   rubber chicken

audience

Figure 17

Figure 18

Figure 19

Figure 20

INSTANT COSTUMES

One way to embellish your kidshow routines is to costume your helpers on stage. In a baking routine, for instance, I've used two very simple apron costumes. These have Velcro tabs at the back, which overlap by six inches to ensure I can fit almost any child. See the photo on the next page. Also, sewn inside a two-inch hem at the waist of the apron is a plastic apron band, available for just a few dollars at fabric stores. This secures the apron to the child's waist.

To quickly put the apron on a child, I have the child face me, and lift her arms. I pull the apron band open, immediately place it around the girl's waist, and let it close. Then I lift the front of the apron up and around her neck where the Velcro overlaps in back.

Removing the apron is as easy as pulling the Velcro apart, then opening the apron waistband. Getting the costume on or off takes less than three seconds.

Using this apron band/Velcro system, you can make other "instant costumes." For a sketch in my "Jungle Tales of Magic" library programs, I made a set of Tarzan and Jane apron costumes.

Apron costumes.

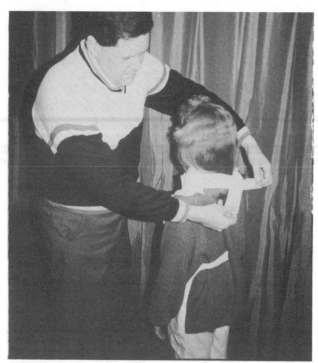

Putting on the instant apron takes about three seconds.

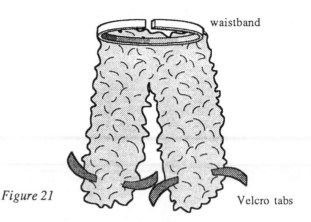

Figure 21   Velcro tabs

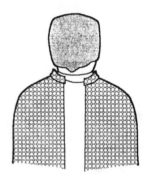

Figure 22

Figure 23

Velcro tabs

Figure 24

Would you like to make an "instant cowboy?" Make a vest for him, then do a set of chaps using the apron band at his waist and perhaps Velcro leg tabs as in Figure 21. A cowboy hat completes the outfit.

You can make a one-size-fits-all shirt, even with tie, as follows: Get a cheap shirt for, say, a 12-year old. Cut the shirt wide open at the back as in Figure 22. Button the front of the shirt and sew it closed. Hem the back and attach Velcro tabs (Figure 23). Then make or sew a clip-on tie in place, permanently attached to the shirt. Short sleeves make it easier, but if you must use long sleeves, eliminate the cuff buttons to facilitate getting the shirt on and off. All you have to do with the shirt is slip it over the boy's arms, then touch the Velcro tabs to each other as shown.

Halloween costumes, you buy and save, could fill the bill. Just figure out ways to get them on and off the children quickly in order to maintain the pace of your performance. If you have to spend time buttoning buttons, snapping snaps, or tying string tie closures, your show will drag. I suggest you convert everything to Velcro.

Here's another way to create an instant costume, depending on what you want the child to represent: Make a simple one-piece cloth costume as shown in Figure 24. All you do is bunch it up, have the child raise her arms, then drop the costume over her head and arms. It falls and

Tarzan and Jane apron costumes.

covers the child almost completely. Again, make it a size that fits an average 12-year old or under. And depending on what color you make it, it could be any number of things:

White	Angel
Purple	Queen, King
Black	Witch, Pilgrim
Brown	Monk, Washwoman
Gray	Shepherd, Hermit
Gold	Statue of Liberty
Blue	Princess
Yellow	Mother Nature
Red	Flame of New Orleans
Green	Swamp Thing

Add some kind of headgear—a hat, a halo, a crown, a wig perhaps—and give the child something to hold— a fake torch, a staff, a magic wand—and you have an instant costume to jazz up your magic routine.

Keep in mind that kids *love* to dress up, and by adding costumes or other props to your show, you add another fun dimension to your clowning and magic. If you've never tried costuming kids for laughs, here's your chance. You'll be pleasantly surprised at the outcome.

THE APPLE/WORM CANS

A few years ago I used this routine in over 50 day care center and kindergarten shows. It uses three children, and though the magic is minimal, the comedy is perfect for kids. The truth is, even though I wasn't wearing makeup, I considered this a clown routine.

Originally, I purchased the apparatus for this routine from Steve Bender at Ickle Pickle Products in St. Louis, Missouri. Since the trick is no longer in production, Steve has given me permission to explain it so you can make it yourself if you desire.

The routine is simple. Inviting three children on stage, the clown explains that he has four canisters—red, yellow, blue, and green—with something inside each, three apples and something else in the fourth. The children choose one can each and open them to find apples. The clown opens the fourth, and a large worm springs out on the clown, much to the delight of the children.

For this routine you'll need four small canisters (red, yellow, blue, green) with lids that screw on or snap on securely. Put a bit of tissue paper in the bottom of each can, and put a nicely carved wooden apple inside each of three cans—let's say the red, yellow, and blue. Inside the green can, put a spring snake covered with green cloth. That's the can that you, the performer, will end up getting.

Now, let's look at how you'll force the green can on yourself while getting the three children to take the other colors.

Cut four pieces of black posterboard as follows: 5 x 8½ inches, 5 x 8 inches, 5 x 7½ inches, and 5 x 7 inches. You'll also need a 6 x 9-inch envelope with an open end. (See Figure 25.) As long as you're buying this stuff at an office supply store, purchase some red, yellow, blue, and green colored stick-on dots, about 1½ - 2 inches in

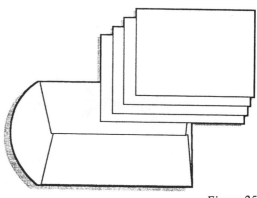

Figure 25

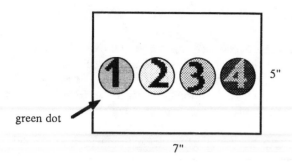

green dot

7"

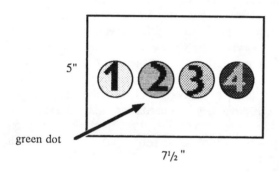

5"

green dot

7½"

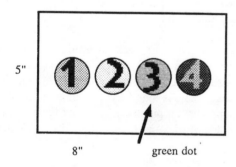

5"

8"

green dot

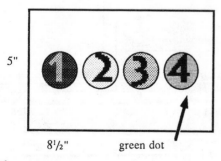

5"

8½"

green dot

Figure 26

diameter, and some black stick-on numbers about an inch tall. You'll need the numbers 1-2-3-4, four of each.

Prepare the cards *exactly* as shown in Figure 26. On the shortest card position the green dot first on the card to the left and the number 1 on it. The second card (5 x 7½) has the green dot in second position with a number 2 on it. The third card (5 x 8) has the green dot in third position with a number 3 on it, followed by the fourth card (5 x 8 ½) with the green dot in fourth position and a number 4 on it.

Place these on top of each other as in Figure 27, the shortest card on top and the longest on the bottom, and slide all four cards into the envelope as shown. This size is fine for birthday parties, kindergartens, and other shows up to about 100 children. For larger audiences, just use a larger envelope and bigger cards, making each card one half-inch larger.

You're now all set to perform, so on with the show.

"Speaking of food, my wife told me to go to the grocery store and buy some apples so she could make us an apple pie tomorrow. Do you know what I did with the apples I bought? I put each one in a separate little plastic canister . . . and here are the canisters."

I bring them out for display in a stand. This is just a board painted black with four holes large enough to slide the cans through; the lids prevent them from going all the way through. This is not absolutely necessary for the trick, but it makes a nice display.

"But do you know what? One of those apples had something wrong with it." I pause to think. "Oh, I know what it was: One of those apples had a little hole in it. What do you think could make a hole in an apple?"

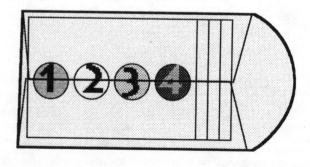

Figure 27

"A WORM!" the kids shout, and I jump back in surprise.

"A worm?" I say. "Now wait a minute! I'm afraid . . . really AFRAID of worms. And my wife is really, absolutely, TOTALLY AFRAID of WORMS. And if I took those apples home, and she found a worm in one, I'd be in HOT WATER. Do you know what that means? It means I'd be in BIG TROUBLE!

"I'd better find out which one has a hole in it and get rid of it. But to do that, I'll need to get some quiet people who are sitting down, raising their hands, without saying a word, to come up here and help me."

At this point I pick three children from various parts of the room. Let's call them Dena, Audrey, and Chip. After learning their names, I proceed.

"Well, I have four cans and only three helpers . . . so I'll be the fourth person. I'll let each one of you pick a number, and that way we'll decide who gets which can.

"Dena, you pick the first number—1, 2, 3, or 4. Which will you have? Four? Okay. How about you, Audrey? You can have 1, 2, or 3. Two? Okay. And Chip, would you like number 1 or 3? Three? That's fine. So Dena has 4, Audrey 2, Chip 3, and that leaves me with number 1, I guess.

"Now here is an envelope, and in this envelope I have a card with some big colored dots on it. And each

David Ginn holding plastic canisters in stand and one of the cards.

colored dot has a number on it, and that will tell us who gets which color."

I've picked up the envelope and reached into it to remove one card. If my number is 1, I remove the first card, the shortest one. If I'm 2, I slide out the second card; if 3, the third; if 4, the longest. Whichever card I pull out has my number on a *green* background, thereby forcing the green color on me. Yes, it's somewhat backwards, but it works in my story.

I display the card so the children and audience can see.

"Now who had number 4?" I ask. "Oh, Dena. So that means Dena gets the red can." I remove the red can from the display stand and hand it to Dena, telling her not to open it.

"Who had number 3? Chip? Okay, that means Chip gets . . ." I pause and let the audience tell me. "Right . . . the yellow can. Here, you hold the yellow can. And Audrey, I believe, had number 2, so she gets . . . right, the blue can. And that leaves me with the green one."

At this point I put the black card back into the envelope and dispose of it along with the display stand.

"All right. Now let's check on all of these apples. Dena, would you open your can and let me see your apple, please." She opens the can, and I take the apple out. "Looks good to me." I sniff the apple. "Smells good, too. Dena, I think you got one of the good ones. Great."

I repeat this exact sequence with the other two children, saying things like, "That's a good one too. I don't see any holes in it. The stem is still in place. Everything's all right."

I ask the kids to put their apples back into the cans and replace the lids.

"Well, that's really neat. You three must be magical or something. I mean, all three of you picked the good . . . uh . . . apples." I stop talking and scratch my head. "Wait a minute . . . uh, just wait a minute." I turn and look at the green can, then pick it up from the table. "Just a second here. Each of these folks got a can with a good apple. Well, maybe I was mistaken."

I start to open the green can, but I stop.

"Tell you what. Would you rather I do a card trick instead of opening this can?"

Everyone shouts "NO!"

"I didn't think so. Okay, I'll open it . . . here we go." I stop again. "How about a rope trick instead?"

"NO!"

"Okay . . . I'll just open it a little bit . . . just take a little peak inside . . . uh . . . there's something green in there . . . it's something L-O-N-G . . . and it looks like a . . . like a . . . like a W-O-R-M!" I yell that last word and release the spring worm straight into the air.

The kids shout. I catch the spring worm, jump around, and yell, finally tossing him offstage or into my case, all the time acting frightened and upset. At last I compose myself.

"Now how did they do that?" I ask the audience. "These three helpers picked the numbers that gave them the cans with the good apples in them . . . and left ME with the can holding that WORM!"

To this, the audience kids laugh really loud. I know, because while writing this, I have just watched a videotape of this routine, and the children really did laugh.

"Well, I think Dena and Audrey and Chip are magicians in disguise, and as they go to sit down, let's all give them a big round of applause!"

Applause follows, then on with the show.

That, then, is the basic routine I used. But what else could be in those cans? How could you adapt this basic idea? Think!

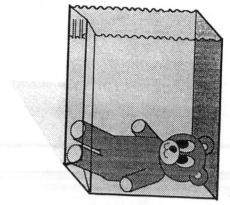

Figure 28

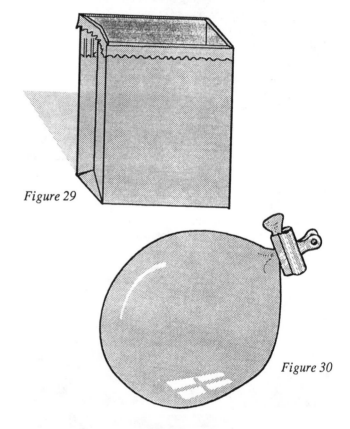

Figure 29

BALLOON BLOW UP

I leave it to other clowns and magicians to do balloon animals. When I do balloon tricks and gags as a magician, typically I blow up a number 9 round balloon, which is very visible on stage. Then I pop it, and something comes out . . . like a selected card, a live dove or rabbit, or in my "Jungle Tales of Magic" show, King Kong's missing head!

If you do sculpture balloon doggies and elephants, you can work my "Balloon Blow Up" right into your routine, perhaps even as the climax. If you don't perform balloon animals, "Balloon Blow Up" will give you a reason to!

The set-up is as follows. Take two paper grocery bags, the kind with flat bottoms, and cut about six inches off the top of one. Place a teddy bear in the bottom of the larger bag (Figure 28) and slide the shorter bag down over it. I suggest you fold the tops of both bags over twice to hide the double edges Figure 29).

You will need three balloons, the same size and same color. I like the number 9 round balloon, which is easy to blow up and will inflate to about 15 inches if desired. You will also need a spring paper clip.

Blow up one balloon to 9-10 inches, tie it off, and place it in a bag. Blow up a second balloon to the same size, twist its nozzle, and clip it with the spring paper clip (Figure 30). Place this balloon in the bag beside the first one as in Figure 31. Have the deflated third balloon nearby, along with a moderately sharp pencil.

This is the routine. "And now, ladies and GERMS

Figure 30

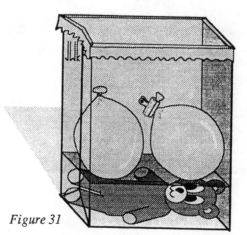

Figure 31

. . . I mean gentlemen . . . I would like to show you a feat of scientific phenomenon, which some less sophisticated persons would even call *magic*. But I am sure you know better than that! An illusion, perhaps, but real magic? Well, I will let you be the judges of what your eyes see."

I deliver this speech in a fake, pompous sort of fashion, performing as Frederick the Great.

"A simple toy BAA-LOON," I state as I hold the deflated balloon up for display. I purposely call it a BAA- (as in the sound sheep make) LOON, which creates humor and makes the kids respond, pronouncing *balloon* the normal way, which I ignore.

"And a paper grocery bag. I am going to drop the BAA-LOON into the paper bag," which I do, "blow into the bag with super human breath . . . I gargled with Lysol . . . I mean Listerine . . . this morning . . . and like magic, the BAA-LOON will automatically IN-FLATE with C-O-2 . . . or for you nonscientific types, it'll blow up. . . . No, no, I don't mean it will EXPLODE . . . I just mean it will fill up with air!"

The kids are usually giggling and laughing over this, but I pompously continue.

"And now, to inflate the BAA-LOON by scientific magic!" Loudly, I blow hard into the open top of the bag. Again the children laugh.

"Laugh if you will! But, wait. I think I will need more air. When I count to three, I want all of you boys and girls to help me by blowing hard at the bag. Ready? One, two, three!"

The kids all blow at the bag.

"Ugh! Choke!" I make the sounds. "Who had ONIONS for lunch?"

I wave my hand in front of my face, fanning the imaginary onion smell away from my nose before I continue.

"The magic is done," I now state boldly, carefully reaching into the bag and grasping the nozzle and paper clip of the second balloon. Slowly I pull out the balloon, holding it up for display. "As you can see, the balloon is filled with air!"

A moment's pause here is fine, but not a long pause.

"But now, I will try to reverse this strange process. I will place the BAA-LOON back into the bag and RE-MOVE the air WITHOUT touching the BAA-LOON! Watch!"

Slowly I slide the balloon down into the bag where it was. I lean over the bag and, with my mouth, pretend to suck the air out of the balloon. I look inside, shake my head from side to side.

"Hmm. It didn't work. It seems I will need your help. When I count to three this time, I want all of you to

Frederick the Great holding the balloon with the paper clip nozzle.

draw the air MAGICALLY out of the BAA-LOON back into your mouths. Ready? One, two, three!"

And the kids suck the air back into their mouths. They love doing this sort of thing, and it's great audience participation because every one of them can help.

Now I reach back into the bag, past the inflated balloons, and bring out the original balloon I dropped inside.

"So you see: There is the balloon once more, without any air. No doubt many of you would like to know how this scientific impossibility really works."

"YOU'VE GOT TWO BALLOONS!" a kid often shouts. If this happens, I smile, ignore him, and continue.

"Back to what I was saying: a scientific impossibility, yes. Perhaps before I explain it, you would like to see me do it again. Oh, yes, I shall. I will place the DEFLATED BAA-LOON back into the bag. Blow in the air like this . . . well, all right, you may help. One, two, three!"

I drop in the deflated balloon. The kids all blow. I take out the inflated balloon with the paper clip on the nozzle.

"And here it is once more, fully inflated!"

"YOU'VE GOT TWO BALLOONS!" someone else shouts. If no one says this, I simply *pretend* that someone did.

"Say what? Two BAA-LOONS? Did you say I had two BAA-LOONS? The very idea! I am, indeed, insulted! I cannot BELIEVE that you would think a thing like that!"

Kids love this sort of thing. It's the clown-in-trouble syndrome at work, so I ham it up.

"It's as if you were accusing ME, Frederick the Great, of trying to pull your leg!" As I say this, I have the bag in one hand and the inflated balloon in my other hand. I am holding the balloon by the spring paper clip nozzle. Just as I utter the words "pull your leg," I squeeze the spring clip, which releases the balloon and it goes flying around the room, to the amazement and laughter of the children.

It takes a moment to quiet them down.

"Okay, okay. Everything is all right. Don't worry," I say, reaching into the bag, "because I have another balloon just like it right here!"

I pull out the original deflated balloon, smiling, and *immediately* I realize what I have said . . . that I've given myself away. I stop smiling. Slowly I turn my head toward the original deflated balloon in my hand. Then I slowly look back into the bag. Then I slowly look back at the audience. Finally, I smile again.

"Uh . . . uh . . . I know what you're thinking. You're thinking I had two BAA-LOONS . . . and . . . well . . . uh . . . you were right. But look: I really can do it, just like I said. And not only can I blow up this BAA-LOON by magic, I can make it into a BAA-LOON ANNIE-MULE! Just you watch."

Quickly now, I drop the deflated balloon back into the bag. I blow into the bag three times, then stop.

"I forgot to ask: What kind of ANNIE-MULE do you want it to be? A BAA-LOON doggie or a CATTY-KIT or an ELLIE-FANT?" I let the kids offer their various replies. "What? Who said a RHI-NOOSEROUS? There ain't no such ANNIE-MULE! Wait a minute! Who said that? Somebody said it. I heard somebody say he or she wanted it to be a TEDDY BEAR! Who said that?"

This is so easy. As the performer, all you have to do is suggest aloud what you want it to be—for some child in the audience will either have already said that (if it's common) or will *admit* to having said it.

"A teddy bear it will be!" I wave my hand over the bag, wiggle my fingers, and pronounce these magic words:

"Mr. BAA-LOON fill right up
But just remember, we don't
              want a pup,
Or even a catty-kit filled with air,
What we want . . . is a teddy bear!"

I smile and boldly reach into the bag, secretly grab the deflated balloon, and wad it up in my hand. Next I remove the inflated balloon, which is knotted at the nozzle.

"And there it is!" I say proudly, "a beautiful balloon teddy bear! See his cute little ears! How about that little tummy! And look at those adorable eyes! And he's so soft and cuddly!" Sometimes I put the bag down, still in sight, at this point so I can handle the balloon and squeeze and squeak it. This is especially funny when I say "he's so soft and cuddly," SQUEAK, SQUEAK!

"IT'S A BALLOON! IT'S ROUND! IT DOESN'T LOOK LIKE A TEDDY BEAR!" The kids' shouting brings me back to reality.

"Oh. Oh. Yes. You're right." Now I act sad. "I wanted so much for this BAA-LOON to be a teddy bear,

Frederick attempting to pop the bag.

I guess I just imagined that it was a teddy bear. I wish it were." As I say this, I pick up the bag, balloon still in my hand, and show it empty.

"Well, this BAA-LOON may NOT be a teddy bear, but this bag is a TRASH BAG! So I'll just use it to trash this BAA-LOON."

Now I put the visible balloon back into the bag, dropping the deflated hidden one in my hand in the bag also. I close the top of the bag.

"Hey, maybe I can blow some more air into this bag and pop it." I blow air into the bag then hold it closed and try popping it. It won't pop. I hold the bag against my chest and squeeze it, but the balloon won't pop. I squeeze the bag with both hands, but still the bag won't pop. By now the children are laughing or holding their hands over their ears or hiding their eyes, waiting for the balloon to pop. But it won't, and that fact creates humor.

Yes, this clown is in trouble again!

"Hmm! Then I'll get something to pop it with. Let's see, how about a sword? Anyone have a sword with you? No swords. How about a bazooka? Is Rambo here? No. Wait! I have a pencil in my pocket. That'll do the trick!"

So I bring out the pointed pencil and wave it around the top of the bag, letting the bag open enough to insert my hand.

"All right, folks . . . here . . . it . . . goes!"

My hand goes down into the bag and pops the balloon with the pencil. When that happens, many of the children shout or laugh. I do too. In fact, I purposely yell "OUCH!" as if I stuck myself.

"Oh, sorry, I thought I stuck myself. But it was only the BAA-LOON." As I say this, I crush the bag. "I guess this bag's no good now." As I crush the bag, I start ripping open the bottom of the bag, and out pops—you guessed it—the TEDDY BEAR!

"I might as well just rip it up and throw the bag away . . . what . . . wait a minute . . . what IS this? . . . Why, it's a R-E-A-L TEDDY BEAR! Hey, it worked! The BAA-LOON did turn into a teddy bear after all. How about that! And I think we should all give our teddy bear here a big round of applause!"

Although it has taken quite a bit of wordage to describe this routine, on stage it runs only three minutes or so. But it contains lots of fun and laughter, involves the entire audience as helpers, and has a genuine magical ending that children enjoy.

On my *Behind the Scenes* videotape, you can see a short version of this which I call "Balloon Bear," illustrating how effective the double bag balloon-to-bear transformation is. Furthermore, the hidden load in the bag could be a gift for the birthday child at his or her party, perhaps something the parents want you to magically produce.

Using this same double bag system, you could also change a balloon dog into a stuffed dog. And I'll bet you could think of a few more uses if you try!

THAT MAGIC FLOWER

One of my basic standbys in children's shows has been a routine taught to me a dozen years ago by my friend Bruce "Sparkles" Johnson. It involves a simple prop, known in magic circles as a *wilting flower* or sometimes called a *drooping flower*. Wilting flowers may be purchased through magic shops or mail order dealers. They range in price from about $3 up to $30 or more. Incidentally, the highest priced ones are not necessarily the best.

The wilting flower is a feather flower on a stem, in the center of which is a spring. A string runs through the flower, out the stem, and is tied securely to a ring at the bottom. (See Figure 32.) To operate the flower, you hold it as shown in Figure 33, pulling down on the ring with your little finger as your other fingers pressure the stem upward as shown. This makes the flower bend as in Figure 34.

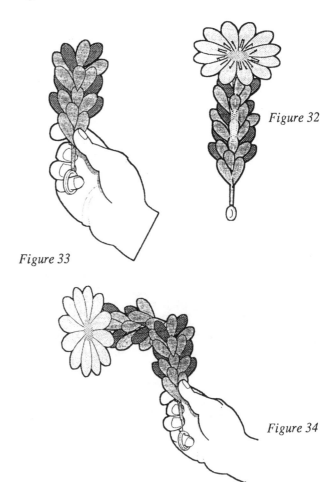

Figure 32

Figure 33

Figure 34

Here is an example of how you can use the wilting flower to create a clever routine.

With the flower out of sight, I invite two children on stage and learn their names. Here, we'll call them Sammy and Laurel.

"Sammy and Laurel," I start, talking not only to the helpers but to the audience as well, "yesterday I stopped at a flower shop to buy a flower for my wife. And in the flower shop I saw this one little flower in a vase all by itself. So I asked the lady, 'What kind of flower is this?' And she said, 'That's a MAGIC FLOWER!'"

I pause for a moment to let that sink in.

"'A magic flower?' I asked. 'What does it do? Does it do tricks?' And she said, 'Yes, it does tricks.' So I said to her, 'Well, let me see it do a trick.' And she said, 'You can't see it do the trick until you buy it.'

"Well, that made me a bit curious, but I gave the lady a dollar bill anyway, and she handed me the flower. I said, 'Okay, now let me see it do a trick.' And she said, 'It already has.' So I said, 'What trick do you mean?' And she said, 'The trick is—I have your dollar bill, and you have that silly flower!'"

After saying that, I start laughing and the audience does too. Then I abruptly stop, saying in mock anger, *I didn't think it was funny!*"

That brings more laughter.

"Can you believe it? That lady had tricked ME into buying this silly flower. And here it is."

I bring out the wilting flower.

"And do you know what else, Sammy and Laurel? As I was leaving the flower shop, that lady had the audacity to tell me, 'Don't forget to water it!'" I say this in a lady's snooty voice.

"By the way, girls and boys, do you know what happens if you don't water a flower?"

The kids begin responding: "It'll die! Drop dead! Wilt! Fall over! It'll droop."

And I say, "That's right. All of those things. But do you know what's strange—in fact, what makes me believe this really IS a MAGIC FLOWER? I haven't given this flower *one single drop of water* since I bought it early this morning . . . and there it stands, straight and tall, like a Georgia pine tree."

I turn to the little girl on my left and say, "You see, Laurel, it hasn't died." As I say this to her, I pull down on the ring of the flower, causing the flower to slowly wilt down to a 90-degree angle. "In fact, it hasn't even wilted or shriveled up or anything." Then I let the flower rise back up.

What's happening in the audience? The children see it fall over, and several of them, sometimes lots of them,

start telling me about it. Naturally, I pretend not to hear them. When I face them again, the flower is standing upright, so there is nothing for me to see.

"Now that I think about it, Sammy," turning to the boy, "this must be a magic flower." As I turn toward him, I hold the flower directly in front of my body and again allow it to fall down. "After all, it's gone over 24 hours without any water, and it sure looks fine to me. Right, Sammy?"

Once more the audience see the flower go down. The kids react, telling me that it is "falling down" and pointing at it. Before I turn back to them, I let the flower stand back up; then I face the children.

"What? What did you say?" I listen to them for a moment. "You say it did what? It fell down? You mean the flower? The flower fell down? It wilted? It died?" They'll be shouting all of that and more. "Well, I didn't see it. Laurel," I turn to my left, "did you see it?"

Down it goes! The girl may point toward the flower at this time, and if she does, I let the flower stand up again before I turn toward it.

"Well, it looks fine to me. Wait a minute. What? You say it fell down when I looked over at Laurel? Oh, okay. I'll just keep my eye on it for a minute."

I hold the flower right in front of me and stare at it intently.

Helper blows on the flower.

"I'm not going to take my eyes off of this flower," I tell them.

Suddenly I turn to Laurel, immediately letting the flower fall, as I say, "And Laurel, don't you distract my attention!"

Up goes the flower, and I turn back to stare at it intently once more. Of course, every child in the house starts yelling on that one.

"What? It did it again? When? When I looked at Laurel? But I just took my eyes off the flower for a second! Isn't that right, Sammy?" I turn to the boy and make the flower fall down.

The shouting starts again: "THERE IT GOES! IT'S FALLING! IT'S DYING! LOOK, LOOK!"

As my head turns back, the flower goes up, and I don't see it.

This is basic look-don't-see comedy, the kind Abbott and Costello were wonderful doing. Now you know what I watched as a kid! You can extend this bit for several minutes if you like, depending on how much your fish . . . I mean audience kids . . . are biting. But let's move on with our explanation.

Sometimes I explain to the kids that it's just an illusion, "something that you think you see, but that is not really there." That's when I finally see the flower fall down myself, and most times I do a double take on that. When I finally see the flower down, you must understand, it is a high point for the children, who have been trying to tell me about it all along.

"Oh, so that's what you're talking about. Why didn't you tell me about it?"

"We DID!" they shout.

"Well, it really is dying, and we'd better do something about it. I guess it needs some water, but I don't have any handy. Maybe we can get some water . . . some moisture . . . right out of the air."

I turn to the girl. "Laurel, when I count to three, you blow some moisture right into the flower."

I hold it toward her. I count to three and she blows. I then let the flower rise back up slowly.

"My goodness! Look at that! Laurel just made that flower come back to life!" Just as I say the word life, I make the flower wilt again, at the same time turning toward the girl and patting her on the shoulder with my left hand. The audience starts laughing right away, and I turn back to see why.

"Oh, no, it didn't work. But maybe Sammy could help me do it. Sammy, when I count three, you blow into the middle of the flower, and we'll see what happens."

I turn the wilted flower toward the boy. I count, "ONE! TWO!" and on the second number I use my right thumb and first finger to twist the flower stem, thus turning the flower around and away from the boy. My audiences think this is very funny, and I act confused. My free hand reaches over and turns the flower back toward the boy.

"Just a moment, Sammy. Let's try that again. Now, on the count of three. Ready? One! Two!"

Once again the flower seems to turn of its own accord away from the boy. I stop the count with "three" halfway out of my mouth, and the kids laugh again.

"Well, Sammy, this flower must not like you! But let's try again," I say, as the audience calms down a little. "I'll hold the flower with two hands this time." So saying, I use my left hand to hold the top of the flower, pointing it directly toward the boy. "Ready? Here we go: One! Two! Three!"

The boy blows into the flower. Instantly I let go with my left hand. My right hand turns the flower directly toward the audience, and I let the flower rise slowly. As it gets almost upright, I cause it to quickly fall down below the 90-degree angle. The audience howls at this.

"Boy, Sammy, what did you have for breakfast? A bowl of ONIONS?" (That's what I say at a morning show. Afternoon show? "What did you have for lunch? A bowl of ONIONS?" Always adapt to the time of day.)

"Well, I just don't know what we're going to do. Oh, wait a minute . . . now it's coming back to me." I pretend I've just recalled something. "That lady in the flower shop told me this flower needs a special kind of water . . . ah . . . something called INDIVISIBLE WATER. And I just happen to have some with me."

I reach into my case or bag and come out with my free hand pretending to hold a glass.

"Here it is . . . a glass of INDIVISIBLE WATER . . . in an INDIVISIBLE GLASS, naturally." Some children always try to tell me it's "invisible," but I just brush past that. "No, I mean INDIVISIBLE . . . can't you spell?" I often remark, jokingly.

"I'll just pour a little INDIVISIBLE WATER right into the flower, and we'll see what happens."

So I pour some "water" from the "glass" into the flower. Then I hold the glass upright again. Slowly the flower comes back to life and stands up straight once more. Often children applaud this.

Once the reaction dies down, I tell them, "Boy, this INDIVISIBLE WATER really did the trick. It brought my flower back to life. Hey, maybe if I drank some, it would give me some extra energy."

Immediately I tilt the "glass" to my lips and proceed to "swallow" all the liquid. I turn and quickly dispose of both the flower and the "glass." Then I face the audience. I make chewing mouth motions for a moment, then I tilt

The magic coloring book can be shown with all the pages blank, with line drawings on all the pages, or with all the drawings colored in.

my head back and pretend to swallow.

The moment my head comes back down to face the audience, I throw my mouth open and my tongue out and yell, "BLAAAHHH!" My eyes go wide. I wrinkle up my nose and shake my head back and forth as though the water tasted extremely bad.

The children scream.

"That's the WORST tasting water I've ever had!" I exclaim. "It tasted just like swamp water!"

Another mild laugh.

"From now on," I tell them, "I'm going to stick to drinking iced tea or a good cold glass of milk!"

Then I thank the two audience helpers, Laurel and Sammy, and send them back to their seats with a round of applause.

This is a simple routine with a minimum of props and a maximum of personality. It can run 3-10 minutes, depending on the audience and you, and it's solid entertainment. I'll always be indebted to Bruce "Sparkles" Johnson for sharing it with me.

COLORING BY MAGIC

One of the easiest tricks in magic or clowning is the three-way coloring book, based on Burling Hull's "Svengali" principle, which he invented with playing cards in 1909.

Basically, this mechanical prop is a child's coloring book which you can flip through and show in three ways—blank pages, pages with line drawings, and completely colored pictures.

Though this book is manufactured in several versions, including the *Fun Magic Coloring Book* and several gospel versions, I have illustrated my routine with *A Clown Magic Coloring Book*, made by Haines House of Cards, Cincinnati, Ohio USA, with permission of Bill and Betty Winzig.

Before we tackle my routine, please study the way I am holding the coloring book in the photos above. I have seen many performers over the years hold such a book to one side, turning their bodies left or right and thus blocking part of the audience from seeing the pages. If you hold the book by the outside of the pages with the spine against your front, everyone can see the pages. The second key is to open the pages and pan your body, turning left and right slowly as you flip from page to page so that everyone gets a partial glimpse of each page. Then you always stop with the book open so people can see two pages at once.

In my routine for children, I use about six children, the coloring book, and a bunch of comedy wands. Let's just plunge into the thing, and you'll see all the fun you can have!

"Now everybody, I want you to know that not long ago I signed up for one of those TV artist courses, the kind where you can become a REALLY REAL ARTIST in about two seconds—as long as you send in ten dollars! They said I could become a real artist like Pablito or Leonardo or Leroy Neiman Marcus, if you know what I mean.

"Well, anyway, I sent in my ten dollars in Monopoly money and look what I got in the mail . . . a COLORING BOOK! It's got all kinds of neat pictures of stuff I love

. . . clowns and magic and circus stuff, see, 'cause it's called A CLOWN MAGIC COLORING BOOK . . . except they forgot one thing:

"They forgot to print the pages!"

I flip through the book and show the blank pages.

"You reckon I should have sent them a REAL $10 BILL? I don't know. All I know is—there aren't any pictures in this coloring book. But never fear! I know magic! And with a little help from the magic AND some of my friends here in the audience, we'll get this book all colored in and maybe all become great ARTISTIC-TYPE PERSONAGES!"

Now I select six children of various ages and sizes, three girls and three boys, to come on stage and assist. I stand three on each side of me, the girls on my left and the boys on my right.

"Now the first thing we have to do," I tell them after learning their names, "is to get some lines in this book so we'll know just WHAT to color in. I want each of you six helpers to reach into your pockets and pull out your imaginary pencils . . . that's right . . . now put them in your imaginary pencil sharpeners . . . yes, right there in front of you . . . and give them ten or twenty thousand turns . . . good, get those pencils real good and sharp . . . great . . . and now stop."

I flip through the coloring book once to show it is still blank.

"Now each of you put your imaginary pencil on the cover of the coloring book and draw one or two pictures like a clown, a magician, a circus tent, stuff like that . . . yes, go ahead, just use your imaginations."

I give the kids a moment to do this.

"All right, now let's take a look." I open the book and flip through pages, showing lined pictures. "Wow! You did it! Didn't I tell you my friends could help me on this? And they sure did!" I continue to flip the pages to let the entire audience see lined drawings on the pages.

"Now for the really difficult magic—to get all these pictures colored in! First, we have to ISOLATE the coloring book, yes, lock it up so nothing or no one can get to it. And here's how—a plastic zipper-top bag."

I bring out a large, clear ziplock-type bag, drop the coloring book into it, zip it closed, and hand it to one girl to hold. This accomplishes two things: (1) It keeps the book in sight the entire time, and (2) it keeps the child from opening the book and possibly exposing the secret during the routine.

"Next I will need a magic wand to make the magic work." I bring out a breakaway wand in its "fixed" position and hand it to the first boy on my right, where it promptly falls apart, creating audience laughter.

Frederick the Great with rollout wand open to reveal message.

"Maybe I need another wand," I say, looking at the boy's plight, so I reach into my bag and take out a *fishing pole wand* and hand it to the second boy, where it promptly falls apart a different way.

"Oh, boy, looks like I need ANOTHER WAND!"

So I pull out a blank rollout wand, immediately letting it tumble open it. On it I have printed some silly message which gets an immediate laugh from the readers in the audience. As a magician I used "WHAT A TURKEY!" and as Frederick the Great, "THE CLOWN IS CRAZY!"

As soon as the audience members read the wand banner, I act confused at why they are laughing. Then I look at it and with mock anger.

"WHAT? Who wrote that?" I look around at my six helpers. "Did one of you write this?" Of course, the kids say NO. "Somebody wrote it!" I exclaim, quickly rolling it back up and putting it aside, bringing out a *spring wand*.

"This is the wand I meant to get!" Suddenly the wand starts to wiggle and wobble in my hand, bending in half, swaying back and forth. "What? What's going on here? This wand is ALL GOOFED UP!"

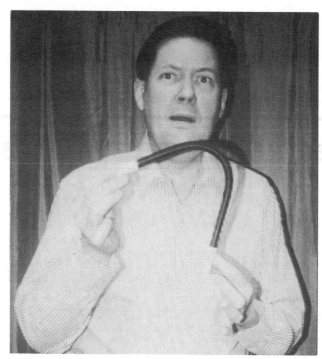

The spring wand.

"I'll just put those colors in my pocket. But I'll need some more." I reach the wand again behind another boy's head, bring it out with the colored feather brush showing, and repeat the taking away and into my pocket bit. I continue this, going behind each child's head, getting colored feathers, pocketing them, doing it all at a rapid pace.

Finally, I decide to try for colors behind my own head. I reach the wand behind my head, pull it out and reveal *nothing*. The kids laugh. I try again and still nothing.

"Well, I'll just get another wand!" I tell them. Immediately I stick the paintbrush wand under my left arm, thumbing open the brush end. I turn my back on the audience and start to reach into my bag, letting them see the feathers. Boy, do they let up a howl!

Immediately I turn back around.

"What is going on here?"

"The colors! The feathers! The paintbrush!" they yell.

I pull the wand out from my arm, closing the brush as I do.

"There's nothing there. It must be your imagination."

Placing the wand under my arm again and thumbing open the brush, I turn my back once more, and the shouting starts. Quickly, I turn back around.

I hand it to the third boy anyway; now all three boys have wands.

"What I really need is a PAINTBRUSH!" I announce.

Now I pull out another wand that I invented about 15 years ago. My friend Phil Thomas made it for me, sort of a takeoff on the blooming bouquet and the old coin wand. I call it a *paintbrush wand*. It's a piece of PVC tubing with a wooden dowel inside as a slide. On the end of the dowel are glued a number of feathers to act as a "brush," and a screw in the dowel acts as a thumb slide in the slit. By thumbing the screw up and down, you can make the brush appear and disappear at the end of the wand. I am currently manufacturing these wands and they should be available from most magic dealers.

So out comes the wand, looking like a wand.

"Let me see," I say, reaching behind one boy's head, thumbing up the brush and showing it. "There's a bit of color!"

Believe me, the children delight in this visual appearance. Immediately I reach up with my left hand, cover the feathers, and simultaneously thumb them down. I pretend they are in my closed left hand and immediately put "them" in my pocket.

A magic coloring book and a paintbrush wand.

"IT DID IT AGAIN!" they yell.

Out I pull the wand (closing it), only to see nothing.

"Are you sure about that? I don't see a thing!"

"YES! WE SAW IT!"

"Well, just let me get another wand," I say, turning around a third time and placing the wand under my arm, thumbing it open.

Off goes the shouting once again.

"WE SEE IT! LOOK!"

I turn around and ask, "Where?"

"UNDER YOUR ARM!"

"Under my arm?" I repeat. Slowly, I pull the wand from under my arm, thumbing it closed and staring at it intently. "Why, there's nothing there." I pause a moment, giving a quizzical look, then raise the wand to the back of my head and pretend to scratch my head, thumbing the brush open. I slowly turn my body around 360 degrees, and halfway through the turn the children start shouting.

"IT'S BACK!"

When I complete my turn with the kids still shouting, I bring the wand with *brush open* from behind my head, holding it upright in front of me and to my right, not looking at it. This is very important for the next laugh. I do not look at the wand. I look at the audience.

"I don't know WHAT you people are shouting about!" I pronounce boldly. Then I turn my head toward the wand, look at it for a split second, look back at the audience and *immediately* back at the wand. A definite *double take*. I open my eyes in wide surprise and *freeze*. Often the kids go bananas at this, just laughing their heads off at me finally seeing the elusive paintbrush.

"So THAT'S what you're talking about!" I exclaim. "Look, we've just gotta get this coloring book colored in today. And I'll use this paintbrush wand to do it. First, I'll wave the paintbrush over the book." I brush the book held by the girl, usually to my far left.

"Next I'll put some color into the air," I explain, reaching up and pretending to remove the brush end of the wand. Actually, I retract it using my right thumb as my left hand pretends to lift it off.

"Watch!" My left hand tosses the "brush" into the air. "Hey! It's gone! But it's somewhere in the air! And I want all of you girls and boys in the audience to help me too. If you are wearing any red, yellow, blue or green, orange, purple, pink or brown, or any other colors . . . just pinch a little of that color off your shirt or pants or sweater and toss it up into the air when I count to three. Are you ready? One! Two! Three! Toss it up! Good, good!

"Now, can all of you see those beautiful colors in the air? You can? Then you're as CRAZY as I AM!" Yes, it always gets a laugh.

A giant crayon, which is handed to the magician's helper, immediately falls apart.

"We have our colors in the air, our coloring book nearby, our three boys have our magic wands ready . . ." I look at the boys, who are holding their wands in various stages of collapse, and that gets a laugh. "I said OUR MAGIC WANDS READY." Whatever the boys do here will be funny, even if they do nothing!

"Huh-hmm," I clear my throat. "But we need one last thing. We need a crayon . . . not just any crayon, but the biggest CRAYON in the world for the biggest magic in the world. And I just happen to have that crayon with me."

Disposing of the paintbrush wand, I pick up my giant clown crayon. It's made of a bunch of cardboard tubes and a cone, with a spring and rope inside. When the knot at the end of the rope is upset, the giant crayon falls apart like a breakaway wand.

"This should do the job," I announce, extending it to the two girls who are holding nothing. "Here, girls, hold this."

Just as they take it, I trip the release and the crayon collapses. I pretend not to notice until the audience laughs and tells me.

"Oh, NO!" I shout. "Everything is falling apart! All the wands fell apart, and now the world's biggest crayon fell apart. I don't know if we'll EVER get this coloring book colored in. But wait—maybe ALL OF YOU can help me! Look, everybody hold up your fingers like INVISIBLE MAGIC CRAYONS. Yes, that's right! And you boys can wave those crazy magic wands, and you girls can try to wave that big crayon. And I'll count to three, and we'll all shout the magic words—PURPLE PUPPY CHOW—and maybe all those colors in the air will fall into the coloring book. Let's give it a try!

"ONE! TWO! THREE!"

Everybody waves, and everybody shouts.

I pause for a moment. Then quickly I gather the three wands and the giant broken crayon, putting them aside. Slowly now, I take back the coloring book, still in the plastic bag, which has always been in sight. Slowly, I open the bag and remove the book. I ditch the bag.

Finally, I hold the coloring book in front of me and flip through the pages, panning back and forth so the kid helpers and my audience can see all the pages colored in the book. Typically, this sets off a chain reaction of applause.

"Look, it really worked. I think we're all GREAT ARTISTS. As they go back to their seats, please thank all my helpers here with a great round of applause!"

If you perform every line and gag of this routine, adding more of your own, it can run up to ten minutes. That may be too long for your situation or clown character. On the other hand, this routine alone could account for one-third of a 30-minute birthday party show, employing six children, and it's packed with entertainment, which is the name of the game.

Other ways to embellish such a routine include adding additional comedy props and possibly costuming some or all of your audience helpers. In a simpler two-kid version, I've dressed the boy like an artist, with beard, vest and hat. There are many fine possibilities for this kind of kid-play. Cook on it, and make it suit the clown in you.

CHAPTER 7

CLOWN STUNTS

Working clowns are famous for their stunts that smack of magic, juggling, and acrobatics with a funny flair. Sometimes these stunts actually work, and the clown looks good. Other times they fail—sometimes miserably—to produce spectator laughs. Clown stunts are meant for fun, and that's what you'll find in this chapter—clown fun!

THE RICE BOTTLE

Many of the easy, yet highly effective tricks and stunts I know, I learned as a beginning magician between the ages of 11 and 14. Mark Wilson and Bev Bergeron (Rebo the Clown) performed this trick on "The Magic Land of Allakazam" TV show in the 1960s, using a small fishbowl filled with rice. Well, I didn't have a small fishbowl, so I tried the stunt with a Coca-Cola bottle, and it worked. I've done it that way ever since.

The performer fills a soda pop bottle with rice, using a funnel as in Figure 35. Then he shows the audience a chopstick, which he pushes down through the bottle's neck into the rice (Figure 36). After saying a few magic words, or calling on the "Rice Genii," the performer lifts the chopstick with his thumb and first finger—and the bottle of rice lifts up with it, magically clinging to the chopstick!

This seemingly impossible stunt is very simple. Begin by filling your pop bottle with rice. Being from Atlanta, I always use a real Coke bottle. Use a kitchen funnel or a piece of stiff paper rolled into a funnel shape. Filling the bottle becomes an actual part of the performance because it allows your audience to see that the bottle is empty at the start.

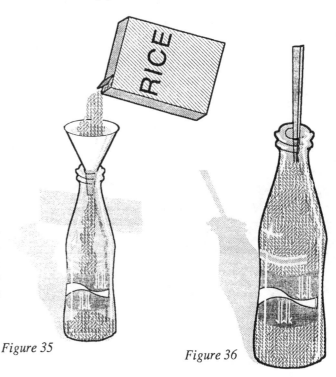

Figure 35   Figure 36

Then press the chopstick firmly into the rice several times, pushing the stick up and down, packing the rice tightly into the bottle. The rice itself does the work when packed tightly. The pressure of the stick will force the rice against the sides of the bottle and actually cause the rice to grip the chopstick. You will feel this as the rice tightens inside the bottle.

When the rice is packed tight enough, you will be able to easily lift the chopstick, and the bottle of rice. Yet here is the amazing part: The chopstick will easily come out whenever you desire. All it takes is a little pull.

Thus, when you conclude the stunt, tell your Rice Genii (or whatever you choose to call him) to let go, and gently pull the chopstick out of the rice. Even though you may have to pull it out firmly, give your viewers the impression that it slips out easily. Then, pour the rice out of the bottle into a glass to show that the rice and bottle are free of trickery.

The story or patter you use to accompany this trick may go like the following:

"You know, some people are afraid of getting bugs in their rice. But not me! You see, I keep my rice in this soda bottle, and a Rice Genii lives in the bottle to protect the rice. Let me pour the rice into the bottle first . . . oh, you didn't see him? That's because he's invisible! Anyway, now I'll poke the rice inside the bottle with this chopstick . . . just like that . . . and then I'll prove the Rice Genii is really there.

"Hello, there! Are you home? If you are, grab hold of this chopstick so everyone will believe you're there. Come on, just do it! What? I feel . . . I feel a grip on the stick . . . yes, he's got it!" Hold the bottle by the stick alone. "See, didn't I tell you he was there? He's holding the stick so tight, the bottle of rice won't even fall.

"Now, I'll get him to let go. Okay, Mr. Rice Genii, would you please release the stick? Come on, let it go." Gently remove the stick from the bottle, display both momentarily, then pour the rice from the bottle.

"You see, he really is there. Thank you!"

If you happen to do ventriloquism, you can make your Rice Genii talk and add yet another comedy dimension to this simple stunt.

Remember, to those who do not know the secret, this is a great mystery. So have fun with it, but keep it a secret!

Lifting the bottle of rice with a chopstick.

BASKETBALL BRIEFCASE

The clown walks onto the stage carrying a thin briefcase or attache case. He sets it down on a thin table top, opens it, and removes a regulation size basketball, which he proceeds to dribble all over the stage. When he tries to put it back in the briefcase, the basketball won't fit!

This stunt will have people scratching their heads in wonder if you don't expose the method. To my knowledge, it was invented by Atlanta magician J. C. Doty for use with a bowling ball. Doty has given me permission to include it in these pages. So please honor the secret I am sharing with you. Here's how it's done.

Using an old briefcase, cut a circular hole in the back as shown in Figure 37. This hole must be large enough for the basketball to fit through. Lay a square yard of heavy black cloth inside the case and over the hole. Place the basketball inside, and close the case. (See Figure 38.) Do this to determine how far the basketball sticks out the back as in Figure 39. Use white chalk to mark the cloth near the hole as shown.

Then open the case, put the ball aside, and trim the cloth *outside* your chalk marks about three inches. Now you must secure the cloth inside the case, as shown in

Figure 37

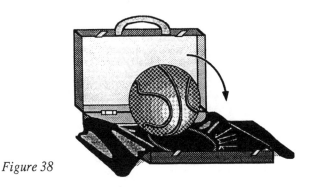

Figure 38

Figure 40, with glue or duct tape. I suggest both. Once the cloth is attached, place the basketball inside, letting it protrude as in Figure 39. You're all set.

The routine would go as follows.

Walk onto the scene carrying the briefcase at your side, just as any businessman would. By having the case against your leg as in Figure 41, you can actually walk directly toward a crowd without them seeing the ball. Your clown costume may cover the bulge even more.

The perfect background music here, by the way, would be the whistled version of "Sweet Georgia Brown," the theme song of the Harlem Globetrotters basketball team.

As you get to your performing spot, turn the case so the top is flat to the audience. Set the case on a thin, uncovered table. (See Figure 42.) If it is covered, your viewers will think the ball came out of the table.

Standing behind the case and table, unlatch the briefcase and open it by swinging the back *down* onto the table as in Figure 43. Do this as naturally as possible, looking into the case as you do.

Scratch your head as though you cannot find something in the case. Fold the case top down onto the

Figure 39

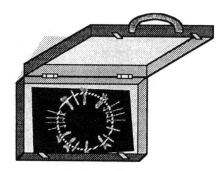

Figure 40

Figure 41

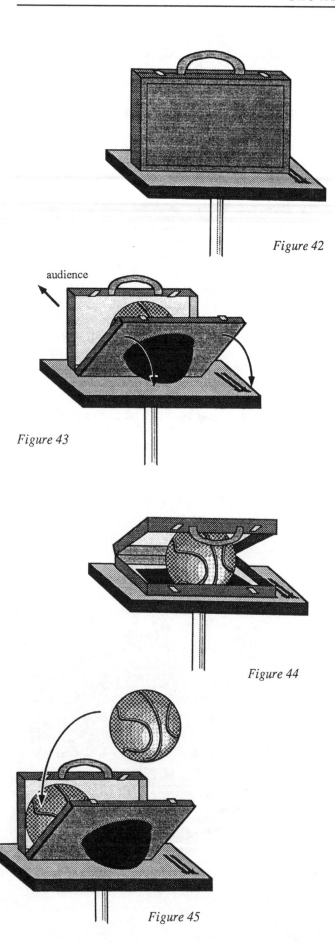

Figure 42

audience

Figure 43

Figure 44

Figure 45

basketball (Figure 44) as if you are about to close the case. Then stop, and open it back up. Scratch your head some more, still looking for something.

Then scoop up the basketball with one hand, lift it out of the case into view, and *immediately* close the case flat on the table. This creates quite a surprise, plus the audience instantly sees the difference in thickness between the basketball and the briefcase. Typically, a briefcase is about three to six inches thick; a basketball 12-14 inches in diameter.

"So that's why I can't find anything in this briefcase," you might remark to the audience. "My basketball is in the way!"

Pause a moment for applause, laughter, or other surprised reactions, then dribble the basketball around the stage to "prove it's real." Believe me, there will be a few skeptics in your audience who will think you're so clever, that you somehow "blew up the ball with a mechanism inside the case" or that it's some kind of fake basketball. It's unreal what lengths some folks will go to in order to figure out our magic stuff!

After you bounce the ball around some, use it for another routine if you like. Be creative. Then decide to put the ball back in the case. Pick up the case, standing it up, and open it in a V fashion as in Figure 45. Put the basketball inside to the left of the hole, and try to close the case, which won't work. Ham this part up for laughs, grumbling the whole time but secretly pushing the cloth bag back inside the case. Now you can turn the case toward the audience as in Figure 46, showing that the ball won't fit while mugging some more.

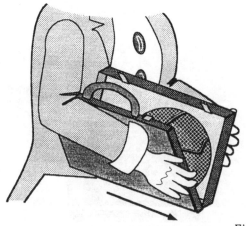

Figure 46

Finally, stop struggling with the ball. Clutch the open case with the ball inside (with the bag/hole against you), and march off the stage or put the case aside in embarrassed disgust.

And there you have a near-complete scenario with beginning, middle, and end, but with enough leeway for plugging in your creative juices to make it you. Think: How would your clown character handle this? What would you do with the ball after producing it?

Several magicians I know perform another version of this trick, using a real bowling ball. So what else could you use? Remember, the large object you remove from the case must be (1) something that is easily recognizable by your audience, (2) something that is easily proven to be real (that's why I dribble the basketball), and (3) something that will surprise people. What will your big object be?

Yet another idea would be to bring in the case filled not only with a basketball, but with other production goods—a rubber chicken, a rubber pig, a rubber fish, boxes, or toys that nest inside each other like the nest of clocks, collapsible pop-up type items. Tell a story about packing for summer camp or a trip and remove the various things you took with you as you mention them. You could even fill a large basket with such production items, finishing your story with the largest item—the basketball.

Hey, it's up to you!

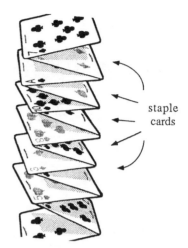

Figure 47

After a response from my spectators, I announce, "I'll do it again . . . and this time I will do it backwards . . . from the Canadian side." (Note to my Canadian friends: You say "from the American side.") I turn the cards backward and once more let them cascade down into my right hand, shouting once again, "NIAGARA FALLS!"

"Would you like to see it one more time? You would? Tell you what: I'll do Niagara Falls in the wintertime. Are you ready? Okay. NIAGARA FALLS . . . F-R-O-Z-E-N!"

HOMEMADE ELECTRIC DECK

I've been showing this simple, do-it-yourself gag for a dozen years, yet many still have never seen it—maybe you! It's a deck of playing cards you can spring from hand to hand, as you see me doing in the photo to the right, without ever dropping the cards on the floor.

Construction is simple: Just staple the cards together as shown in Figure 47, using one staple per joint. By using only one staple, you can fan the completed deck. Also, be sure to use the entire 52 card deck for more springiness.

Typically, I hold the cards in my right hand and quickly pull up on the top cards with my left hand, springing them upward or sideways then closing them back together quickly, accordion-fashion. This makes eyes open wide because the movement seems so impossible.

Besides bouncing the cards from hand to hand, however, my favorite gag with my homemade electric deck is to drop the cards from the left hand straight downward into my right shouting, "NIAGARA FALLS!"

The homemade electric deck.

Niagara Falls!

I let the cards cascade down from my left hand as I shout the word "FROZEN," but I purposely hold on to the top cards, causing the cards to stop in the attached condition. After a split-second pause, I let go with the left hand and let all the cards drop, catch them, and toss them aside, often to a humorous round of applause.

SAWING A GOAT IN HALF

"I will now attempt a great A-FEET of magic," you announce in your boastful fake radio voice. "I will actually saw a GOAT in half!"

Look around the crowd.

"Does anyone have a goat handy?" No. "Well, what about a horse? Did anyone ride to the show on a horse today?" No. "Hmm, no horse. Well, how about a dog? What? No dog, either? Well, then, I'll just saw a balloon in half, and we can pretend it's a goat or a horse or a dog."

Pull out a long red balloon at this point, and blow it up.

"I know—it'll be a HOT DOG! Anyone got any mustard or ketchup?"

Tie the balloon, which is maybe three feet long, and have two audience children come up to assist you. Stand

one child on each side of you, learn their names, and proceed.

Have one child hold the balloon while you pull a plastic toy saw out of your bag or pocket. Give the saw to the other child, and retrieve the balloon. Twist the balloon several times in the center as in Figure 48, and have the child with the saw actually cut through the balloon between your fingers as in Figure 49. If he has trouble sawing through it, you can simply break the balloon at the twist, making sure you pinch the twisted ends tightly as shown. Whatever you do, *don't let go of those ends.*

Figure 48

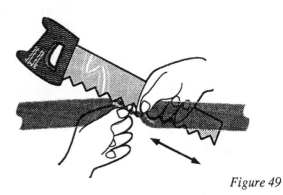

Figure 49

"Well, what a great job," you say to the boy sawing. "Leon here did a really fine job when he SEWED the dog in half . . . I mean he SUED the dog in two . . . I mean he SAWED the dog and now it's SEWN . . . I mean SAWN . . . I mean— HE CUT THE THING INTO TWO PARTS!

"Whew, I'm glad that's over!

"Now, since we have two halves of this LONG, LONG HOT DOG, I'll give one to Leon and one to Linda to take home. Or maybe I should just make them both vanish and give my two helpers some better balloon doggies. Okay, on the count of three, I'll make the SEWED, SUED, SAWN DOG DISH-APPEAR! Everybody, help me count.

"ONE! TWO! THREE!"

At this point, let go of both pinched balloons simultaneously so that they go flying off into space.

"Well, whatta ya know—DOG GONE!"

Figure 50

Figure 51

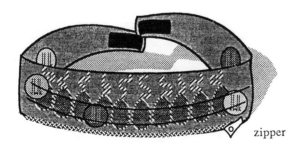

zipper

Figure 52

Rapidly make each of your two helpers a nice balloon dog or horse or goat, and send them with the balloons back to their seats with a round of applause.

MAGIC EGGS

"I will now magically produce the MAGIC EGG laid by the golden goose. I will do it eggs-actly right with no fuss or muss, no fumble or bumble! You will be surprised, delighted, enthralled, and entwined as well. All I have to do is reach under this cloth and say the magic words— DENVER OMELET!"

Basically, this is a bumbling clown magician routine. The clown tries to produce an egg from beneath a large cloth draped over one arm. (See Figure 50.) He or she fumbles under the cloth as though searching for something, which can't be found. More fumbling, while smiling to the audience, but no egg.

"You probably think I am having a little difficulty. You are WRONG! I am having a LOT of DIFFICULTY! But clown magic will prevail!"

Finally, the clown smiles and nods his or her head in triumph. Suddenly, a dozen eggs come tumbling out from beneath the cloth, hanging down on a dozen long strings. (See Figure 51.) The clown acts embarrassed.

"Uh, uh, anyone want a 12-EGG OMELET?" He exits rapidly.

Now let's look at the how of it:

Using cloth that will match or complement your costume, make a double-thick cummerbund as shown in Figure 51. Attach long strings or Velcro to secure the cummerbund at your back waist.

The double thickness at the front is a pocket about as wide as you are. In it you hide a dozen plastic or wooden eggs, each attached to a string about two feet long. The other end of each string is sewn or pinned inside the cummerbund. The bottom of this cummerbund bag is closed with a zipper. (See Figure 52.)

In performance, you drape a cloth over your arm as shown and try to produce an egg, to no avail. After all the fumbling, you unzip the cummerbund bag all the way across, causing all the eggs to fall out and down. Due to their weight, wooden eggs are probably better for this, but plastic would work as long as you can quickly and easily loosen the eggs from the cummerbund and make them drop. The key is to have all the eggs resting on the zipper and the cummerbund not be too tight.

When all the eggs fall down, act surprised. Look down, get embarrassed, run off, and ditch the whole thing.

Since the cummerbund is attached with Velcro or strings at your back, you can easily discard it and continue your performance, even up on the stage if you wish.

Figure 53

CRAZY MAGAZINE

The clown holds up an auto magazine. Suddenly, a horn starts honking. The clown looks around surprised. He wonders where the sound is coming from. Then a honking horn pops up from behind the magazine as in Figure 53, dancing and honking across the top of the magazine before the clown puts the magazine aside in fright.

This one is an adaptation of the old daylight seance cloth used by magicians. One of the hands is a fake one, and if you're wearing gloves in your clown character, it's all the easier.

To prepare this trick, open an auto magazine to the center and spot glue all the pages together in the open position (Figure 54). Cut a piece of corrugated cardboard the same size as the open magazine, and score it down the middle (see Figure 55) so it will bend. Then glue the cardboard into the magazine.

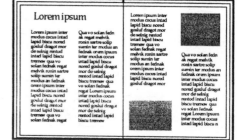

Figure 54

Next, attach a fake hand (rubber or plastic) to one side of the magazine as shown in Figure 56. If you perform in gloves, cover the fake hand with a matching glove before securing it in place.

Now glue or tape an elastic band or rubber band to one side of the cardboard so you can hide the honk horn there. (See Figure 56.)

In performance, you can enter carrying the magazine open with your hand over the fake hand. As you face the audience, turn slightly away, slip your hand inside the magazine, and face the front again. Pretend to read the magazine while getting hold of the horn, honking it, and making it dance across the top of the magazine without letting viewers see your hidden hand. After you've done the gag long enough—and I suggest you keep this short—turn back to the right and put the magazine aside in a bag or under your table out of sight.

Perhaps with a bit of ingenuity, you could make the magazine foldable, yet stiff enough to stay open when desired. That way you could bring it out folded, with the fake hand away from the audience, getting your hands in the proper places as you opened it.

Recently another version of this trick appeared on the magic market under the title of "Newspaper Seance," a foldable newspaper with fake hand gimmick so you can do the same type of thing. This trick is available through many magic shops and mail order magic companies.

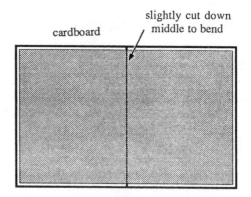

cardboard

slightly cut down middle to bend

Figure 55

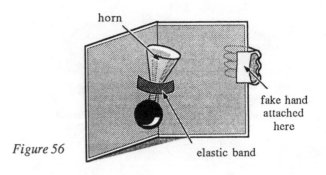

horn

fake hand attached here

Figure 56

elastic band

BOOK GAGS

Using gimmicks similar to the Crazy Magazine, you can have fun "pun"-ishing your audience with book titles that lend to logical, though often unusual interpretations.

For example, when I use the *hot book* or *fire book* sold by magic dealers—the one you open and flames leap out—I often refer to it as the life story of Smokey the Bear. "It's called HOW TO PREVENT FOREST FIRES," I tell my audiences, and then the flames leap up as a surprise.

One basis for creating book gags is the cut-out book. Just visit flea markets or garage and yard sales to cheaply purchase some old, thick hardbound books. I've bought dusty tomes at less than a dollar each, then put them to work for laughter.

Use a razor knife or an electric drill to hollow out the book as shown in Figure 57. Once your book is hollowed out, decide on a title and what you'll put in it.

Figure 57

Here are some examples, and then I'll leave others to your creativity.

HOW TO COOK CHICKEN SOUP. Open your cut-out book and pull out a rubber chicken.

SOUTHERN BARBECUE. Pull out a rubber pig.

HOW THE WEST WAS WON. Pull out a toy cap gun.

TARZAN AND THE JEWELS OF OPAR. Pull out a string of beads or pearls.

AIR CONDITIONING FOR AMATEURS. Pull out a hand held fan of some sort and start fanning yourself.

TWENTY THOUSAND LEAGUES UNDER THE SEA. Pull out a rubber fish.

ROCK MUSIC OF THE 1990s. Mount a small tape player or radio inside your book. When you open the book, push the play button. Let the audience hear it for a few moments, then shut it off as you close the book.

HOW TO FEED YOUR CAT. Take out a can of cat food.

Figure 58

BEAST WITH FIVE FINGERS. Cut all the way through the book. Show the front cover only. When you open the book, stick your free hand from the back of the book through the book, grab your throat and start choking yourself, monster-like. Mug this up, gasping, then finally shove your hand back inside the book and slam the book shut. If you like, glue a monster rubber glove into the book, inserting your hand into it from the back. (See Figure 58.)

GROWING FLOWERS. Open the book and let a load of spring flowers blossom out, filling the open book as in Figure 59.

Figure 59

OPTICAL ILLUSION NUMBERS

Now for a simple stunt you can make at home, in small, medium, or large stage size according to your needs. This trick was shown to me at a Georgia Magic Club meeting by Nolan and Mark Robinson (father and son magicians), and served as a part of my "Seeing Is Deceiving" eyesight show several school seasons ago. It never failed to work.

First, you'll need to make a poster with the numbers shown exactly as in Figure 60. My wife Lynne hand-lettered these using a black marker on a sheet of 22 x 28-inch white poster board. I made mine specifically for large school show audiences. Yours could be smaller if you're doing birthday parties and smaller groups.

```
         1000
           40
         1000
           30
         1000
           20
         1000
           10
         4100
```

Figure 60

Second, you'll need an envelope to conceal the poster. We made one out of brown paper and package sealing tape.

With the poster in the envelope, here's how I used it.

"I have a large poster in this big envelope, and I want all of you to see it. Now I am going to pull the poster out of the envelope SLOWLY, and each time you see a number, I want you to add it to the other numbers and SHOUT your total out loud. The first number is 1000."

I pull the post up just enough to show 1000.

"Now when I show you the next number, I want you to shout the TOTAL."

I lift the post to show the number 40, and the kids shout, "ONE THOUSAND FORTY."

I lift the poster again, showing the next number (1000), and the kids shout, "TWO THOUSAND FORTY."

Then: "TWO THOUSAND SEVENTY."

"Good," I say. "Keep going."

"THREE THOUSAND SEVENTY. THREE THOUSAND NINETY. FOUR THOUSAND NINETY. FIVE THOUSAND!"

Envelope and poster.

I stop short of my printed total and ask, "What was your total again?"

"FIVE THOUSAND!" they shout.

Now I pull out the entire poster and stand it in front of the envelope. "Better check your addition again," I reply, "because the actual total is FOUR THOUSAND ONE HUNDRED."

Here I pause a moment so each person can re-add the figures in their own heads. As the group realizes the answer is really 4100, a bit of laughter and amazement sweeps over the audience.

"You see, what really happens is that your mind is racing so rapidly ahead that when it gets down here to 4090, your brain jumps TWO DIGITS, making you think the total is 5000 instead of the correct number 4100.

"So SEEING CAN BE DECEIVING, but remember this: It's not really your eyes playing tricks on you. It's your brain, because eyesight takes place NOT in your eyes, but in your BRAIN! And today we're going to have fun with some funny, clown magic that may play tricks on your eyes as well as your brains. Are you ready for more funny magic? Well, let's go!"

I find this a good stunt for early in a show because it's fun and educational at the same time. You can make it small or large to suit your needs. I saw it originally as a pocket trick, which makes me think of the next chapter.

CHAPTER 8

MAGIC UP CLOSE

Close-up magic uses small props such as coins, cards, glasses, and other everyday objects. Because the items used are relatively small, close-up magic is performed for a limited number of observers. Birthday parties and walk-arounds usually provide small audiences for which to work these types of tricks. May I offer you some comedy magic for that purpose?

HOUDINI STRAWS

As a teenager I learned this trick at a Georgia Magic Club meeting. I have no idea of its origin, but it's so adaptable that it's great for an impromptu performance. This trick works with paper or plastic drinking straws, the kind you find at all fast food restaurants, or you can even do it with pipe cleaners.

You simply twist two drinking straws together in a way that binds them to each other. Then, with a sharp tug, you pull them apart so they seem to penetrate each other yet remain whole.

Start by holding one straw upright, and place the second straw in front of it as in Figure 61. Twist the vertical straw down around the horizontal one and back up as in Figures 62 and 63.

Next take the right side of the horizontal straw and twist it around the vertical one. (See Figure 64.) Bring it all the way around the vertical one, being sure it passes *underneath* itself as in Figure 65.

Then bring the two ends of the horizontal straw together to the right as in Figure 66. Close the vertical straw ends together also. (See Figure 67.) With your left hand holding the vertical ends and your right hand holding the horizontal straw ends, show the straws seemingly joined as in Figure 68.

Suddenly tug them apart as in Figure 69. This separates the straws. Immediately let go of one end of each straw, causing the straws to open and pop up. This part works better with plastic straws; with paper straws you'll need to work the straws open with your thumb and fingers.

My basic story line involves the Great Houdini. As I wrap the straws around each other I say, "You know, they say the Great Houdini could escape from anything . . . rope, chains, even boxes nailed shut and thrown into the river. Let's pretend one of these straws is Houdini himself and the other one is a chain. Look, I'll wrap this straw around Houdini so he can't get away. And just to make doubly sure, I'll wrap Houdini around the chain like this.

"Now I'll take Houdini in one hand and the chains in the other hand. Looks like Houdini is securely bound . . . but wait . . . Houdini, can you do it? Can you really

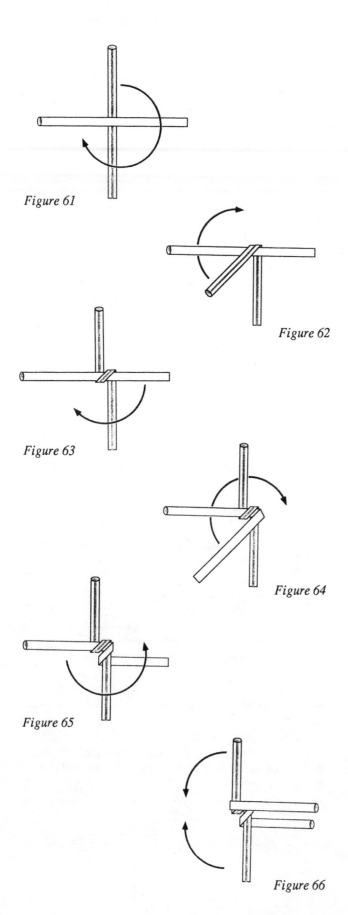

Figure 61

Figure 62

Figure 63

Figure 64

Figure 65

Figure 66

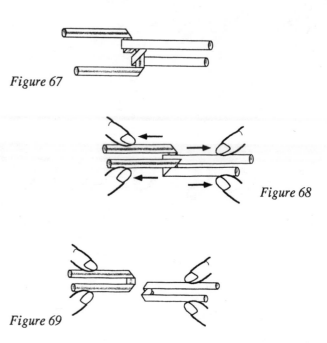

Figure 67

Figure 68

Figure 69

escape? Watch!" Here I pull the straws apart dramatically, pause a moment, then let them pop up as illustrated in the photo on the opposite page.

"Well, Houdini made it! He escaped from the chains, and both Houdini and the chains are still in one piece. It's magic!"

COKE FLOAT

"Most people think that drinking a diet soda makes you lighter. But it also helps to have *light ice.* In fact," you tell your spectators, "that's exactly what I have in my cup . . . *light ice.* It's so light . . . that it almost floats." As you say this, your paper cup appears to float up between your hands.

This is a good little stunt to pull at the end of a meal in a fast food restaurant. Wait until you've finished the liquid in your wax paper cup and there's still a bit of ice in the bottom. Secretly punch a hole in the back of your cup using your car key, a sharp thumbnail, or any silverware (even plasticware) on the table.

Hold the cup in your hand as in Figure 70, and insert your right thumb in the hole, jamming it in tight. With your hands cage-like around the cup, shake your thumb and make the cup move mysteriously. Then let the cup "float" upward from your hands, opening your fingers at the same time.

Letting go of one end of each straw causes the straws to open and pop up.

As the cup begins to float upward, move your arms up as you grab it and then bring it back down. Let it "float up" and bring it back down again. Repeat this a third time, finally holding the cup still.

"Wow! This is the lightest ice I've ever seen. I'd better get rid of it before it floats right off into space!" Saying this, walk over to a trash receptacle and dispose of the gimmicked cup, thus keeping it a secret.

COIN UNDER THE CUP

Place a coin or any small object on the table. Cover the coin with a paper cup, hat, book, or whatever is handy. Tell your friends you can pick up the coin *without touching the cup*—which you do by magical trickery!

How? When you say you will pick up the coin without touching the cup, you begin to make magical passes by waving your hands mysteriously and humorously over the cup. After a few moments of this, you tell your friends, "I have done it! You may look and see!" Then you wait.

The moment someone lifts the cup to look, you quickly grab the coin with your hand.

"See—I told you I could pick up the coin WITHOUT TOUCHING the cup!"

Yes, it's a cute little table trick that kids, in turn, can play on other friends and relatives.

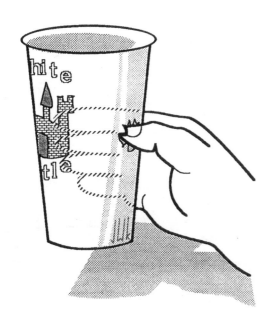

Figure 70

Cup floating between the hands.

COIN GONE TWICE

Kids love to see coins appear and disappear, especially if you pull the coins out of their ears or hair. Now this is not the place for a course on sleight-of-hand with coins, but let me share just a quick little coin interlude that will take a minimum of practice and perhaps make you a hero, in or out of makeup.

You drop a coin on the floor, pick it up, cause it to vanish in your hand, then reappear under your shoe. You pick up the coin, vanish it again, but this time it's not under your shoe. You reach behind a child's ear and find the missing coin.

Let's learn this one step-by-step.

First, show a coin large enough for kids to see. "Accidentally" drop it on the floor near your shoe.

As you reach down to pick it up, slide the coin under your shoe, but come up as though you picked up the coin. Most everyone will assume you did.

Now pretend to place the coin in your other hand. Wave your empty hand over the closed coin hand, making magical passes. Then open your closed hand to show the coin is gone.

"Where did it go?" Point to the floor and move your shoe. This often gets a laugh when your spectators realize you just slid the coin under your shoe. "Would you like to see it again?" you ask. "Yes," they answer.

Reach down to get the coin. As you pick up the coin, toss it behind your leg, catching it with your other hand. Continue upward with your coin hand and make the coin vanish again.

When everyone looks down to see if it's under your shoe, raise your foot. No coin!

Finally, reach behind a child's ear with your hidden-coin hand and reproduce the coin to the magical amazement of the child.

YOUR DOLLAR—MY DOLLAR

"And now, friends, I will perform a bit of mind reading coupled with a few keen insights into the obvious!"

Ask someone to take out a dollar bill. "Notice the bill has all kinds of numbers on it. Like one and one and one and one . . . a one in each corner. The bill also has a serial number. Not the kind of CEREAL you eat, of course. The other kind of serial."

Have him look at the serial number without letting you see it.

"Humor me a little. If I can tell you that exact serial number, can I have the dollar?"

Wait until the person agrees.

Then close your eyes and wave your fingers over the dollar while the person holds it stretched between his hands. Mumble some silly magic words. "Aruba! Jamaica! Chocolate cake bake-uh!" Suddenly, grab the bill from the person's hands and quickly read the serial number out loud.

"There! I did it! And your dollar is my dollar now!"

It's a quick gag, which you admit as such, and a great lead-in to a real trick with a dollar bill. Like the one that follows.

EAT A DOLLAR

Okay, here's another simple one I learned as a teenage magician, but I'll tell you this—I've used it for over 20 years to baffle thousands of people of all ages. And you can do the same.

The effect is straightforward. You fold a dollar bill, tear a chunk out of it, put the chunk in your mouth and chew it a bit, then instantly restore it to the dollar bill.

Before I explain the trick step-by-step, let me suggest that you put a crisp, relatively new dollar bill in your right pocket. I always do this so I'll have a good finish to my routine. Now, let's go.

Start by folding the dollar bill as shown in Figures 71 and 72.

Figure 71

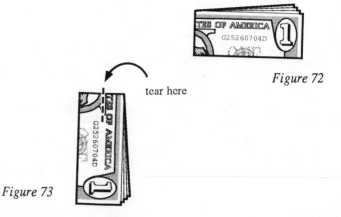

tear here

Figure 72

Figure 73

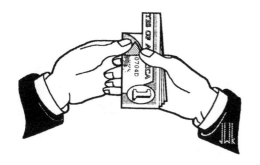

Figure 74

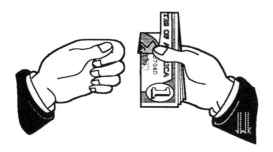

Figure 75

Figure 76

is necessary. During this chewing, you hold the torn dollar with the missing piece in front of you.

Now take the pretend, nonexistent piece from your mouth with your left fingertips and place it back on the dollar bill, immediately flipping the folded-down piece upward as in Figure 76. Rub on the bill corner as though trying to restore it. Blow on it momentarily.

Then open the dollar bill and hold it out flat to show it is in one piece. From just a short distance the torn area cannot be seen—yes, even up close!—due to the lines alongside the tear. Believe me, this works! But the problem now is that you cannot hand this bill back to the volunteer.

So here you say, "Who GAVE me this dollar?" Emphasize the word *gave*. The volunteer usually says, "I did." And you say, "Thank you!" Immediately put his dollar in your right pocket, switch it for your dollar bill, and bring it out laughing. "I'm only kidding. Here's your dollar back . . . thanks a lot!"

If you're concerned that a volunteer might check the serial number because of the previous dollar trick, just give that bill back and borrow another one from someone else. Tell them you need a newer bill, "something a little more clean and crisp, like lettuce. After all, I'm hungry." Then proceed with the trick as described. You'll like it, and so will your spectators.

CARD STICK

Card tricks are fine for clown comedy as long as you don't do too many of them. Even in my magic shows at schools, I limit myself to *one card trick* per show. Here's an easy one you can "ham it up" for laughs.

Glue a card onto a flat wooden stick, the kind the doctor puts in your mouth and tells you to say, "Ahh." (See Figure 77.) Glue a different card on the back of that card and stick. Now you have a card-size old-fashioned fan. Let's say your back-to-back cards are the three of hearts and king of spades. We'll call this your card stick.

Hold up a fan of real cards with your card stick behind it. (See Figure 78.) Ask someone to touch a card. As the person reaches for a card, slide the card stick up into view as in Figure 79 so the person touches that card, the three of hearts. This will get a laugh. Your job is to act as if everything is ordinary.

"Remember your card," you tell the spectator. Then slide the card stick back down behind the fan. Close the fan, with the card stick hidden in your hand. Turn slightly left and slip the card stick behind you and into your back

Now tear the bill as in Figure 73, right beside George's head. Use your left thumb to fold the torn portion down as in Figure 74.

Pretend to tear the piece of bill out now as illustrated in Figure 75.

Immediately place the pretend piece in your mouth and chew on it. I've seen a few magicians purposely have green chewing gum in their mouths at this point; they open their mouths and show briefly what appears to be a chewed piece of dollar in their teeth. Personally, I don't think this

Figure 77

Figure 78

Figure 79

Figure 80

pocket so it sticks up as in Figure 80 with the king of spades showing.

Now turn back to the spectator. Say you'll make her card vanish. Slap the deck three times. "There—it's gone!" Hold the deck facing the audience and fan the cards bit by bit so the spectator can see her card has vanished. (You removed the three of hearts before the trick started.)

"Now, I bet you wonder where it went. I'll show you."

Turn your back halfway around so the audience can see the card sticking out of your back pocket, showing the king of spades.

"See—there it is, in my back pocket!"

When the spectator says that's not her card, you face her again and act puzzled. "Not your card?" Quickly reach into your back pocket and pull out the card stick, bringing it into view with the three of hearts showing.

"Gee, that's strange—I thought your card was the three of hearts!" you exclaim, tossing the card stick and deck into your bag for a laugh.

THUMB OFF

Another trick kids love to see is the one where a magician or clown pulls off his thumb. I do this as follows.

Holding my right hand as in Figure 81, I bring my left hand around it as in Figure 82. As I wrap my left hand around the thumb, I swing my thumb down as in Figure 83. Then I immediately pull up the left hand as in Figure 84.

To the children, it looks like I've pulled my thumb right off. Their eyes and mouths open wide, and often they laugh in amazement as well.

After a moment's pause, I bring the left hand back down to the right, swing the right thumb back up inside the left fingers, and pull my left hand aside to show the right thumb is back.

Now, if you're clowning in gloves, you can do this just as easily. But you can even go a step further. Get a three-inch piece of wooden dowel, whittle it into a thumb shape, then cover it with white cloth to match your gloves.

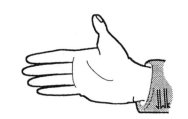

Figure 81

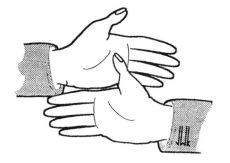

Figure 82

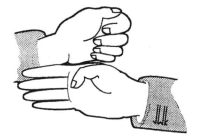

Figure 83

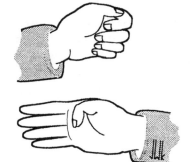

Figure 84

Have this thumb gimmick in your left pocket.

Proceed with pulling off your thumb as I already described. While the kids laugh and maybe even try it themselves, secretly slip the thumb gimmick out of your pocket into your left hand. Tell the kids you'll do it one last time if everyone will watch very closely.

Hold up your right thumb. Bring your left hand over the right, swing your right thumb down into hiding, and twist your left hand around so they can see the thumb gimmick inside. They'll think they are seeing your real right thumb.

Now pull off the fake thumb, pause a moment to look at it, then toss it aside into your bag or pocket it. Immediately reach your right hand behind your head and pretend to pull out your thumb, which is now back on your right hand.

"Whew! I thought I lost it there for a minute! That was THUMB FUN, wasn't it!"

PENETRATED THUMB

As long as we're on thumb tricks, here's an oldie but goodie from the magic of kidhood. Play it for comedy, and you'll have a real winner.

The clown drapes a handkerchief over his thumb, then proceeds to stick hatpins or straight pins through the hank into his thumb, yelling "OUCH!" with each pin. Finally, he pulls the hank off to reveal his thumb unharmed and a piece of carrot as the real victim of the pins.

What starts out as "magic" becomes a gag at the end. Hide a four-inch piece of carrot inside a handkerchief. Tell the audience you're going to practice the ancient art of acupuncture by sticking pins into your thumb. But since it's too gruesome to watch, you'll cover your thumb with this handkerchief.

Hold up your thumb and cover it with the hank, grasping the carrot. Now for the pins. Stick about a dozen pins into the carrot through the hank as in Figure 85, hamming it up with fake pain as you do. After the last one, tell the audience you have survived.

Pull the hank off your hand, turning it over as you do, not only showing that the thumb is okay, but also revealing the carrot with pins still inside it. Flex your thumb, smiling, then notice the carrot.

"Uh . . . uh . . ." You don't know what to say. Then take a bite of the carrot and say, "Ehh—what's up, Doc?" It's a joke!

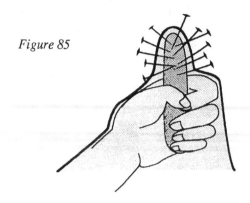

Figure 85

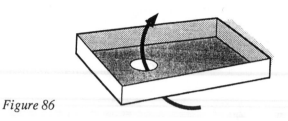

Figure 86

Figure 87

THE MUMMY FINGER

I love this one. Maybe that's because it goes back to my early days in magic with my friend Marty Walden, doing shows in our basements and having the thrill of learning new tricks. It's another simple trick, but one that could easily be used in many close-up situations, depending on your character and presentation.

Let me first give you the basics, then we'll clownize it.

Take a small cardboard jewelry box and cut a hole in the bottom large enough for your finger. (See Figure 86.) Place your middle finger in the hole and bend it over as in Figure 87. A little cotton around your finger to cover the bottom of the box creates a better illusion.

To enhance the effect, sprinkle a little talcum powder or dusting powder on your finger and rub it in to give the finger a lifeless appearance. Then place the cover on top of the box.

As a kid magician, I would tell my audiences of friends and relatives that I dug up this strange thing out in the backyard, and I put it in this box. Then I would remove the lid and show the finger, which appeared to be cut off.

"Maybe it's a real mummy's finger," I suggested.

Then I would raise my finger up and wiggle it for a laugh, making them realize it was my own.

Now let's adapt this old trick to clowning. In a similar fashion to the trick of pulling off your thumb, whittle a piece of wooden dowel into the shape of your middle finger, from the big knuckle to the fingertip. Cover this with white cloth to match your gloves. Then prepare a little box as described, but put black felt or some color in it for contrast instead of the white cotton described

earlier. Lay this fake finger in the box and close it.

In performing, open the box to show the "clown mummy finger." Remove it with your free hand, show it around, and tell some wild story about locating it in "Indiana Jones' lunch box." Be sure the viewers do not see the hole in the box.

As you go to place the fake finger back into the box, secretly insert your gloved finger from underneath, and steal the fake finger away with your other hand. Reach into your pocket for the lid, dropping the fake finger. Put the lid on the box.

Now have everyone concentrate while you chant to the "mummy clown spirit." Say something like, "Oh, Boris, Karis, Doris. Give your clown mummy finger the energy of a bowl of Wheaties and an ice-cold Coca-Cola, and bring it back to life."

Then slowly lift your finger so the lid rises up and falls off.

"Look—it worked—the lid came off by itself!" you say dramatically, or better, melodramatically.

Then let your finger slowly rise up and start wiggling around. Smile, let go of the box, and hold up your entire hand wiggling your fingers and the box at your friends. "It's a J-O-K-E!"

SMELL THE FLOWER

Prepare a long-stemmed yellow rose that will come off the stem easily. Paint a 15-18 inch piece of wooden dowel green for the stem. Get an artificial cloth flower from the store. Glue a heavy paper or cardboard tube to its bottom as in Figure 88. Paint the tube green to match the stem. Now set the flower onto the stem.

Inside the cloth flower attach a piece of double-stick tape or an O-ring of regular tape (Figure 89). Walk around with the flower, displaying it. Then bring it up to your nose as though to sniff it.

As you do this, press the yellow flower to your red clown nose, where the flower sticks and stays. Pull the stem away as in Figure 90, not looking at the stem and "not realizing" that the flower is now on your nose. Smile a lot.

Finally, you look at the stem and see that the flower is gone. You look all around for the flower . . . left and right and under your arms, check your pockets. Nowhere can you find the flower. If kids tell you it's on your nose, ignore them at first, but finally listen them. Then you try to back your head away from your nose to look at the flower. If you can cross your eyes, now's the time to add that bit of comedy.

Seeing the flower, you carefully pull it off your nose, and holding your head high in the air in a snooty fashion, you place the flower back on the stem and walk on.

I like it. It's simple and easy to repeat if you are in a crowd at a picnic or other event. And little kids think it's R-E-A-L funny!

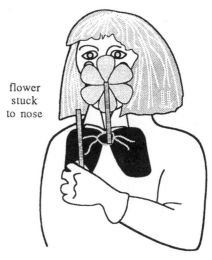

flower
stuck
to nose

Figure 90

SQUEAKER GAGS

One of the great comedy devices to appear on the magic/clown market in the last few years is a little gadget called a *squeaker,* or *hand squeaker.* The photo on the right shows me holding one. All you do is squeeze this plastic, nearly flat bulb, and it makes a loud squeaking,

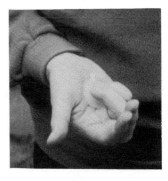

whistling, or chirping sound. These devices come in different sizes and thus make different sounds.

By hiding a squeaker in your hand or even inside your glove at the palm (see Figure 91), you can make it squeak using your middle two fingers. This you do unknown to the audience. Therefore, you can make anything you touch appear to squeak.

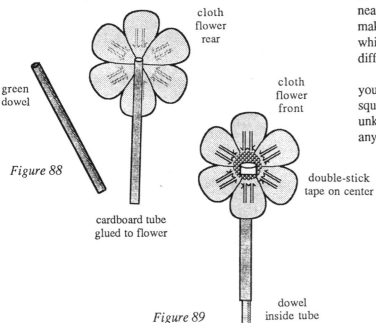

cloth
flower
rear

green
dowel

cloth
flower
front

Figure 88

double-stick
tape on center

cardboard tube
glued to flower

dowel
inside tube

Figure 89

squeaker in glove

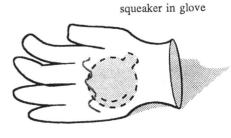

Figure 91

You can also sew squeakers into hidden pockets in your costume. Then, when you touch your knee, shoulder, or elbow, you cause that part of your body to squeak.

"Talk about squeaky joints," you remark, "listen to this elbow." Tap the elbow a few times with your free hand to make it squeak.

With a squeaker palmed, reach over and touch a child's nose. Make it squeak for a laugh. Squeak the child's ear, elbow, head, shoulder. The uses for this device are limited, truly, only by your imagination.

Here are a few more ways to have fun with squeakers:

- Squeak as you wind your watch. "Hmm, I really need to oil this thing!"
- Hold a squeaker and a fly swatter in the same hand. Squeak repeatedly as you swat an imaginary fly.
- Make any toy or stuffed animal squeak, whether your own or a child's. You can also cause a puppet to squeak.
- Have a child reach into your change bag. Make a squeaking sound as he does, and jump back slightly. "What's in there?" you say. Then pull out something silly or funny, like a toy mouse.
- Squeak your own nose. This is really funny if you are wearing a big red clown nose. You can even pretend to sneeze, building up slowly like this: "Ah, ah, ah . . . ah . . . SQUEAK!"
- Touch a kid's hair and make it squeak. Say, "I guess you just washed your hair—because it's squeaky clean!"
- Remove the squeak device from three child's rubber toys. Using your hidden hand squeaker, play a "three shell game" using the toys, showing that one squeaks and two do not. Then move them around, and let the kids try to guess which one does squeak. Of course, you're always under control over which one squeaks. Have all three toys squeak for your ending.
- If you use any kind of live animal in your show, use the squeaker to cause that animal to make sounds. Kids love this.
- Press the spots on a playing card, and make them squeak. "Hey, it's a playing card." Push a pip and remark, "See—the pips squeak!"
- Use the hidden hand squeaker to make balloon animals squeal and squeak. Kids will go crazy trying to make theirs do the same thing!

With these ten ideas for starters, I'm sure you can think up dozens of other squeaker gags. Just carry one or two squeakers in your pockets at all times, and look for opportunities to use them for fun. The chances are endless. And thanks to Bruce Johnson and Paul Diamond for the ideas.

CHAPTER 9

SUPER SIGHT GAGS

What are sight gags all about? Sight gags are props, objects, or acts that are instantly, or nearly instantly, funny. Some are clever, some are corny, but the humor depends on some visual incongruity. Many of these gags can be done as walk-arounds where you would go into the audience before the show begins or at picnics, parades, business grand openings, and the like. Let's take a look at a few sight gags to give you the idea, and start you creating your own.

SUITCASE GAGS

Suitcase gags have been a circus standby for years, and they're great for walking around in parades and at picnics. Bruce "Sparkles" Johnson, my clown friend from Lexington, Kentucky gave me a bunch of new and old suitcase gag walk-arounds which I'll share with you here. Bruce's thoughts on walk-arounds, suitcase gags, and parade clowning in general, are based on over 30 years of performing experience. You can make up any of them for your own use but also use them as springboards to creative clown thinking. Here we go, more or less in Bruce's own words.

Make the inside of your suitcase gags with bold, contrasting colors so they may be easily seen and read. Do the same thing with the sign on the front. I strongly suggest that you use all the same color letters for readability. Using different colored letters makes signs hard to read. Get professional lettering, or buy stick-on letters from the office supply stores, but whatever you do, *do not* magic marker your signs by hand on white poster board! It looks homemade and unprofessional.

As far as placement goes in a parade, I always try to get behind a marching band. First, so I won't interfere with their music or pace, but second, so I can use their music and work to the beat of it. It's like I have my own background music.

During the parade, I show my suitcase or sight gags to one side of the crowd and get my reaction. Then I go to the other side of the street and repeat the same gag for that group. I continue this pattern behind the band, zigzagging my way back and forth. In an auditorium situation, I do the same sort of thing, working the aisles back and forth with different gags.

Now, I've made my suitcase gags interchangeable, so I only have to carry one case, even for an event where I have to use three or four gags. My outside signs have Velcro tabs (found in cloth stores) on the backs to match up with his suitcases. Same for the inside. Then I carry all my props and signs in one big case, interchanging them offstage.

Bruce "Sparkles" Johnson doing some clown magic.

Where do you get ideas? Go to a shopping center, walk through store after store, and look for ideas. They're everywhere, just waiting to jump out at you if you keep your eyes open and your mind working on gags. Flea markets, salvage stores, Salvation Army and Goodwill stores are great sources for these sight gags. You can find cheap old cases there that you can paint and fix up for suitcase gags, as well as for carrying your show items.

In many stores you can often find large items on display. I usually ask the manager if I could possibly have the large display item (such as a giant toothbrush) when they're finished with it. I'll give him my card, and he'll often give it to me on the spot. Other times he'll save it for me or tell me how to contact the distributor.

By the way, if you write to such a distributor, address your correspondence to the Public Relations Department. They always respond if you tell them you're a clown and entertain children in hospitals, picnics, and the like. Many times they'll send me the prop free; other times they'll just charge me for shipping.

Another note: If it's a good prop you think you'll use, try to get two of them, one for backup and future use.

Practice handling your suitcase so it will open and close easily and quickly, thus allowing you to move on. One simple clasp is best, especially if you make your own. A simple door hook on the side works well for me. Some clowns use magnets to keep the case closed; then they use an extra handle on the side or top to pull the magnets apart and thus open the case.

Make sure the audience sees clearly what you're doing so they will understand the bit. Don't parade around with an old beat-up suitcase gag. If it needs repainting or fixing up, *do it*. The way it looks reflects on you. Make the suitcase gag as crisp and clear as possible.

Be sensitive as to how you perform your gags. I've seen clowns parading around with beer bottles and questionable inflatable objects I would not use. Some of these things turn people off and hurt not only your image, but clowning as well. Throwing or squirting things into a crowd are *no nos*. Many people don't like that, especially older folks and the parents of little children.

If you're working with a group, be sure to talk over what you're going to do so there's no duplication of gags. The second time around, it's not so funny. Keep the gags varied so that each clown uses different types of props.

Another important point: Try to create gags that require no resetting so you can do them one after the other without any hesitation. That makes parading easier, plus it's less work on you. Too many clowns try to carry too many props for these situations. After all, you're only there for a short time with each group, so don't try to do too much.

One last thing: *Please* look as professional as possible with good, clean, crisp makeup and clean colorful costumes because your first impression is so important to people. Remember, in most cases, people look at your makeup and costume *before* they see your gag, so you must make a good impression. In fact, often they'll come up to you and ask for a business card, asking if you do parties and so on. If you just look run-of-the-mill, they won't even talk to you. I can't stress that enough—you have to look good!

Thank you, Bruce, for those words of advice. And now let's check out Sparkles' list of suitcase gags. Maybe there's something here for you!

FIRST DOG IN SPACE. Have these words on the front of the suitcase. Open the suitcase to show a toy dog suspended inside the case from a clear fishing line.

HOW'S TRICKS? Open the case and pull out a box of Trix cereal. Open the box and eat some, then say, "Mine are fine. How's tricks with you?"

HAVE YOU EVER WALKED ON WATER? Take out a sign that says "WATER," lay it on the floor, and walk across it.

FOUL BALL. Open case to reveal a rubber chicken with a ball in its mouth.

MY BEE COLLECTION. Open the case to show lots of letter Bs printed on a board inside.

MY DIAMOND COLLECTION. Have all the diamond cards in the deck—ace of diamonds, king of diamonds, etc.—pasted inside on a black background.

MY FAMILY CREST. Open to reveal a jumbo size of Crest toothpaste glued on a dark background.

ORIGINAL ROCK AND ROLL. Inside reveals a rubber rock and a rubber or plastic roll (bread). You can use a real roll if you spray coat it with clear lacquer or varnish.

MY ANT COLLECTION. Open the case to show pictures of old ladies, as in your "aunts."

PAIR OF BLOOMERS. Two little pots inside the case with plastic flowers growing out of them.

DANGER BABY RATTLERS (with picture of snakes on front). Open the case to show two pink and blue plastic baby rattler toys. I've also done this with a wicker basket to carry out the snake theme. In addition to the words I had a skull and crossbones on the front. When I lifted the lid, it had a ribbon dangling from it with the two baby rattlers on it.

MORNING PAPER. Open the case to show a roll of toilet tissue.

SILLY SIGHT GAGS

Here are some more sight gags from Bruce Johnson that can be used as suitcase gags or to accompany your silly talk or magic antics. By using an idiom book, which offers alphabetical listings and explanations of thousands of common expressions. You can stimulate your thinking and create additional sight gags. You'll find such books at the library or bookstore. Just read through them and let your mind play on the words. Who knows? Maybe your ideas will be better than these!

HAIR SPRAY. Hide a water-filled syringe inside a fake rabbit, with the nozzle pointing out of its mouth. Ask someone, "Have you seen my hair spray?" When they say no, pull this rabbit out and squeeze the syringe so it sprays water out of its mouth.

FOOTLOCKER. Hold up a rubber joke foot or shoe with a padlock hooked through it.

SWEET TOOTH. A large sponge tooth with packets of sugar glued onto it.

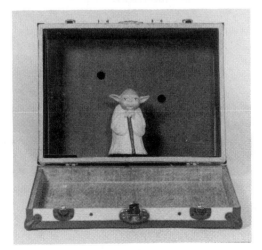

My Toyota is a "toy Yoda."

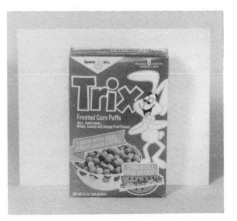

My box of tricks is a box of Trix cereal.

GREEN THUMB. Spray paint a giant rubber thumb green. Use this to remark about your gardening skills.

GIVE SOMEONE A BLACK EYE. Reach in your pocket and take out a black cardboard letter "I."

GIVE SOMEONE THE THIRD DEGREE. Pull out a cardboard number 3 with a degree sign on it.

GIVE SOMEONE THE LAST WORD. Pull out a sign with the last word in the dictionary printed on it.

RING AROUND THE COLLAR. Hold up a dog collar with a bell attached to it, and shake it to ring the bell.

ACE IN THE HOLE. Take a rubber donut (found in children's shops), and stick a jumbo ace of spades card in it. When you tell them you've got an "ace in the hole," pull out the ace and show them.

BESIDE YOURSELF. Hold up a mirror and look at your side.

CATCH SOME ZZZs. Pull out some paper or cardboard letter Zs and gently toss them to a few people.

CHEER UP! Hold up a box of Cheer washing detergent as you say that, and toss it up into the air.

PRETTY PENNY. Glue lace and ribbons around a jumbo penny (novelty shop item).

DRY BEHIND THE EARS. Take a piece of rubber or plastic corn on the cob, and use a towel to dry the back side of it.

FLIP MY LID. Take the lid off any prop, and flip it into the air.

BOOK . . . WORM?

Buy a cheap, thick book at a flea market or garage sale. Drill or cut out two holes large enough to mount a couple of cans inside, similar to my "Comedy Lunch Box." Compress a couple of spring snakes into the cans as shown in Figure 92, and hold them in place with a steel coat hanger pin as shown. Using office supply stick-ons, label the book "RAISING WORMS FOR FUN AND PROFIT." (See Figure 93.)

Show the book, read the title, and open it up. The coat hanger holds the snakes in place. Pretend to read the text. Then close the book. While holding it shut with one hand, slip the coat hanger pin out the bottom. Then say, "I wonder how big those worms grow?"

Now open the book, and let the snakes pop out on you, shouting with surprise and mugging (making funny facial expressions) and so on.

"About that big, I guess!"

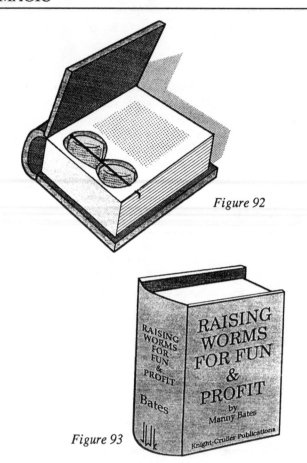

Figure 92

Figure 93

COMPUTER BABY

Years ago a college student named Scott Miller showed me an interesting item during a convention in Gatlinburg, Tennessee. I liked it so much I made arrangements with Scott to use it in my shows, then in my book *Kidbiz*, and later I even manufactured it, in addition to showing it on my *Behind the Scenes* videotape. Here's how it looks to an audience.

The performer tells the audience he has his computer baby along tonight. "I wish you could see him, but he's asleep."

About that time the audience hears a baby crying. The performer reaches into his case and brings out a diapered tape recorder/player, as in Figure 94, announcing, "Well, he woke up. Here he is, my computer baby, Little Hershel."

"WHAH! WA-EH! WAH-EH!" the baby cries.

"It's time to feed the little guy," says the performer. "Better get his bottle." Out comes a baby bottle, and the performer starts feeding the little guy. "This is not ordinary milk. It's milk mixed with machine oil. It greases him good . . . so good, in fact, that he can calculate and compute all day long. He can even tell you PIE ARE SQUARE!"

All this time the baby computer is making slurping sounds. Finally, he stops.

"Well, it looks like he drank it all." Bottle aside, the performer turns the computer to his shoulder. "Gotta burp the baby now. You always have to do that."

After a few taps on the back, the baby computer lets out a loud BURP sound, which causes audience children to laugh every time. Then the baby starts crying again, and the performer rocks him to sleep until the crying subsides.

This entire bit is an acting job on the part of the clown. Little Hershel is merely a tape recorder partially covered with a cloth diaper, Pampers, or even a white pocket handkerchief.

Inside he contains an audio cassette tape that has crying, slurping, a big burp, and more crying, timed to certain lengths and with blank intervals in between. The first ten seconds of the tape are blank so that the performer can hit the play button as he puts a prop down, move back to center stage, and talk for a few moments before the crying starts and interrupts him.

The recording can be made at home if you like, providing you can do a baby cry voice or have a real baby who will cry on cue. Also, these recordings are available commercially. You can change the skit to suit your needs and clown character.

One lady clown I know in Texas wraps her computer baby in a small blanket, never letting the viewers see it. She tries to feed it a rubber hot dog and a hamburger, but the baby keeps crying. Finally, she offers it a two-liter bottle of 7-Up, complete with baby nipple top. But she keeps the baby a mystery. Others have opened the baby blanket to reveal a rubber pig or chicken for an additional laugh. This could also be a neat walk-around for picnics.

Figure 94

BIG BAND MUSIC

Charlie Sable, a clown from Fitzwilliam, New Hampshire, is responsible for this gag. We met at the Clown Fest in Asbury Park, New Jersey, several years back, and during a lull in activities, Charlie began telling me about his newly acquired musical taste.

"I'm into BIG BAND MUSIC," he told me, "the kind our parents listened to back in the 1940s. You know, what they call the BIG BAND SOUND."

"Yes, I know what you mean," I replied, though that music wasn't my cup of tea, so to speak.

"I started listening to some of it not long ago," Charlie continued, "and I've really gotten into BIG BAND MUSIC. You ought to try it. You might find you like it more than you think. Of course, the real key to playing BIG BAND MUSIC and enjoying it is to have a BAND BIG ENOUGH to produce that kind of music—in fact, I think the bigger the band, the better the BIG BAND MUSIC sounds."

At that point, Charlie dug into his pocket and pulled out this very large *rubber band*. He stretched it between his fingers and started plucking the two strands like bass strings.

"Twang! Twang! Twang!" it went, as Charlie smiled and remarked, "Yes, I really do love that BIG BAND MUSIC!"

I flew home and found the biggest rubber band I could locate so I could pull the same good, clean, corny joke on everybody I know. And so can you just lay the verbal buildup on thick, then hit them with the visual!

RAPID BALLOON SCULPTURE

While I've been having fun with his Big Band Music gag, Charlie "Cecil" Sable has cooked up another gag that he uses on a regular basis amid his balloon sculptures.

"In addition to performing magic," he announces, "I am also a balloon sculptor. That means I can make balloon animals out of balloons and lots of hot air.

"Now, there are two important things in making inflated animals: Speed is important, but people MUST be able to recognize WHAT the animal is. I know one balloon artist, for instance, who can inflate, tie off, and twist a balloon in THREE AND A HALF seconds. Of course, the balloon doesn't look like anything, but the guy has speed.

"However, you must also have ACCURACY. And that is what I, balloon sculptor CECIL, have perfected. In fact, I have honed my skill to the point where I can perform FOUR balloon creations in the time it takes most people to do just one. Yes, that's right—four balloon animals in the time most clowns can do ONE!

"Would you like to see me do that?"

Of course, the audience says YES.

Quickly Cecil pops out a surgical rubber glove which was concealed in his hand. He blows it up and holds it over his head.

"A CHICKEN!" he shouts.

Immediately he brings the glove just below eye level and turns his head sideways.

"A TURKEY!" he exclaims.

Then he turns the glove upside down and uses his free hand to tug on the fingers.

"A COW!" he explains.

Now he lets the glove deflate and the fingers dangle. He shakes the glove and makes it quiver.

"A JELLYFISH!" he says loudly with a big grin.

That's right, folks—four sight gags with one rubber glove in about three seconds. According to Charlie, it never fails to get an assortment of laughs and groans. It's clean, it's corny, and I'll use it!

Thank you, Charlie!

COMEDY DOVE APPEAR

Announce that you will miraculously produce a "real dove" from a handkerchief. Secretly have a packaged bar of Dove soap folded in the corner of a handkerchief.

Wave the hank around in the air several times. Then bunch it up, and fiddle with it as though a live dove (bird) is fluttering around. Work the bar of soap up and out of the handkerchief, revealing it to the audience.

"And there it is—a REAL DOVE from the handkerchief!"

You could also perform this corny gag with an empty container from a Dove ice cream bar or other common product available in your area. Either way, it's a real "dove!"

DOG IN THE SHOE BOX

I've saved one of the best walk-around gags to close the chapter. I've seen magicians and clowns perform it, and it always gets a lot of laughs and comments.

When I attended my first Southeastern Magician's Convention in Chattanooga, Tennessee, veteran school show performer Paul Smith, professionally known as Elmer, was doing this one all over the convention. In more recent years, Atlanta magician/clown Clint Hope performed this as one of his favorite walk-arounds.

In effect, the performer walks around with an ordinary shoe box, and from the box comes sounds of a dog squeaking. "You wanna see my little dog?" he asks the curious kids or adults. Of course they do.

Then he opens the shoe box . . . but before he gets the lid completely off, the dog starts squeaking in a loud racket, as though someone stepped on his tail. This often makes kids jump back.

"There he is," says the performer, "my little dog."

Now the kids look inside the shoe box . . . and see . . . a rubber hot dog glued to the bottom of the box.

The performer covers the box again and continues on to the next group for a laugh. I suppose I've seen this performed over 100 times, and I've never seen it fail to attract attention and get laughs from young and old. So how is it done?

First, the rubber hot dog is glued to the shoe box bottom so it will stay in one place and not roll around and make noise.

Second, the sound may come from one of two sources: (1) a mouth squeaker or Swiss bird warbler, or (2) a hand-held squeaker, operated under the shoe box by the hand holding the box. In either version, the audience is not aware of where the sound comes from or how it is produced. They must assume that it comes from within the box.

When you start pulling off the lid to show the "little dog," kick your squeaker into high gear, like a dog in pain or fright, and extend the box toward someone as you make these sounds. Your audience may back off at first, but as you tilt the box and let them see the hot dog inside, they'll feel silly and begin to laugh.

It's a harmless trick, but sure lots of fun, and easy enough to repeat again and again right away.

CHAPTER 10

RUNNING GAGS

What is a running gag? According to author Henning Nelms in his book *Magic and Showmanship*, "A running gag is a bit of comedy which is repeated several times during an act, and which becomes funnier with each repetition."

Repetition is the key word. When something happens over and over in your clown act, either exactly the same way or similar in format, each time getting a few more laughs, you're doing a running gag. Hopefully, by the end of the act or show, that running gag will reach a climax, possibly due to the use of magic.

In this chapter we'll take a look at some classic running gags, both to educate you and to stimulate your thinking. And we'll cook up a few new ones to spark your own creativity.

WATER OF THE CHATTAHOOCHEE

Great magicians of the vaudeville era used this one as an out-front bit while illusions and scenery were being changed backstage. I'm sure I even saw it performed at my first magic conventions. And it's perfect for clowning, inside or outdoors.

Magicians like Dante performed it this way: Walking over to the side of the stage, the magician would pick up a large metal vase and pour water out of it into a bowl or bucket, announcing loudly, "WATER OF INDIA!" Between scenes in the show, the pouring would be repeated, and the vase always held more water, much to the crowd's amazement. The water vase was virtually inexhaustible, and this repetition caused lots of laughter.

Not wanting to copy Dante or any of the others (and I've seen that done), I took the trick and localized it. In my home state of Georgia, right beside Atlanta, is the Chattahoochee River, made famous by a Sidney Lanier poem. When I perform this feat of mystery, I call it "Water of the Chattahoochee," and my audience can identify with that.

So my first suggestion to you is to localize this trick using the name of a big river, lake, pond or even ocean in your area. I'll leave that up to you.

Second, let's look at the modus ap . . . modas opera . . . let's look at how it works. In a nutshell, this is a mechanical trick vase called a *lota bowl* or *lota vase*, depending on who makes it and what size it happens to be. It is a double-walled vase, these days typically made of aluminum, which contains water in both the inner and outer chambers. (See Figure 95.)

When you pour out all of the water from the inner chamber, the water stays in the outer chamber due to air pressure. Most often you control this with a finger or thumb over an air hole inside or outside the top of the vase. Once you have emptied the inner chamber, you set the

Figure 95

Bubbles pours water from lota vase while Ruffles watches.

vase upright once more. When you release the air hole, water flows from the outer to the inner chamber, partially filling it again. This way you can pour again moments later.

Most lota vases can pour six or seven times or more, the amount of water diminishing each time. This also depends on the size of the outer chamber. Indeed, the better stage lota vases have an outer chamber *larger* than the inner chamber.

Third, we must look at the showmanship, or clowning, side of this effect. Obviously, using it just as described works fine for magicians or clowns. But I feel that a clown performing it must do more with it than a magician. A clown must deliver this one with his or her voice, mannerisms, and movements.

Saying the same thing each time, "Water of the Chattahoochee," for example, is fine, but you need to pronounce it dramatically the same way each time. I prefer a hokey, high-brow but corny delivery.

Gesturing with your hands the same way each time helps too, setting up the repeat situation in gestures as well as words.

Finally, walking over to the vase, picking it up, pouring it out, and setting it down—all the same way each time—hammers the gag home.

And last, all that you do with this gag will depend on your character. How will he or she deal with this situation?

Another possibility is to work the lota vase with a second clown. Perhaps you show your clown friend how to water the flowers with magic water. "But you don't pour it right onto the flowers. Oh, no. First you pour it into this bucket (bowl, glass, etc), like this." And you say these words: "Oh magic water flow for me. Grow my flowers magically."

Your friend now protests that you've used all the water, but you explain that by saying those magic words, the water will flow again. To prove it, you pour the water.

Immediately your friend picks up the vase, putting her thumb or finger over the hole to stop the vase from filling. When she tries to pour, very little comes out. Once she sets the vase down and lets go, it will start filling again. You explain the magic words, say them, and make it work once more.

Does that have you thinking? I hope so because I'm going to let you finish this routine on your own. Good luck!

OLSEN AND JOHNSON'S GROWING PLANT

Back in 1938-39 a Broadway show, later turned into a movie, had millions of people in stitches. Walter Winchell said it was "the funniest show he had ever seen." It was Olsen and Johnson's *Hellzapoppin!* For my money, the whole thing walked the fine line between clowning and comedy because it was one sight gag, one pun, one groaner, one slapstick gag, one everything funny after another. Absolute nonstop hilarity, like being in a machine gun blitz of humor. I mean this as a sincere compliment, if you have any doubts.

Moviewise, Olsen and Johnson followed *Hellzapoppin!* with another Broadway show, *Sons O' Fun,* and then a movie called *Crazy House,* which is exactly that. Shemp Howard, of Three Stooges fame, is actually the main running gag man in *Crazy House,* constantly trying to sell Olsen and Johnson something crazy at every lull moment, making no lull moments in essence. Examples:

"Ya wanna buy a deck of cards?   It's a good DEAL!"

"Ya wanna buy a clock? On TIME?"

"Ya wanna buy an anchor? Straight off the BOAT!"

You should check for these movies on TV. They'll get you thinking funny!

Why did I mention all this? Because unknown to me at the time, magicians and clowns were doing Olsen and Johnson stunts at conventions when I was a budding teen magician. And my personal favorite came right out of *Hellsapoppin!* Here's how it went.

Thirty minutes prior to the evening show, a man dressed like a bellhop came walking through the theater with a small potted plant.

"Mrs. Jones? Delivery for Mrs. Jones!"

All through the aisles he went, never finding the lady and finally leaving. But ten minutes later he was back— same thing, "Mrs. Jones!"—carrying the same pot, but the plant had grown by about a foot. No, he didn't find Mrs. Jones this time either, and the next time he came through, the plant was two feet tall . . . and then three feet tall.

Just before showtime, the bellhop came through one last time, carrying the same pot with a tree about four to six feet tall, which he could hardly carry, still looking for the elusive Mrs. Jones. Finally spotting her he says, "Oh, Mrs. Jones, I'm so glad I finally found you! Here's your plant!" He sets the tree right in her lap! (See Figure 96.)

The audience just loved it. It had a beginning, certainly a middle, giving them something to talk about and be amused about prior to showtime, and finally an ending. Of course, when the show started, the bellhop quietly came back and retrieved the tree.

What a great audience running gag! I've always wanted to use it in one of my "big shows." And it's so perfect for clowning, whether you employ it in the audience or on the stage throughout a program. Just have one clown continually coming onto the stage between skits or acts carrying the growing plant, trying to find someone, at last locating the right person on the stage or even in the

Figure 96

audience and presenting that someone with the plant, now a small tree.

But let's look at this creatively for a moment. What other ideas could fit the pattern? Could a clown come on carrying a baby, feeding it with a bottle, and with each return visit the baby (a doll) grows bigger and bigger? How about walking a little dog across the stage, remarking that you have to "go feed him," and each time you return, do so with a bigger dog, ending with a Saint Bernard? If using real dogs won't work for you, how about stuffed animals, dogs or cats, using the same format? The final cat could be a huge stuffed tiger!

Being creative sometimes means asking the questions, "What else could it be? How could I change it to suit my act or a particular need? How could I adapt it to be me?"

Think about it!

NEWSPAPER SWINDLE

Recently, reading Ralph Dewey's book *Dewey's Clown Gags & Giggles,* I came across this interesting skit, reprinted here with Ralph's permission.

A newsboy enters holding up a newspaper and yells, "EXTRA! EXTRA! Read all about it! Con artist swindles 250 clowns!" The clown is interested and buys a newspaper for a dollar. The clown opens the paper and finds it totally blank. He is angry and complains to the newsboy, "This is a gyp, the paper is blank." The newsboy turns and walks away, yelling, "EXTRA! EXTRA! Read all about it! Con artist swindles 251 clowns!"

Actually, I thought this was a pretty good gag on its own, but then I started thinking: What else could I do with this skit? Where else could it go? Why not treat the gag described as the first scene of a running gag?

The question then became: Where do we go next?

Well, how about this:

The newsboy returns with the same "EXTRA! EXTRA! 251" announcement. The clown reacts with skepticism, saying the last paper he bought was blank and getting the reply that this one is "completely printed." He scratches his head, then buys the paper for another dollar. He opens the paper and tries to read it. "Wait a minute! I can't read this paper! It's written in Chinese!" He opens the paper to show its insides printed with Chinese characters. The newsboy then walks off shouting, "EXTRA! EXTRA! Con artist swindles 252 clowns!"

Third time around:

"EXTRA! EXTRA!"

The clown says, "Not this time! Oh, no! You sold me a paper that was blank, then you sold me one written in Chinese. You're not gonna swindle me a third time."

Newsboy clown: "But this paper is printed so that even a *child* can read it. You won't have a problem! Trust me!"

So the clown buys the paper and opens it to reveal drawings of stick figures, A-B-Cs, and other childlike scribbling.

"EXTRA! EXTRA! Con artist swindles 253 clowns!"

How far can we go with this? I'll list a few more possibilities for you to consider:

• Newsboy promises that the paper is printed in English. Clown opens it to reveal large boldface words: GOTCHA AGAIN!

• Newsboy states, "It's a Sunday paper . . . it's holy." Clown opens paper to find it full of holes.

• Newsboy states, "Look inside. It shows how Moses crossed the Red Sea." Clown opens paper to find large red letter C with a black X crossed over the C.

• Newsboy states, "Look inside. It'll teach you how to house-train your new puppy." Clown opens paper to read in large bold letters: "PUT DOG HERE!"

• Newsboy, "Inside you'll find the location of Blackbeard the Pirate's buried treasure." Clown opens paper to reveal HUGE letter X inside. Clown says, "What is this?" Newsboy replies, "X marks the spot!" Then newsboy clown reaches inside the pocket at the paper's center and pulls out a string of beads (jewels) and walks off.

Where else could you go with this gag?

An important question is: How does it all end? Here we go again, trying to wrap it up!

Maybe the clown gets tired of being swindled and determines to trick the newsboy this last time. He gets a cream pie or a glass of water and holds it behind his back.

When the newsboy clown appears selling papers, the other clown asks if the paper has a food section.

"Yes," he answers.

"Will it teach me to make a COCO-NUT CREAM PIE?"

"Certainly."

The clown buys the paper but has trouble opening it with one hand because his free hand is holding the pie behind his back. So he asks the newsboy to open the paper, which that clown agrees to do.

He then takes the pie and hides it behind the paper. He looks at the audience, shows them the pie, and laughs to himself, getting ready to throw the pie at the newsboy. Then he says, "I can't find the recipe. Could you help me find it?" The newsboy approaches, says "It's right there!" and pushes the newspaper toward the clown, "accidentally" shoving the pie right into the clown's face.

The clown mugs for laughs, foaming and fuming, wiping his face in disgusted anger.

"EXTRA! EXTRA! Read all about it! Con artist swindles . . . "

Clown shouts, "I'M GOING TO SWINDLE, FOLD, MUTILATE, AND SPINDLE your red rubber NOSE!" And chases the newsboy clown off the stage.

So that's my idea of an ending. What's yours?

SCARVES THAT WON'T STAY TIED

Basically, all you need for this routine are two silk handkerchiefs, bandanas, or scarves.

Giving this a big verbal buildup, the clown announces he will tie these two scarves together and something magical will happen. Yet each time he gets them tied and counts to three, the scarves come untied and nothing happens. Each time the scarf knot dissolves, the clown says the same thing: "Well, it never was a very good trick!"

Delivering the line in the same manner each time builds up the gag. Use it enough and you'll have the whole audience, especially the kids, saying the line with you. An audience participation running gag, no less! Not bad for having done nothing yet!

But to my way of thinking, such a running gag needs an ending. I end it by picking up a duplicate of one scarf on the last go-around. This duplicate is located with a picture silk (see Appendix A). When I tie the scarves together this time and pull them apart, the picture silk appears as in Figure 97. The audience is impressed and typically offers applause.

How does it work? I'll explain in two parts.

Figure 97

Silk Unknotting

I prefer the easiest way to make silks unknot, as follows:
With one silk in each hand, twist their corners together as in Figures 98 and 99 as though you are actually tying a knot. Then tie a real overhand knot as in Figure 100 directly on top of the twist. The finished product appears in Figure 101. From a short distance it appears to be a real knot, but with a slight tug on each scarf, the knot will unwind itself and fall apart.

Yes, it's that simple, but boy, is it effective!

Big Silk Appear

Take a large picture silk (I use a 36-inch silk) and fold it in half, keeping track of the top corners. Fold it in half again and again until it is about three to four inches wide. (See Figures 102, 103, and 104.) Then roll it up as in Figure 105. Tie one of the top corners to an 18-inch silk as in Figure 106 and roll it inside the silk as shown in Figure 107. Be sure to pull up the other top corner of the big silk as shown. Place this aside.

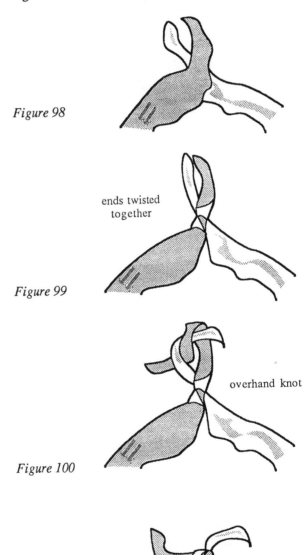

Figure 98

Figure 99

ends twisted together

overhand knot

Figure 100

Figure 101

Figure 102

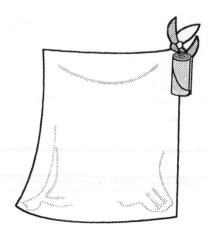

Figure 106

Figure 103

Figure 104

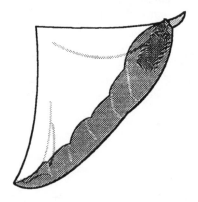

Figure 107

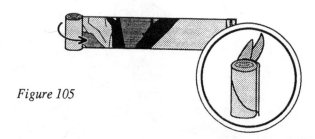

Figure 105

Figure 108

Perform the unknotting part as described. On the last time around, switch silks by picking up the loaded duplicate. Tie the big silk's top corner to the other unprepared silk. (See Figure 108.) Count to three or do your buildup, then pull the silks apart to make the big picture silk appear as in Figure 109.

It makes a nice magical ending to a simple running gag. But what really sells the gag to your audience is the way your clown character puts it across in the presentation. That makes it or breaks it. Think funny, and make it happen that way!

Figure 109

SILK TOSSED UP

While I'm thinking about it, I'll offer you another running gag along the same lines. Yes, another "Well, it never was a very good trick!" I used to perform this one a lot at home birthday parties.

I would pick up a white silk and announce that when I tossed it up, it would magically change into a bird. I tossed it up, but it fluttered to the floor, and nothing happened. I repeated this several times during the show, often to humorous mixed reactions from the children.

At the end of the show, or near the end, I picked up what appeared to be the same white silk . . . but this one had an appearing cane attached to it. I went through the same buildup and finally tossed the silk upward, releasing the cane as I did. The cane instantly opened in midair, falling down into my outstretched hand so I could style for applause.

It always goes that way. The silk-to-cane effect, performed with the midair toss-up, always gets 'em. In fact, the day I wrote this section I performed two library shows in the morning, using silk to cane in the second show only. Right after the show it happened: A boy came up to me, said how much he enjoyed the show, then asked, "But how did you throw that rag up into the air and make it change into a stick?"

I decided to tell him the truth, "You see, I had this invisible box hanging up there in the air with a little man in it. When I threw the rag up, he caught it, and then he threw the stick down so I could catch it. But please don't tell anybody. It might put him out of a job!"

GLASS OF WATER

As one clown speaks to the audience, another clown rushes onto the stage, interrupts him, and asks for a glass of water. The first clown tells him to go out to the kitchen, so the second clown hurries off the other side of the stage.

Later in the show the second clown rushes back on stage, interrupts the first clown, and says, "I got the water!" Then he hurries off in his original direction.

Now, this can be repeated throughout your act or the entire show. The blow-off comes when the second clown comes on with the last glass of water.

"I got another glass of water!" he exclaims

"Wait a minute!" says the first clown. "All during the show you've been back and forth with all these glasses of water. Are you thirsty or what?"

"Thirsty? No!" shouts the second clown. "Your DRESSING ROOM is ON FIRE!"

And with that, he hurries off, followed quickly by the first clown.

TREE OF INDIA

I'll end this chapter on running gags with what may be my favorite.

"Over 500 years ago, East Indian magicians would sit in the dirt on the streets of Calcutta, Bombay, or New Delhi performing their street magic for the passersby. The magician would pile a mound of dirt in front of himself, pretend to plant a seed in the dirt, then cover it with a ragged cloth. When he pulled off the cloth, a small plant would be growing out of the dirt. A little mango tree. The tree of India!

"Today I would like to duplicate that feat but in a more modern manner, not using dirt or a seed or a ragged cloth. Instead, I am going to use this thin wooden tray . . . and this empty metal can . . . and in place of the seed, a little feather flower. I will drop the flower onto the tray through the metal can . . . and when I remove the can, the one single flower will bloom into a beautiful ROSE BUSH . . . my modern-day version of the ancient TREE OF INDIA!

"And now, it will happen . . . on the count of three . . . ONE! TWO! THREE!"

I pull off the metal can, the feather flower falls over limply and nothing else happens. Yes . . . "it never was a very good trick!"

Thus begins my running gag "Tree of India" presentation of the *botania* effect. This effect is a tube magicians show empty, drop a flower inside, then cause to spring open into a huge bush of two dozen or more feather flowers.

A good version of botania is expensive, especially since the basic trick lasts only two seconds, so I decided I'd get my money's worth by using it as a running gag. My botania, by the way, is Abbott's super botania. It contains 24 blooms, which hide in an 18-inch can some five to seven inches in diameter yet spring open to nearly 30 inches across. There are versions of this trick on the market that are smaller and cheaper, and others that are larger and more expensive.

Here's what happens when I count to three: I immediately pull off the metal and look at the flower in shocked disgust. Then I slowly shake my head and put the tray, flower, and can aside, finally making it back to the

"It never was a very good trick!"

The tree of India finally appears.

microphone to announce, "It never was . . . a very good trick."

On the final try—usually the third, and near or at the end of the performance—I pull off the can to let the rose bush spring open, much to the surprised, ooohs and ahhhs of the audience. I often perform this with music the last time, getting the kids to clap their hands and working up my courage to the point of pulling off the can. The buildup certainly helps, and the trick typically goes over great. In fact, when I'm not concluding my 45-minute show with a live rabbit trick, I often close with the "Tree of India."

But so far, I have not shared with you the little bit of business that really *makes* this routine so effective. And as I sit here and write this, I've just had a change of heart: *I'm not going to!*

Okay, okay, it's a joke. Of course I'm going to share it! Do you think I can do all the kidshows in the world? You've got to do them too!

Each time I say the words "tree of India," I clap my hands dramatically on the word "tree," then extend my hands upward, slowly and reverently, the backs of my hands to the audience with fingers closed. My head and eyes also turn upward as you see, and I give the entire gesture a *long moment's pause* before I resume my speech. In the opening description, I do this gesture twice—once as I describe the original dirt/seed version and again as I

explain my modern day version. Midway through the show, I do it again. And on the final go, at or near the end, I say the words dramatically one more time.

This gesture and the solemn pronunciation of the words create a definite humorous effect on my audiences, particularly school show crowds, and gives them something to talk about—even to imitate—after the show.

One other bit of humor I add on the second time around: I announce that I will count to three in three foreign languages.

"UNO!" I shout, waving my arms and hands in a mystical gesture over the can.

"DUO!" I shout, waving some more.

"TRIO!" I shout, turning to the audience for a moment, raising my head and eyes toward the ceiling as if to say, "What did you expect?" then pulling the can off the lone feather flower, which may even be standing up on the board this time. Still no flower bush, and so I repeat "it never was . . . "

The proof of anything's effectiveness comes from how it affects your audience. I had my proof of this presentation ten years ago. As I was leaving the school where I had performed, I passed the baseball field. The moment they saw me, all the students playing ball, some three dozen of them, dropped what they were doing, raised their heads and hands to the sky, and shouted: "TREE OF INDIA!"

It made my day.

CHAPTER 11

CLOWN MAGIC ON STAGE

For me, as a comedy magician (and occasional clown), entertaining a crowd from the stage is more fun than almost anything else. I would rather perform for a thousand kids in a school gym or auditorium than, say, a handful of children on a living room floor birthday party. The bigger the crowd, the more laughter, the more applause, the more fun—and the more people I can affect with any message I'm trying to convey.

Performing on the stage means you must do routines that are big enough to be seen as well as heard. For example, you may perform a chick pan trick at a party, producing a cupcake for the birthday child, but on a school auditorium stage, the chick pan just wouldn't show up. Instead you'd have to use a dove pan and produce something larger, like one of Peachey Keene's sponge birthday cakes, which pops up to 15 inches tall.

In other words, on the stage your props must be visible to a large crowd. You're fooling yourself—and making your audience unhappy—if you perform a silk routine with six-inch or nine-inch silks in a stage show when you could be doing the same trick with 18- or 24- or 36-inch silks.

It amuses me highly when I see a prop advertised in two sizes (or more): "Stage size" and "parlour size." A good example is the great kidshow trick Hippity Hop Rabbits. The parlour or close-up size is six inches tall; the stage size is 12 inches tall. Yes, there is a price difference,

but let's put that aside for a moment.

My point is: The small size is fine for a birthday party with 20 kids, but it is too small for a stage show, even a small stage show in a church basement. Having such a prop *limits* you as a performer. On the other hand, the stage size can be played on big stages and small, and, at the little birthday party size shows as well.

Now, which one do you think I advocate purchasing? The stage size, of course, because you can use it anywhere!

That's your philosophy point for this chapter. No more preaching—on with the comedy magic!

MY TIE TIDE

Here's a stage routine that can also be played close up if the necessity arises. In fact, it's a pretty good show opener if it fits your clown character and your costuming. All you gotta do is adapt!

The bare bones of the routine goes as follows: The clown draws attention to the wild tie he is wearing, then surprises himself by making the large part of it vanish. The tie returns, and the clown says it's too tight, so he unties the tie. Now the tie stretches to eight feet long, with both parts hanging all the way to the floor. Finally, he pulls the tie off his neck, and a Tide detergent box appears hanging from the center of the tie: *He finally got his tie TIDE (tied)!*

Preshow Preparation

You can construct this trick at home. Begin by making a cloth tie about eight feet long, the first three feet of it three to five inches wide and the other five feet about two inches wide. Then cut the cover from a Tide detergent box, about an 8 x 10-inch size or larger for visibility. You may wish to laminate the box and tape the edges to make it last. At the same time, secure two rings about two-inches in diameter to the top of the Tide box as shown in Figure 110.

Now, I will give you the basic setup, but you will have to adapt this to your own clown costume, as each performer's clothing will be different.

First, slide the Tide box onto the center of the tie as in Figure 110. Then place the Tide box down inside your shirt, vest, coat, apron, or even in a large pocket in the front of your costume. The large part of the tie should be on your right side.

Second, lay both parts of the tie over your shoulders. Tuck all but about two feet of tie down the back of your shirt at the neck.

Third, with the remaining footage of each tie part, tie a loose tie knot (four-in-hand or half Windsor) at the front of your neck. (See Figure 111.)

Now you are all set to perform.

The Show

"Greetings, everybody! How do you like my new tie? You know what? This tie is *hand painted*. It really is! I know, because I hand painted it all by myself . . . with a can of spray paint! Check out all these neat colors. In fact, this is a new color of paint they have at K-Mart. It's called *flower color*. That's why my tie looks like all kinds of flowers."

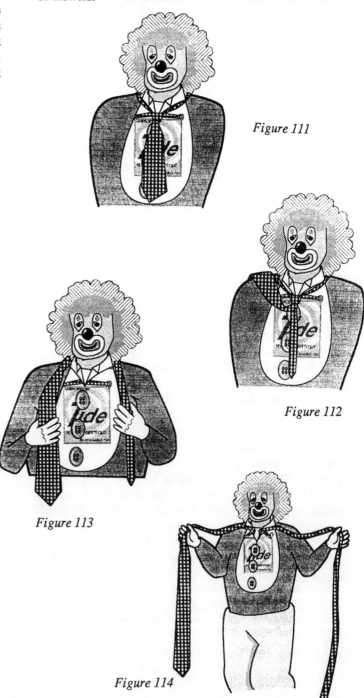

Figure 111

Figure 112

Figure 113

Figure 114

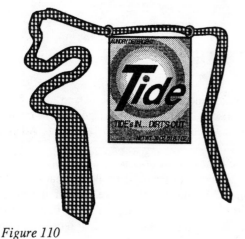

Figure 110

Start the routine by drawing attention to your tie, telling something about it to give the skit personality. If your tie isn't flower-colored, think up something to say that fits your tie pattern. ("It's a new color they call *Midnight in a Candy Factory!*" How's that for a helpful aside?)

"As you can see, like all ties, my new tie has a BIG PART," which you point to on top, "and a LITTLE PART," which you indicate underneath. "The big part is here." Hold it up and wave it. "And the little part is here." As you hold up the big part and mention the little part, flip the big part over your right shoulder as in Figure 112, purposely looking down at the little part. Due to its length, the big part stays over your shoulder. If it doesn't, you should use more tie length before making your knot.

"Now, the way you know the DIFFERENCE . . . between the BIG part and the LITTLE part is that the LITTLE part . . . is SMALLER . . . and the BIG is LARGER." Say this silly speech slowly, emphasizing the words in all caps, looking directly at your audience without smiling. You will get laughs if you can keep a straight face. Having given this little speech, look down at your chest and notice the absence of the big tie part.

"Wait a minute! Something is wrong here! The BIG part is gone! It's missing! Someone has STOLEN the BIG part of my tie! Who could have done such a thing! I can't believe it . . . and right here in plain daylight! I've got to find the rest of my tie! It must be somewhere! Have any of you seen it?"

Believe me, kids in the audience, especially those under eight years old, think this is very funny. As you make this speech, turn right, then left, looking for the tie, and then turn your back on the audience to look behind you. Of course, the kids already know you flipped the tie over your shoulder, but the sight of the tie hanging down your back usually kicks them into gear and they shout to tell you. If your tie is of a contrasting color or pattern to your costume, all the better.

"Where is that thing? I don't see it anywhere!"

"BEHIND YOUR BACK!" the kids shout.

Act ignorant for laughs, turning around, looking here and there, but don't draw this out too long. Finally, find your tie.

"Oh, there it is! How silly of me to do that. I guess I just got carried away with showing you the little part of the tie. Anyway . . . hum . . . I think I tied this tie TOO TIGHT. It's sort of SHOCKING my neck." Purposely say the wrong word. "In fact, boys and girls . . . or should I say, GUR-RELS and BAW-EES . . . *ladies first,* you know . . . in fact, you should never tie anything tight around your neck to the point where it SHOCKS you . . .

because that could really HURT you BAD. In fact, it might SHOCK you to death, and you couldn't eat candy anymore!"

Worked into this little safety lesson is the comedy of saying a similar sounding, but wrong word, and waiting for the children to correct you.

"You mean CHOKE," someone will finally say.

"Anyway, never play with rope or fishing line or string around your neck, because I wouldn't want any of you to get SHOCKED."

"It's CHOKED!" they may shout.

"What?" you say. "CHOKED? Of course, you wouldn't want to get CHOKED either. I thought that's what I said! Anyway, don't play with ropes or stuff around your neck. Not even neckties. If you wear a real TIE-TIE, like to church or someplace, just make sure your mom or dad helps you with it so it won't be too tight, like the one I'm wearing now."

Fiddle with the knot a bit.

"I think I'll loosen this knot. Maybe I'll even untie it and tie it again so it isn't so tight."

Untie the knot and separate the tie as in Figure 113. Pause a moment to let the audience see how far down the tie hangs, a little below your waist.

"Let me see . . . how does that go?" Reach up near your neck with both hands, grasp the tie on both sides with each hand, and pull upward about a foot. This makes about a foot of each side of the tie come out of your shirt. Then drop the tie parts so they hang down again, a foot longer than before.

"Now let me think . . . about how you do that."

Look down and notice the tie parts are longer.

"Hey, what is happening here? This tie is now hanging nearly down to my knees! What is going on here?"

Saying that, you repeat the lifting at the neck move, pulling about another foot of tie out on each side, dropping both tie parts once more (Figure 114).

"Hey, my tie's stretching! Look! Now it's down below my knees! Oh, boy, I'll never get it tied again! What AM I going to do?"

All this is said, of course, amid lots of children's laughter.

You can repeat the pulling from the neck once more if necessary, but don't do it unless some of the tie is still tucked in your shirt at the back. Now for the finish.

Say, "I don't know how I'm going to do it . . . but I'm going to get this tie TIED if it's the last thing I EVER DO!"

Grab the tie parts near your neck. Pretend to struggle with them, pulling on them but without accomplishing anything. Finally, lift both hands straight up, pulling the Tide box front right out of your costume and displaying it.

"Hey, didn't I tell you I'd end up with my tie TIED! Well, there it is—in black and white and orange and yellow . . . my tie is TIDE! And I want to thank all of you who really believed I could do that . . . give yourselves a big round of applause!"

Well, yes, it's sorta silly, but oh, so much fun! What? You don't want to go the Tide Detergent route? Well, then, think: What else could that sign say? Could it be your clown name? Or some other message you're trying to get across to the audience? Then change it to suit you—yes, adapt!

SIREN FLASHLIGHT

Years ago I ran across an unusual item, sold in stores, that struck me as having potential comedy magic use. It was a flashlight that also housed a rather loud siren. When the switch was pushed forward, the light came on. One notch back made the light go off, but a third notch back activated the siren, which sounded like a police car.

Having used Trevor Lewis' "Blooming Bouquet" routine so much in years past, and having read that Trevor had also used a torch (the British word for flashlight) with the same kind of routine, I decided not only to buy this flashlight, but to use its siren for an extra kicker.

In addition to the flashlight, I made three magic wands: six-inch, nine-inch and 12-inch, actually wooden dowel rods with black and white tape covering them.

Now, here's how I employed the siren flashlight to entertain over 100,000 children in my "Great Magical Inventions" school assembly program. It is reprinted from *Laugh-Makers* magazine, with the permission of Cathy and Bob Gibbons, editor and publisher, respectively. This "Siren Flashlight" routine certainly became an effective way to get my audience kids "warmed up" to enjoy the rest of the show.

The Show

"I just bought this new flashlight, but it doesn't seem to work," you tell the kids. "Maybe the batteries are dead. But that's all right. I'll make it work by magic."

So saying, you dramatically wave your free hand over the flashlight and pause. Nothing happens, so the kids laugh. Clown in trouble again!

"Well, I'd better get my magic wand," you explain. Tuck the flashlight under your arm as you speak and, in doing so, thumb on the light switch. The beam now shines out from under your armpit toward the back curtain or wall.

Turn around 180 degrees and pick up the shortest wand, completing your 360 degree turn all clockwise. That way everyone gets a glimpse of the shining flashlight.

The kids start getting vocal now, telling you that the light is on. Reach under your arm and pull out the flashlight, flicking the switch off as you do. Be very careful *not* to flick the switch too far, which would activate the siren.

"What?" You act ignorant of what is happening. "The light was on?" Look at the light. "Hmm. No, it's not on. You must be seeing things. But that's okay. My magic wand will do the trick."

Wave the little wand over the flashlight. Pause for dramatic effect. Nothing happens, so the kids laugh again.

Explain that you think the magic wand isn't big enough, and you need a larger one. Here you repeat the business of flashlight under the arm, switching it on as you turn around to get the second wand, switching it off as you turn back, then remove the flashlight. More laughs and shouts from the children. Of course, the second wand doesn't make the light work either.

Make excuses and repeat all the business a third time and have the third wand fail too. Then "remember" that you will need *them* to shout the magic words. I use funny magic words here, like "big baloney sausages" or "purple puppy chow." Make up some original funny words of your own to customize your routine to your character.

When the kids shout the words on a three count and you wave the wand, do so with hand movements, leading them like a choir director or a conductor. This allows you to flick on the light switch unnoticed, which you do.

"Hey, look! It worked! Give yourselves a big hand for such a good job!"

Applause follows. But the fun isn't over.

"Now, let's see if you can turn the light off. Just shout the magic words again on three. One! Two! Three!"

They shout, you wave the wand, and as you do, flip the light switch all the way back to siren. Immediately the loud siren noise sounds.

Play ignorant again. Look around. You hear noise, but you can't figure out where it's coming from.

"What? What's that?"

The kids are shouting.

You discover that the noise is coming from the flashlight and crazily try to turn it off, to no avail.

"Help! How do you stop this thing? Turn it off!"

The kids are laughing and shouting more.

I tell the kids, "Shout the magic words again, fast. One! Two! Three!"

They shout again, you wave the light and turn off the switch. The siren dies amid their laughter.

"Wow!" you exclaim. "I thought a POLICE CAR was driving through here!"

That's basically the routine. You can do the first parts with a regular flashlight, but if you can find one with a siren in it, so much the better. A few years ago I paid less than $10 for my flashlight in a hardware store. You might look for one in a department store or appliance store as well. With a couple of alkaline batteries, you'll be set for at least a hundred shows.

No, it's not "sophisticated magic," but *yes,* it is entertainment to kids. This is an excellent example of clown magic.

OOEY GOOEY

During my childhood, Atlanta had a children's TV show called "The Popeye Club," which ran for about 15 years, five days a week after school. The show was hosted by Don Kennedy, known to a million kids as "Officer Don." Not only did Officer Don appear on the show, but he also made personal appearances at schools, shopping malls, fairs, and festivals. In greater Atlanta, he was a kids' folk hero.

During my last year of college, I made a half dozen appearances on the show performing my magic. I also interviewed Don Kennedy about his work on the show and his work with children for my master's degree thesis in journalism. It was a fun time of learning, and both Don and his staff were good to me, helping me learn bits of the TV craft.

At least once a week, as well as on live appearances, Officer Don played the kids' favorite game (and my favorite too)—Ooey Gooey. Now this game involved a Lazy Susan turntable about 18 inches in diameter and five brown paper bags with flat bottoms. Don placed the five bags, which looked exactly alike, on the turntable. In two bags each, he placed a bag of potato chips. In two more bags, he put candy bars. And in the fifth bag, he made Ooey Gooey.

Ooey Gooey was made by pouring half a cup of mud into a bag, followed by a raw egg and a third ingredient such as applesauce which made the kids wince, as in "Yuck!" Officer Don called this concoction "Ooey Gooey."

Then he slowly rotated the turntable. Round and round it went, mixing the bags up quite well. He'd invite a girl and a boy up to play the game.

The girl picked a bag and had to stick her hand down into it to get her prize. Somehow, Don always managed to "let" the girl get the candy or potato chips.

Next, the boy had four choices left. Don turned the Lazy Susan around a few more times, then let the boy pick a bag. Most of the time he "let" the boy get the other good prize. I suspect that since Don was tall enough to see down into the bags, he knew which was which. If the boy, for instance, started to put his hand into the Ooey Gooey bag, Don might wince and make a face, telling the boy that was the wrong bag. Then the boy would change his mind and select the candy or chips.

Finally, Officer Don arrived at the part the kids loved so much: It was his turn. He had someone spin the table around while he looked the other way or covered his eyes. Then he held up a hand over the bags, said some encouraging words about how easy it was, and plunged his hand into a bag.

The look on his face told the whole story. His smile turned sour and he would yell, "OH, NO—OOEY GOOEY!" Then he would slowly lift his hand out of the bag, his fingers dripping with mud, raw egg, applesauce, and anything else he had put in the concoction that day.

Believe me, the children watching this—at home, in the TV studio, and at the live appearances—absolutely *loved it! Yes, it was* my early introduction into the Performer-in-Trouble Syndrome used as a comedy technique on kids. And it worked! They laughed and laughed and laughed . . . and all Officer Don had to do was stand there with Ooey Gooey dripping from his hand . . . and mug!

Officer Don acted upset . . . angry . . . crying . . . yelling . . . pouting . . . all the emotions to make the children laugh in this comedy situation.

After getting the most laughter out of the situation, Don wiped his hand off with a convenient towel (always nearby) and sent the two child contestants back to their seats with their prizes.

How much more do I need to tell you? Wouldn't this be a great game bit for a clown show? If you're working alone, play it like Officer Don did. Of course, you'll want to remove your gloves. If you work with a partner, play it so that one of you gets the Ooey Gooey and make the kids laugh. Know what? I may even start using this routine myself, as a comedy magician!

I know it will play because I was there and I saw it and I heard all those children laugh.

ANY-COLOR CRAYON

This is a quick magic trick, fine for stage, that every child will enjoy. Open a top wire-bound pad of paper so the kids see a blank page. At the same time, pick up a black crayon.

"Now, do you all see this crayon? Well, let me tell you—it's a magic crayon, and it will write ANY COLOR in the world. I can see you don't believe me . . . so I'll prove it to you!

"All right. Somebody . . . anybody . . . just name me a color. What's that? RED? Okay, I'll use this BLACK crayon to write RED."

Turning the pad back toward yourself, you write in bold letters the word RED. Keep the pad facing you as you continue to talk.

"Now, let's try another color. Somebody name another color. What? BLUE? Fine! Now the BLACK crayon will write BLUE."

Boldly now, write the word BLUE.

"And one last color . . . any color . . . green? Yes, that will do. I will now write GREEN with this BLACK crayon." Write the word GREEN as shown in Figure 115.

"There! I did it," you say, admiring your work without showing the audience. "My magic crayon wrote in all three colors—red, blue, and green. What? Who said that? You want to see it? Don't you believe me? You don't? Then I will show you! Here—take a look—RED, BLUE, and GREEN!"

Immediately turn the pad around and show the audience what you have written. Be prepared for laughter, groans, and maybe even some booing. As the performer, you should smile as though you've done real magic,

expecting applause. Then you realize that you're not getting applause but laughter and groans instead, so you act insulted. (For my magician friends, imagine the Great Thomsoni mugging anger. For clown friends, think of Leon "Buttons" McBryde doing the same.)

"Well, I am insulted!" you exclaim as if angry and close the pad as in Figure 116. "I can't believe it! Here I stand and do REAL MAGIC, and all you people can do is laugh and make naughty noises! I am thoroughly embarrassed! In fact, furthermore, I think you people are just plain COLOR-BLIND! Are you? Is that what the problem is? Are all of you COLOR-BLIND?"

"NO!" the kids will shout, even if the grown-ups don't.

"You're not?" you reply. "Then why CAN'T you SEE these three colors YOU asked me to write . . ."

Quickly lift up the cover of the pad to reveal the same words as before, but this time the RED is written in red crayon, the BLUE is written in *blue crayon*, and the GREEN is written in *green crayon*.

". . . RED, BLUE, and GREEN!"

Folks, it will take your audience a moment to recover from the shock, but the applause will come. If you want to really kick it into gear, just add this remark:

"Those who are NOT color-blind may now clap their hands in applause!"

Now let me explain how to work the trick. Purchase two wire-bound notebooks or sketch pads with the binding at the top. If they have 50 pages each, you have enough paper for nearly 100 performances. Try to get paper that cannot be seen through easily.

Carefully remove the top cover from one pad, along with one or two pages. Do not tear them out. (See Figure 117.) Remove them from the wire, or take the wire off

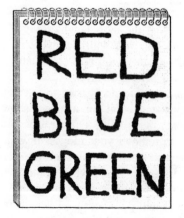

Figure 115

Figure 116

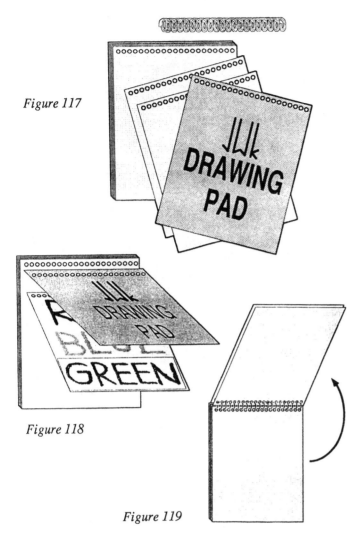

Figure 117

Figure 118

Figure 119

When the audience wants to see what you've written, you turn the pad around to show them the color names written in black. As they offer their reactions, you close the top double cover from the back directly toward them in one smooth movement. A moment later, after the color-blind remarks, you lift the real top cover only. Hold the bottom of the second cover down with your thumb as you display the words written in three different colors.

Accept your applause, then put the pad aside. Before your next show, open the pad and tear out the page you wrote on in black crayon, discarding it. Now you're ready to perform again.

RIBBON AND BALLS

I cooked this one up about 20 years ago as a teenage magician to perform at children's birthday parties. Well, maybe it was more than 20 years ago, but who counts anymore?

The idea came to me after seeing some cotton ribbon in a fabric store. The ribbon came on long spools and had cotton balls sewn onto it as in Figure 120. I bought a yard and cut it in half. Now I had two 18-inch lengths with about a dozen cotton balls on each piece, all colored red. I cut the cotton balls off one ribbon and put them in a clear glass, followed by the ribbon.

Then I took a plain brown sack, cut a piece from another sack, and glued it into the first sack to make a hidden pocket. I hid the ribbon with balls still attached in the pocket inside the paper sack.

Basically the trick works as follows: Show a ribbon and a dozen cotton balls, drop them into a paper sack, then pull the ribbon out to show the balls attached to it. With this in mind, I'll lightly sketch for you my birthday party kid routine and add a two clown routine. Keep in mind, that to make this bigger for stage, you might consider purchasing more ribbon, perhaps doing the trick with a six-foot length of ribbon (which means you will need to purchase four yards).

(depending on which type of wire binding you have). Carefully glue one page to the loose cover; if there is any see-through, glue another page atop that one. Once this is dry, use three crayons of the colors red, blue, and green to boldly write those colors on the glued page. Then carefully remove the wire from the second pad, and insert this prepared page right under the cover as shown in Figure 118. Then wire this gimmicked pad back together.

In performance, display the pad as you talk and lift the double cover, flipping it over the back as in Figure 119. In doing so, it is obvious that you're going to write on the first page of the pad.

As you ask for colors, pretend to hear red first. Turn the pad toward yourself and write R-E-D in about the same place you secretly wrote it on the gimmicked page. Then do the same with blue and green, without turning the pad around for the audience to see. Holding the pad this way also shows the audience the inside "top" of the cover, so they can see there are no other pages above the one you're working on. You never say anything about this; it's just there.

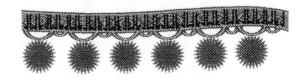

Figure 120

The Show

Invite a child up to help you. Let's call her Mary.

"How do you do, Mary? Are you quite contrary? Mary? It's just a joke!

"Anyway, Mary, today I brought along this piece of MAGNETIC ribbon. I bet you didn't know that COTTON ribbon was magnetic, did you? Of course, this magnetic ribbon won't pick up nails or screws or metal objects. It just picks up COTTON. So I guess you could say . . . this is a COTTON-PICKING RIBBON!"

I laugh out loud heartily at what I've said, though few others laugh as loud. Then I quickly remark, "It's a JOKE!" I stretch out the word on purpose for humor.

I shake my head, then continue.

"Here, Mary, you hold the cotton-pick . . . I mean, the RIBBON . . . and let me show you what else I have in this glass. Look! I have lots of little cotton balls in here . . . one, two, three . . . six . . . nine . . . why, I must have at least a dozen . . . and maybe even TWELVE little red cotton balls in here."

Purposely I pull out a few cotton balls, showing them and letting them drop back into the glass. It is important that the children see that the balls are separate.

"Most of the time cotton grows WHITE on cotton plants, but when my cotton plants were just little seeds, I colored them RED with a crayon . . . so when they grew up and made cotton, the cotton came out *RED*. Now wasn't that clever of me? Ha, ha, ha!" I pause, smiling.

Then say, "It's a JOKE!"

I pick up the paper sack and immediately pour all the cotton balls into the sack. They go into the empty side compartment.

"Now I will prove to you, Mary, that this ribbon is really magnetic. I want you to drop it down into this paper sack with the little red cotton balls. That's right." She does it. "Oh, I forgot to tell you to hold on to one end of the ribbon. Let's see . . . here's an end for you to hold."

The moment she drops the ribbon inside, I make my statement and reach into the loaded side of the bag. I quickly pull up one end of the ribbon with balls attached, just to the top of the sack. That's where I have the girl hold the ribbon, pinching the sack so she will not pull it out prematurely.

"Now, to make the magnetic properties of the ribbon come to life, all you have to do, Mary, is say the magic words. Do you know what they are? No? Well, just repeat these words after me so everyone can hear you:

"OH-WAH!" She repeats it. "TA-GOO." She repeats it. "SIAM!" She says that too. "One more time, so everyone can hear: OH-WAH! TA-GOO! SIAM!

Figure 121

Again, please, and faster this time: OH-WAH! TA-GOO! SIAM! Oh, what a goose you are? Is that what you said? It's not? Well, it sounded like it! Let's see if the ribbon became magnetic, Mary . . . just pull it out slowly."

She pulls on the ribbon and out it comes, covered with little red balls, much to her delight. (See Figure 121.) Tell the audience that Mary made the magic work, and have them give her a good round of applause.

Two Clowns On Stage

Set up the props in much the same way, but in the loaded side of the bag, have a length of ribbon about six feet long with balls attached. The plain ribbon in the glass should still be 18 inches.

Use some of the same patter explanation as I described above, but have the first clown boast that all twelve cotton balls will appear magnetically attached to the ribbon.

"I want you to count them," he says to the second clown, "as you pull them out of the bag."

After the magic words, have the second clown start pulling the ribbon out, counting the balls as they pop into view: "One, two, three . . . six . . . nine, ten, eleven, twelve . . . THIRTEEN, fourteen, fifteen . . . twenty . . . fifty . . . eighty . . . ninety . . . a hundred . . ."

The first clown acts angry, grabs the bag and all the ribbons, and storms off the stage, muttering about the other, "He has to be a show-off!"

Either way, have fun with it. In fact, it just goes to show you how much fun you can have with simple props!

MECHANICAL TOY TAKES OVER

Kids love seeing a performer get in trouble. They love seeing us goof up, make mistakes, or even get hurt, in a slapstick sort of way. And you can use this fact in many ways as a clown or comedy magician; understand that *when a performer gets in trouble, CHILDREN LAUGH!*

In my book *Kidbiz,* I talk at length about what I call the Magician-in-Trouble Syndrome, which may also be called the Clown-in-Trouble Syndrome. In that same book, I describe an opening comedy warm-up I used one year. It employed a mechanical monkey I called Eddie, a store-bought novelty item originally titled Jolly Chimp.

When switched on, this monkey clapped symbols in his hands and if you tapped his head, he bared his grinning teeth and make a horrible noise that amused the children.

During the show, I acted as though the monkey was alive and had him teach the children how to clap their hands. When the monkey "took over" and kept clapping despite my telling him to stop, the children howled with laughter. When I finally tapped his head, he grinned his teeth at me and shrieked at me, and the kids laughed all the harder.

Finding a Jolly Chimp like Eddie seems nearly impossible these days. I've had folks write or call me from all parts of the world about acquiring one, but I don't know where to get them anymore. But the point is—this same routine will work with any mechanical toy.

Just take a trip to your local toy store and take a good look at the mechanical, battery-operated toys. Look for toys that make noise and have movements, are easily visible, and audible from a distance. See if the toy has an on/off switch you can work with one hand, preferably with your thumb or first finger, without the children seeing you do it.

Once you have such a toy, create your own routine following these bare bones.

Show the children the toy, and show them what it does, then switch it off.

Start talking about the toy or about anything else, and secretly switch the toy back on. The kids will laugh when it interrupts you.

Fiddle around trying to turn the toy off, which you finally do. Apologize to the audience for the interruption, then continue your talk.

Secretly switch on the toy again and have it interrupt you once more. This creates more laughter

Turn it off, having more trouble this time, taking a bit longer. Act as though the toy is alive.

Start talking again, on comes the toy—but this third time you cannot shut it off. It seemingly "takes over," and you can't make it stop. The children will be roaring with laughter by now, especially if you ham it up and act mad, angry, upset, embarrassed, and so on. You can compound the humor of this part by pulling out a rubber or sponge hammer, hitting the toy to make it stop (but it won't!), and doing any other thing along this line to make it stop.

Finally, you must end the scenario in some way. You could, for instance, have a small child come on the stage and show *you* how to turn off the toy, especially if it is a toy that all the kids are familiar with. When the child does this successfully, all you have to do is mug, playing straight man to the child, then voice a Jack Benny, "Well!"

Or perhaps your toy has some other movement, which you haven't shown to the audience, that kicks in at the end, drives you crazy, and finally forces you to remove the toy from the stage.

Or maybe you finally shut the toy off, and a different toy on the stage starts up.

Or—now it's time for you to be creative.

HANK BOX

What starts out looking like magic, in this sketch, becomes crazy clown comedy!

Your setup goes like this: Spread a typical red/white checkered tablecloth over a card table. Tie five or six silks or bandanas end-to-end, and pin the last one to the center of the tablecloth. Place a wooden box with no top or bottom in the table's center, with the silks in it. (See Figure 122.)

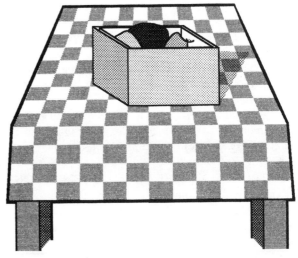

Figure 122

Next, take six to ten more silks of various colors, and put them one by one into the box. As you push each silk inside the box, twist the corner of the next silk to it. This will make another silk pop up and out each time you remove a silk. Let the last silk hang part way out of the box, but do not twist it to the second silk.

For an extra funny reaction, spray paint three or four empty metal cans in different colors, and have these sitting on the table.

The Show

"Ladies and GERMS. Sorry . . . gentlemen. I will now perform my PAH-EEECE DAY RAY-SISTER. Say, does anybody know Ray's sister? I don't even know Ray! But never mind. I am going to do the 'Great Handkerchief Out of the Wooden Box Trick.'"

Gesture to the table.

"On this table you can see a small wooden box, and coming out of it is a single silken handkerchief once owned by a beautiful French lady named MARY HAD A TOE-NET. That's Marie Antoinette in English. Anyway, I will remove this handkerchief . . . as you can see, it is PURPLE in color . . . and when I count to three, the handkerchief will fly into the air and return to the little wooden box on the table. Watch! One! Two! Three!"

On three, toss the silk into the air, over your head, where it flutters to the floor behind you.

"VOILA!" you shout, oblivious to the fact that the silk is on the floor behind you. "And now, I will BOLDLY reach into the little wooden box and remove the handkerchief."

Step over to the table and slowly pull the second silk out into view, but not all the way out. You don't want to expose the third silk, which is twisted to the second.

"You see—there it is, and it has magically changed to ORANGE!"

Often the children will already be telling you that it's the wrong color, but with this statement, you cover your mistake.

"Isn't that amazing?" you say, now pulling the silk out of the box, toward the audience, which makes the next silk (let's say yellow) pop up and hang over the front of the box.

"THERE'S ANOTHER ONE! A YELLOW ONE!" the kids will shout, and you act ignorant of the fact.

"A what? A yellow one? No, no, this is an ORANGE handkerchief. It's not yellow. What? Where? Over there?"

Now you spot the yellow one coming out of the box.

"Say, you're right. It looks as though this orange handkerchief has brought a friend with it. A yellow handkerchief! I'll take it out."

Pull this one out, moving immediately toward the audience and the next one, say blue, pops out without you seeing it. The children shout again, and you repeat this pulling out part of the routine for each silk you have twisted.

Finally, you get to the first of your silk chain, knowing its color and also knowing you have six silks tied end-to-end.

"Hey, what's this?"

Now you start pulling the knotted silks out of the box, one after the other, faster and faster.

"Another one . . . and another one . . . and another one. . . ."

Just as you get to the last one, turn your head directly toward the audience and jerk the last silk, pulling the tablecloth with it, lifting the box with it, and flipping all the cans onto the floor. The children will start laughing right away at the stupid blunder you've made.

Furthermore, if your box is small enough and your tablecloth is thick enough, the box will lodge on the middle of the cloth, and you can swing the cloth over your shoulder. Look around at this point, amid the audience laughter, and act confused, baffled, and disgusted.

"How do you like that?" you might say with a Jimmy Durante slant. "The box went and disappeared too!"

Turn your back on the audience and walk away. This could be the finish of a short act, especially if you made a big mess with cans on the floor. If there is not too big a mess, just put the cloth and box away, and proceed with your next routine.

IT'S EMPTY! IT'S GONE!

You can perform this routine on a stage if you like, but be prepared to mop up afterward, or do it outdoors at a picnic without the cleanup. Get six paper or plastic cups and razor-cut the bottoms out of five of them. Stack the bottomless cups inside the one good one as in Figure 123. Have a small pitcher or bottle of water nearby.

"And now folks, the Mystery of the Magic Water!" Hold up the stack of cups in one hand. "In one hand, I hold a stack of plastic cups." Pick up the water. "In the other, a container of AGUA, or as they say in Spanish, WATER."

Swish the water around to show it's clearly the real thing.

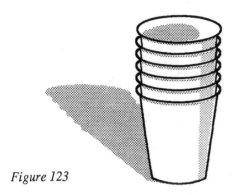

Figure 123

"I will now pour a small amount of water into the top plastic cup." Do this then put the water container aside.

"And now, the Mystery of the Magic Water! I will wiggle my fingers over the water to commence the mystery. Wiggle, wiggle, wiggle. Who's giggling? This is NOT funny! I did not say giggle, giggle, giggle."

Which, of course, makes little kids giggle.

"Never mind. Now the water has VANISH-DAPPEARED! That means it is gone, gone, gone. I'll show you."

Lift the top cup slowly out of the stack so the water goes right through its bottom into the next cup. Hold it up to your face and look through it to the audience.

"See, I told you—IT'S EMPTY! IT'S GONE!"

Place this empty cup now on the bottom of the stack. Lift the next cup, repeating the look-through, saying, "See, I told you—IT'S EMPTY! IT'S GONE!" Encourage the audience to join in saying this. Repeat this with three more cups, always putting them on the bottom of the stack.

You now have the "water cup" on top. Lift it up and out, and immediately turn the mouth toward your face to look through it, splashing yourself in the face with all the water.

"See, I told you . . ."

And hopefully the kids will shout, "IT'S EMPTY! IT'S GONE!"

All you do is stand there and mug, as the children and parents laugh at the clown with water running down his face.

The Clown-in-Trouble Syndrome strikes again!

ANOTHER VERSION. You could also work this routine with two clowns, the first clown pouring the water to make it vanish, then showing the second clown cup by cup that the water is gone. When the second clown decides to check the final cup himself, he gets the water in his face.

Here is another way to play it. Pour the water into the cups, then try to drink it yourself as you lift each cup and

discover it is empty. After going through five empty cups and not finding the water, you basically give up. Then you decide to try one more, and that one splashes you in the face with water.

THE APPLE CANS

Take five vegetable cans, strip off the paper and clean them, then spray paint them all the same color, perhaps blue. Place an orange in one can and a pear in another can, then hide these two cans on the shelf of your roll-on table as in Figure 124. If you don't work with this type of table, you can perform this routine on a box turned sideways. You can use plastic or wooden imitation fruit for this.

Place the other three blue cans on top of the table, *mouth up*. Inside the center can, place an imitation apple. Now you're ready to have some clown/magic fun!

The Show

Start this one off like a wisecracking carnival barker.

"Step right up, folks, step right up! We're going to play a little game today . . . with not ONE, not even TWO, but THREE BAH-LOO metallic cans, which were actually RUH-ED until I spray painted them this color!"

Swiftly move the cans around like a pitchman performing the old three shell game, only these cans atop your table or box are easier to see.

"One, a two, a three little cans . . . back and forth they go. But wait! I forgot to tell you there's something inside one of these cans. Is it this one? No." Hold up one can and show it empty. "Perhaps this one? No." Show that one empty.

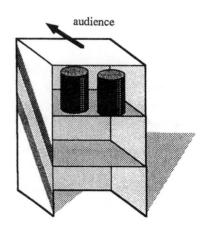

audience

Figure 124

"Yes, you guessed it, each and every one of you—it's this BAH-LOO can right here." Hold it up. "And what's inside, you may ask?" Tilt the can and make the apple roll out into your hand. "A nice, healthy, delicious juicy apple, that's what. I think I'll take a bite out of it . . . but if I do, we won't be able to play my little game."

Drop the apple back into the can.

"So I'll drop the apple back into the can . . . put the can on the table . . . and mix the three cans up a little, like this . . . a one . . . mix 'em up . . . a two . . . a little more mixing . . . and a three . . . and there we are . . . or should I say, there YOU are!"

Stop and look around for a member of the audience.

"Perhaps that young lady in the pink dress. Would you like to play my apple game? Good! Come on up here and help me."

Have the little girl, somewhere between four and seven years old, come up and stand to your right front as in Figure 125.

"What's your name, Hortense?"

"My name is not Hortense!"

"It's not? Well, what is your name?"

We'll call her Chelsea.

"Okay, Chelsea. Which can do you think the apple is in?"

Let her guess. If she gets it right, congratulate her and get her some applause. If not, give her a second guess. If she misses on the second guess, show her the apple, put it back in a can, and perform the mix again slowly so she will get the right can.

"Hey, young lady, that's very good! How did you do that so well? Do you have X-ray vision like Super Girl? Can you actually see through these cans? No, I don't think so either. Tell you what.

"Let's try the game again, just a little faster, and see how well you do. One can empty, two cans empty . . . " Show them as you go, "and here goes the apple into the third."

Mix them around, making sure the girl knows the right one. Ask her to point to it. As she does, pick up that can with your left hand, dump the apple into your right hand, and hold the apple up for all to see.

"She did it again!"

As you hold up the apple this time, drop your left hand down under the table or box, and switch the empty can for one of the loaded cans.

"Applause once more!"

As the audience applauds, naturally bring your left hand with the loaded can back into view. Set the can on the table.

"Let's try it one more time."

Drop the apple into an empty can, mix them again,

Figure 125

and let the girl get it right. Repeat the can switch move as you hold up the apple and get her applause from the audience, which is also for misdirection. Now you have two loaded cans on the table, and you drop the apple into the empty can.

"Now Chelsea, this time I am going to make it very hard. You'll have to watch very, very closely. Get ready! One, two, three, GO! Back and forth they go . . . in and out . . . out and in . . . looks like Atlanta traffic during rush hour! Now they're all mixed up. Now which one do you think contains the fruit?"

Have her point once more. Then, according to her response, go for one of two endings.

ENDING ONE. If she picks the apple, dump it out into your hand, give her applause, then turn the other two cans over, revealing the orange and pear.

"Now I've figured out how she knew the apple was in here," you tell the audience, just before revealing the other fruit. "Because the apple wouldn't fit in here with this orange or in here with this pear. Hey, it looks like FRUIT SALAD! And let's give Chelsea a big round of APPLESAUCE as she goes back to her seat!"

ENDING TWO. If she picks the orange or the pear, dump that fruit out.

"What? An orange? Well, Chelsea, I asked you to tell me where the fruit was, and this orange is certainly fruit." Look inside the pear can. "And hey, what's this?" Dump it out. "A pear! And here's the apple! Well, whatta ya know—FRUIT SALAD! And let's give Chelsea a big round of APPLESAUCE for being a great helper!"

CHAPTER 12

CLOWN SKITS

Just as illusionist David Copperfield weaves magic into vignettes on TV and stage, clowns can inject magic into skits and stories on the stage, in the circus arena, at shopping malls, even at parties and outdoor picnic situations.

In these next few pages, I'll share with you how that has been done and might be done by you!

THE SPLIT UP

Leon "Buttons" McBryde and Jim Howle used to clown together at shopping malls across the United States. Posters told people that clowns would be performing, but they needed more than that to draw a good sized crowd. Therefore, Leon and Jim would often open their programs with an audience warm-up they called "The Split Up."

Rushing onto the mall stage, Buttons would start shouting, "Hey, hey, hey! All right, we're going to start the show . . . we're going to do it right now. Come on, Jim!"

Now on the stage, Jim asked, "What are we going to do, Buttons?"

"Well, we're gonna split up the crowd here and see who has the best people. I'll tell you what, Jim, I'll take all the people right here . . ." Buttons gestured with a sweep of his arm to *the entire audience,* "and you take all those people back there." Buttons gestured to the area behind the crowd, where nobody was.

"Wait a minute, Buttons. There's nobody back there," said Jim. "Where's my part of the audience? I'm supposed to get HALF!"

"Oh, well," said Buttons, "we'll do it a different way. We'll make sure you get half. Tell you what—you take all the ARMS and the LEGS . . . and I'll take the HEADS!"

By now the crowd was gathering and laughing.

"No, no, no, Buttons!" said Jim. "That won't work either. We can't split up these people like that! You'll have to take half the audience on one side, like over there." He gestured right. "And I'll take the other half over here." He gestured left.

"Oh," replied Buttons, "okay. I've got the people on the right, and you have the ones on the left." Buttons smiled and nodded his head. "I like my people better than yours!"

Jim said, "And I like my people better than yours. Why do you like yours better?"

"Because my side can count LOUDER than yours!" Buttons announced boldly.

"Oh, no they can't!" Jim replied.

"I'll prove it," Buttons came back. "I'll give my side the signal, and they'll count to three louder than your side. Here we go, people . . . when I give the signal, all of you shout ONE, TWO, THREE! Ready? Now!"

Jim Howle and Leon "Buttons" McBryde.

"ONE! TWO! THREE!" they shouted.

"See, I told you!" shouted Buttons, laughing as usual. "I told you they could do it!"

"Hold it! Hold it!" Jim injected. "You haven't heard MY SIDE yet!"

"It won't do any good," said Buttons. "I won't even be able to hear them when they shout."

"Just you wait and see. All right, everybody on my side, shout ONE, TWO, THREE when I give you the signal. Here we go—NOW!"

"ONE! TWO! THREE!" shouted Jim's side.

"How about that, Buttons!" said Jim. "Did you hear that?"

"Hear what?" Buttons replied. "All I saw was mouths opening . . ." He flaps his hands to demonstrate, "and NOTHING came out!"

Jim said, "What do you mean, NOTHING came out?"

"I mean, I didn't hear NOTHING! Anyway, the next time my side shouts one, two, three, I AM going to STAND on ONE FINGER!"

Jim looked skeptically at Buttons. "You? As big as you are? YOU are going to stand on ONE FINGER?"

"That's what I said," Buttons replied.

"I don't believe it. That's absolutely impossible. I'd like to see you do it."

"Okay," said Buttons. "I'll give my side the signal to count to three, then I'll stand on one finger. Ready, my side? Okay—NOW!"

"ONE! TWO! THREE!" they shouted, and as they did, Buttons leaned down, put one finger on the floor and put his giant clown shoe on top of his finger, therefore *standing on one finger.*

"Oh, no!" shouted Jim. "I can't believe you did that!"

"I did it! I did it!" Buttons shouted back.

"Yeah, yeah, all right. But that's not what I thought."

"Look, Jim, maybe we shouldn't split up the audience like that," said Buttons. "Maybe we should get them ALL TOGETHER like ONE BIG FAMILY. Then if we did something that they ALL liked, they would all clap their hands together, laugh together, and have FUN TOGETHER."

"Hey, Buttons, that's a good idea. Let's see if they can all shout ONE, TWO, THREE together!" Jim exclaimed.

"And at the same time too!" commented Buttons. "Everybody ready? Let's all shout one, two, three together. Here we go—NOW!"

"ONE! TWO! THREE!" shouted the entire audience.

"And now," said Buttons, "we can really start the show."

By that time the clowns had gathered a crowd. So they plunged into their comedy routines as planned, and just had a "real large time" of it. But remember, without this warm-up or ballyhoo, the crowd would not have been there. And those who were, would not have been with them to the same extent. Believe me, you gotta warm 'em up!

CHICKEN OR THE EGG

"Which came first—the chicken or the egg?" you ask your kidshow or family audience, holding up a wooden or plastic egg in one hand and a rubber chicken in the other hand. Accept the first answer you hear, and roll with it, like this.

"The chicken? That's right!" Hold up the rubber chicken to gesture. "The chicken did come first. That chicken was walking around on the earth millions of years ago . . . but wait. I wonder where that CHICKEN came from? Where do you think it came from?"

Wait a moment until someone shouts, "An egg!" If

Which came first?

no one says that, just pretend you hear someone say it.

"Ah, yes, you're right! An egg!" Hold up the egg. "The chicken came from an egg! So that means the EGG came first. Not the chicken! The egg came first."

Stop and stare at the egg.

"But wait a minute. Where did that egg come from? What? From a chicken! That's absolutely right! So that means the CHICKEN came first." Hoist the chicken up once more and lower the egg.

"And of course, that chicken came from where? An egg!" Hold up the egg again. "So the egg came first . . . and that egg came from a chicken . . . and that chicken came from an egg . . . and that egg came from . . . OH, NUTS! Forget the egg! Forget the chicken! I'm going to get something to eat!"

Saying that, pull out a Kentucky Fried Chicken bucket, toss the egg and rubber chicken inside, and walk away.

Once I was doing this warm-up with a group of kids, going back and forth between the chicken and the egg, finally saying, "And where did that chicken come from?" That's when some kid in the crowd shouted, "From GOD!" I thought: That's so true, how can I top it?

Another time, when I asked where "that chicken" came from, a kid shouted, "Kentucky Fried Chicken!" And that's where I got the idea for the ending written above.

But let's look at the creative side of this, with that good old question: What else could it be? How can I adapt it? Oh, sure, you can use it just as I've written it, but give those questions some thought. How about a variation along the following lines.

"Which rises first, the sun or the moon. The sun? That's right! The sun comes up in the morning. Then it goes down at night, and out comes the moon! But wait a minute. If you were born at night, you would see the moon first, so you'd think the moon came up first. So that's the answer: The moon comes up first, then goes down each morning, and the sun comes up."

Can you think of other variations that you might work into your clowning?

SINGING WITH CAKE

Remember in an earlier chapter how I said you could get some pretty funny ideas from old movies? Well, here's another one, and you'll find it in the first five minutes of *You'll Find Out,* a 1940 Kay Kyser movie.

Kay Kyser was a gentleman band leader of the 1940s with a quick wit. Just watching one of his movies is an education in many types of comedy. This movie is a haunted house spoof which features Boris Karloff, Bela Lugosi, and Peter Lorre, as well as Ish Kibble and the rest of the Kay Kyser crew.

The opening scene in the movie takes place during a radio broadcast of Kay Kyser's "College of Musical Knowledge," and Kay has a man from the audience on the stage, asking him to name three of the Seven Dwarfs. After the man does that, with a bit of humor thrown in, Kay announces that now this fellow will have to sing a song. The song will be "My Bonnie Lies Over the Ocean," and Kay hands the man a piece of paper with the words on it.

"And just in case you are nervous," says Kay, as an assistant hands Kay a piece of uniced sheet cake about 6 x 8 inches, "we're going to give you a bite of this cake every now and then, just to help you along. And whatever you do, DON'T STOP SINGING!"

The band strikes up the tune at a moderate pace and the man sings the first line: "My Bonnie lies over the ocean."

"A bite!" says Kay, and sticks the corner of the cake up to the man's mouth.

The fellow bites the cake, then sings the next line: "My Bonnie lies over the sea."

"Another bite!" Kay offers.

The man bites the cake again, then sings: "My Bonnie lies over the ocean."

"A bite!" says Kay, and gives the guy more.

"Oh, bring back my Bonnie to me," sings the man.

"Another bite!" And the man bites more cake, trying to chew it up and continue singing at the same time.

Now the tune changes to shorter lines.

"Bring back—" sings the man.

"A bite!" Which he takes.

"Bring back—"

"BITE!"

"Bring back my Bonnie to me—"

"BITE!"

"To me—"

"BITE!"

"Bring back—"

"BITE!"

"Bring back—"

"BITE! BITE! BITE!"

"Bring back my Bonnie to me!"

By the time the fellow gets to this point, his mouth is absolutely full of cake, and he can hardly sing at all—but the audience is laughing their heads off because this is a very funny sight!

Well, the moment I saw this, I thought, CLOWN-ING! I could see myself as Frederick the Great working this gag (pardon the pun!) with a clown like Earl Chaney as Mr. Clown. I could see working up an entire skit with a quiz show theme and this being the blow-off. I could even see myself saying, as a final line, "Well, Mr. Clown, I guess you TAKE THE CAKE!"

I'm not so sure I'd use this gag with an audience volunteer as Kay Kyser supposedly did. I'm afraid there might be negative feedback with giving anything edible to a child or even an adult on the stage. You wouldn't want someone getting sick, then suing you.

Probably the best thing would be to use a partner clown or a prepared stooge from the audience (be he clown or not), someone already "in" on the routine and familiar with whatever song you have him sing. Pick a simple song like "My Bonnie," then have someone play the first verse and chorus for you on the piano while you tape record it. You won't need more music than that, obviously, because your cake-mouthed singer cannot keep singing that long.

Remember what I said earlier about good taste. Pulling things out of the mouth is *not* good family entertainment. But this bit does not bother me because you're putting food into the guy's mouth. Sure, when he takes bites and when he's trying to chew and sing, some cake is going to drop out, which still does not bother me.

But whatever you do, do not have your singer spit out the cake on stage! That, my friends, would be going overboard and would ruin the skit for a lot of people. And, furthermore, it would make you, the performer, look bad because it happened in your act.

This can be a very funny skit if you use good sense.

How about this for another ending: Announce that the fellow has done a wonderful job of singing, and as a special prize, you're going to award him with—you guessed it—A CAKE!

You could go several ways with this.

One idea would be to produce a cake by magic is my first thought, using a dove pan and Peachey Keene's rainbow birthday cake, a commercial product made of sponge which expands from two inches up to 15 inches tall. The moment your singer sees your cake production, have him shake his head, scream if possible, and run off the stage with you hurrying behind trying to give him the cake.

Another idea would be to produce a real cake, or just bring out a real cake. As you start to award it to him, have him scream "OH, NO!" and raise his hand to gesture, "accidentally" bumping the cake up into your face.

Still another idea would be to announce to the singer that "His Bonnie" has just returned from across the ocean, and "here she is—with a freshly baked CAKE for you!" At this point, a very ugly girl or ugly girl clown runs out from the wings with a large cake (real or fake). The singer shakes his head, somehow voices "OH, NO!" and runs off the stage.

So that's it. Thanks to Kay Kyser for a funny bit that we can adapt to clowning.

MAGA-SOUNDS

In the same way I came up with the book sight gags earlier, I cooked up what I call Maga-Sounds—magazines that make appropriate *sounds* when you open them. Sounds logical to me! Anyway, the idea is simple.

A clown enters the stage, which is made up like a doctor's waiting room. There's a chair and a table, and the nurse indicates that he may sit down and read a magazine while he's waiting.

He picks up one magazine after another, and each time he opens a magazine, he hears sounds associated to the theme of that magazine. The sounds are prerecorded on a tape, played offstage but over the sound system. The clown knows the order; in fact, the magazines can be stacked in that order, and it's just a matter of opening the magazines and reacting.

Here are some samples of magazine titles followed by suggested sounds:

PEOPLE. Have a clip of Barbra Striesand singing the song "People."

GOLF DIGEST. Someone shouts, "FORE!" Then the sound of a golf club hitting a ball: "Whack!"

BRIDES. Wedding March "Here Comes the Bride" plays.

POPULAR MECHANICS. Sounds of a drill, saw, hammer, and other tools.

OUTDOOR LIFE. Various animal sounds.

VOGUE. From *My Fair Lady,* play a line of the song, "The Rain in Spain."

SEVENTEEN. Voice counts aloud: "Thirteen, fourteen, fifteen, sixteen." Clown stops reading. Looks at cover, which says *SEVENTEEN.* Then continues reading as voice continues: "Eighteen, nineteen, twenty, twenty-one."

STEREO. Any kind of music plays loud, ending as clown closes the magazine. A matter of timing.

ROLLING STONE. Sound of a landslide, rocks tumbling down.

BUSINESS WEEK. Voice announces: "The Dow Jones averages for the week are as follows . . ."

FIELD AND STREAM. Bird calls, followed by running water.

TIME. "Tick, tick, tick . . . chime, chime, chime . . . bong, bong, bong." Sounds of various clocks. End this sequence with an alarm clock.

CRICKET. A chirping cricket, what else?

MONEY or *FORTUNE.* Cash register sound, with coins rattling around.

MUSCLE AND FITNESS. Sounds of working out, drill instructor counting pushups, aerobic lady counting exercises, and so on.

CAR AND DRIVER. Race car sounds, horns, speeding, crowd cheering.

WESTERN MAGAZINE. Cows, horses, sheep making their noises.

SOUTHERN LIVING. Play "Tara's Theme" from the movie *Gone with the Wind.*

These are enough titles to get you started. See what magazines you have around the house. Check with friends for used copies. Don't go out and buy any unless you can't find a specific one you need for your skit.

Then make up your own skit. Once you get it together, you can number the magazines lightly in pencil somewhere on the covers, so you can easily reset them.

Record your sound track accordingly, at home or professionally, depending on how much you plan to use it. And be sure you have a way to end it.

Do I have a creative thought on that?

You bet I do!

What I haven't told you up until this point is this: Personally, I think a running gag would make this routine really fun and funny. And my number one thought involves using a love/romance magazine such as *Modern Romance* or *Soap Opera Digest* to get this across. Here's how it would work:

About every third or fourth magazine, the clown picks up the soap magazine, opens it, and the voices of a man and woman would be heard. The man would say, "Oh, Marsha, please!" And the woman would say, "No, John, no!" The clown wipes his brow, mugs a shocked reaction, then puts down this magazine. Later, however, he picks it up several times between other magazines, and the romance magazine's sounds would always be the same.

Finally, as the clown is called into the doctor's office, he picks up the soap magazine again and opens it. The man's voice says, "Oh, Marsha, please!" And the woman's voice replies, "Oh, all right, John—we'll EAT at McDonald's for supper!" Or anything else totally unromantic that will get a laugh.

At this point, the clown would slam down the magazine and stalk off the stage.

That, of course, is how I would do it.

How would you?

KARRELL FOX'S HANDY DANDY EARPHONES

Back in the early 1940s a young Karrell Fox worked in a Detroit, Michigan, magic shop, along with Mickey O'Malley. One day, while they were playing their show in town, comedians Olsen and Johnson walked into the shop to buy a blank gun, which they wanted to have demonstrated.

Karrell was in the back room at the time, but when Mickey fired the blank pistol, Karrell did what they always did for a gag: He tossed a spring duck into the room so it appeared the gun had shot the duck from the air. Olsen and Johnson loved sight gags, so one of them asked: "Do you sell those spring ducks too?"

"Of course," the guys replied.

"We'll take a HUNDRED of them!" said the zany pair of comedians.

The next thing Karrell knew, Olsen and Johnson had adapted this bit to *Hellzapoppin*. One would fire a pistol on the stage, and instead of one duck falling from the sky—*100 DUCKS fell from the sky!* Then one of the guys would say, "You're sure lucky that COWS don't fly!" About that time a huge dummy cow would fall from the rafters.

Well, I had to tell you all that to tell you this:

Karrell Fox has been one of my favorite comedy magicians since my first IBM (International Brotherhood of Magicians) convention as a teenager. He has a reputation for effective magic that is secretly very simple, allowing the performer to easily master it and spend practice time on the presentation. From his first book, *Kornfidentially Yours* in 1948 to the more recent works such as *Clever Like a Fox, Another Book,* and *For My Next Trick,* Karrell has shared a lifetime of comedy magic experience in print, in lectures, and in performances at magic conventions.

Therefore, it is my pleasure to include here, with Karrell's permission, one of his best comedy bits and one that I consider perfect for clowning. Believe it or not, this appeared in his *Kornfidentially Yours* nearly 50 years ago! And it's still great. How do I know? In the past 25 years, I've seen Karrell perform it at least a dozen times with hilarious results!

All Karrell uses for props in this bit are a pair of red thimbles and an ordinary deck of playing cards. Clowns may wish to substitute a set of earmuffs or something larger for visibility for the thimbles, but the bit will be basically the same. It all starts by making fun of the act presently on the stage. I'll describe it as I've seen it performed by Karrell and his buddy, Duke Stern. It goes like this:

As Karrell stands at the microphone talking, a fellow dressed as a newspaper photographer comes onto the stage, carrying a camera and camera bag. This part is played by a third person, perhaps even a stagehand. He tells Karrell that he works for some local paper.

"Do you mind if I shoot your picture?" he asks.

"You want to shoot my picture?" asks Karrell, acting flattered.

"Yes, I'd like to shoot your picture," says the photographer.

"All right," says Karrell, standing up straight in a pose. "Go ahead, shoot my picture."

Immediately the photographer pulls out an 8 x 10 photo of Karrell Fox in one hand and a blank pistol in the other hand.

"BLAM! BLAM! BLAM!" goes the pistol, fired point blank at the picture of Karrell Fox.

The photographer hands Karrell the photo of himself,

which he holds up to display full of bullet holes (previously punched). Then the photographer exits.

And all Karrell Fox has to do at this stage is stand there, mugging, as the audience laughs.

As the laughs subside, Karrell begins talking once more to the audience. Then he realizes that he can't hear anything.

"Oh, I guess those gunshots have hurt my ears. I can't hear a thing. Those shots must have made me temporarily deaf. Nothing to worry about, because I have my handy dandy earphones right here in my pocket." He pulls out the two red thimbles and inserts one in each ear. "They fit in your ears just like this. There. How about that! I can hear fine now."

He proceeds to select a volunteer from the audience, in this case a prepared volunteer "in" on the bit. So onto the stage comes Duke Stern, playing a humble, quiet, oddball character. He stands to Karrell's right.

Karrell says, "Would you like to see a card trick?"

Duke just stands there, looking at the audience and smiling, saying nothing.

Karrell repeats, louder, "WOULD YOU LIKE TO SEE A CARD TRICK?"

Duke makes no reply.

Finally, Karrell taps Duke on the shoulder. Duke looks at him.

"Sorry," Duke says, pointing at his ears, "I'm a little hard of hearing."

"Oh, you are?" Karrell remarks. "Then you ought to have some of these handy dandy earphones. They're wonderful."

"What?"

"I said—oh, let me show you," says Karrell, and he removes the thimbles and puts one in each of Duke's ears. "Now can you hear me?"

"Yes," Duke replies, shaking his head affirmatively, "that's wonderful. I can hear every word you say."

"Good," says Karrell. "Now, I'd like to show you a card trick."

Duke says, "Can I shuffle them?"

Supposedly not hearing Duke, Karrell keeps talking about the card trick, completely ignoring his helper because now Karrell can't hear.

"Can I shuffle them?" repeats Duke.

Karrell continues talking.

Finally, Duke shouts, "CAN I SHUFFLE THEM?"

Then it dawns on Duke that Karrell cannot hear. He taps the magician on the shoulder, transfers the earplugs (thimbles) to Karrell's ears, and asks his question again. "Can I shuffle them?"

Karrell hands Duke the cards and answers, "No, but you can cut them."

Karrell Fox.

Duke taps him on the shoulder to get his attention. Then Duke transfers the plugs to Karrell's ears.

"RED!" says Duke.

"All right," says Karrell. "Now, as I deal the cards into my other hand, one at a time, you say STOP, and that will be your card."

Immediately Karrell starts dealing cards, one by one, face down into his other hand. He deals all the way through the deck as Duke looks off into space because he hasn't heard the instructions. When Karrell finishes dealing, he looks at Duke and realizes the guy cannot hear. So he takes the earplugs from his ears and puts them into Duke's.

"Now," Karrell repeats, "as I deal the cards into my hand, you say STOP, and that will be your card."

Karrell starts dealing the cards again.

"Stop!" says Duke.

Karrell keeps dealing.

"Stop!" Duke repeats.

Karrell keeps on dealing the cards.

"STOP! STOP! STOP!" shouts Duke. Then he realizes the problem. Quickly he removes just one plug from his ear and places it in Karrell's ear that is on Duke's side. Then he leans over and speaks directly into Karrell's plugged ear. "I said STOP!"

Magician Karrell, now very disgusted, shouts into Duke's plugged ear, "I would just as soon forget the WHOLE THING!"

Duke shouts into Karrell's ear, "That's OKAY by ME!"

Karrell shouts back into Duke's ear, "SWELL!"

Duke shouts into Karrell's ear, "SO LONG!"

Magician Karrell shouts into Duke's ear, "GOOD-BYE!"

And both exit to thunderous applause amid uproarious laughter.

Notice that the entire sketch runs only about three minutes. After all, it's a bit based on one joke, and therefore you need to keep it short and tight. Believe me, it plays better that way.

Question: How would you and your partner clown handle this? Would you eliminate the gunshot on the stage? If so, how would you account for one clown being suddenly deafened? Sure, one of the clowns can be hard of hearing, but not both. How about a loud explosion (on tape?) offstage? Maybe one clown was playing with dynamite? You have to THINK about these things to make the bit logical.

Next question: What would you use for earplugs? With clown wigs, thimbles would not even show up since most clowns' ears are covered. How about some sort of earmuffs? But then you run into the problem of splitting

Immediately Duke starts shuffling the cards, as rapidly as possible.

In panic, Karrell says, "I said, just cut them!"

Duke keeps shuffling. He can't hear.

"I said," Karrell repeats, "just cut them!"

Duke keeps shuffling.

"I SAID—oh, wait a minute." Karrell removes the thimbles from his own ears, taps Duke on the shoulder, then inserts them into Duke's ears. "Now, I said—just cut them."

"Oh," says Duke. He immediately cuts the cards once and hands them back to the magician.

Now Karrell states, "I want you to take a card, look at it, and return it to the deck."

Duke carries out this procedure; after all, now he can hear.

Then Karrell asks, "Was your card red or black?"

"Red," answers Duke.

Karrell repeats, "Was your card red or black?"

"RED," Duke repeats.

"WAS YOUR CARD RED OR BLACK?" Karrell shouts.

them at the end of the sketch. How would you work it out? Change the end of the sketch? Or use separate earmuffs with double-stick tape? Velcro?

I'm not giving out answers to this one—mainly because I haven't thought them up! But also because I want you to do some creative clown thinking. So if you like Karrell's basic idea, get to work adapting.

And thank you A-GINN, Mr. Karrell Fox!

THE CHAIR

This is a one-man or one-woman skit involving nothing more than a straight-back wooden chair. The chair must be sturdy, but lightweight. Although I designed this as a one-clown skit, you could change it to include one or two others if you like. Even with the one-clown aspect, you might wish to have two more clowns enter at the end.

Here it goes, step-by-step.

A wooden chair sits at center stage. A clown walks onto the stage, sits in the chair and faces the audience as music plays slowly in the background.

Suddenly, the music changes to the "William Tell Overture," often know as "The Lone Ranger music." The clown jumps up, turns the chair backward, straddles the chair, and pretends to ride it like a horse, yelling, "Hi-yo Silver, away!"

Then the music changes to a violin solo, and the clown pretends to play an imaginary violin.

That stops. A lion or tiger roars. The clown jumps up and uses the chair like an animal tamer in the circus, pretending to fend off the lion or tiger with the chair and an imaginary whip.

Slow music comes on again, and the clown sits down on the chair in side-saddle fashion like a lady rider, holding his head up high.

Next we hear traffic noises, like horns honking and brakes screeching. The clown assumes the pose of a taxicab driver and plays that part for a few moments.

Now comes electric guitar music, and the clown picks up the chair and pretends to play it like a guitar.

The music stops. The clown turns the chair upside down to use it like a speaker's stand. The clown gestures like an orator.

Now the clown holds the chair upside down and pretends he is pushing a grocery cart. A child's voice says, "Mommy, I want candy!" And the clown mimics her voice as she replies, "Sit down in the basket—you can't have any candy, it'll spoil your supper!"

Shots are suddenly heard, then a cowboy voice:

"Hurry, boys, and we'll head 'em off at the pass!" More shooting, and the clown pretends to be shooting too, ducking behind the chair for cover.

Now the clown sits on the back of the chair, with his feet on the seat. (Be careful not to lean back in doing this; keep your center of gravity over the chair seat.) Sounds of chewing popcorn are heard, and the clown pretends he's at a movie. "Oh, Rhett, what will I do?" "Frankly, my dear, I don't give a . . ."

From this position, the clown squats down onto the chair seat with his legs crossed, imitating Buddha, as symbols clash and chimes are heard.

Suddenly a baby cries, and the clown picks up the chair and rocks it like a cradle, side to side.

The clown turns the chair around and sits in it backwards. He pretends to cast a fishing pole, fishing off the dock as Otis Redding or Michael Bolton sings "Sitting On the Dock of the Bay" and whistling along.

Suddenly trumpets blare. The clown gets off the chair, turns it to face the audience, then stands on it like the Statue of Liberty, as a voice says, "Give me your tired, your poor, your hungry . . ." and the last line of the "Star Spangled Banner" plays.

As the national anthem finishes, the clown drops down quickly into a sitting position in the chair and bows to applause, as two clowns or stagehands pick up the chair with him on it and carry him offstage.

All in all, depending on the length of each sound effect, this skit should run about three minutes. It's one of those things that once you have it taped and rehearsed, all you need is the audio tape and the chair. And you.

Now let's talk about you. Certainly the taped sound track will carry this entire sequence, but what will make *it* *work*, indeed, make it pass or fail with the viewers, is you. You must think and practice and carefully act out each and every part of it. After all, you won't be doing any talking during "The Chair," just a few lip-sinc words and the rest is pantomime acting and pantomime clowning.

Can "The Chair" be a winner for you and your audiences? That depends on how much thought, skill, and practice you put into it. Give it a try, though. Change it according to your needs and tastes.

I've just given you the start.

CLOWN CAMERA

One of the highlights of Clown Camp has been a class taught by Bill Rath of Vista, California. Bill and his wife Jean are teachers in "real life," so Bill's classes were not

Jean and Bill Rath.

only fun, but very organized and educational. So it is with pleasure that I share with you Fumbles (that's Bill) and Cinnamon's (that's Jean) routine with their instantfunatic *camera*, expanded from Bill's lecture notes with his permission.

The best place to start is with the list of props you'll need; after that, the performance will make lots more sense.

Instantfunatic Props

1. The camera. This is made from a 3-D bunny box rabbit production Bill bought from Magic, Inc., in Chicago. There are many bunny production boxes available on the magic market (try your local magic shop first) which will do. Bill painted his box black.

2. A snake can. This Bill also painted black and attached to the camera as its lens. By unscrewing the cap, you cause a spring snake to jump out.

3. A *long hare*, from Supreme Magic in England. This is a silk-screened rabbit printed on cloth about three to four feet long. You could make this yourself with white cloth and a magic marker.

4. Boy-to-rabbit wand. Dealer prop in which a magic wand unrolls to show a rabbit in the hat picture with a hole cut out for a kid's face to fit.

5. A monkey picture mounted on heavy cardboard.

6. A large comb.

7. Large sunglasses.

8. A large powder puff with powder or confetti on it.

9. A rubber chicken or rooster.

10. A giant toothbrush.

11. A honk horn or noisemaker for the sound of taking a picture.

12. A small squirt camera. Ickle Pickle Products of St. Louis used to make these (see Appendix B).

13. A glossy photo of Fumbles and Cinnamon.

Instantfunatic Setup

Put a handle on the bunny box camera so you can carry it. (See Figure 126.) Paint the word "INSTANTFUNATIC" on the side of the camera. Weld a nut to the snake can so it can be attached to the front of the camera for a lens. The box is set up so the doors swing sideways, away from the audience. The slit in the side also points the same way.

Attach a horn or noisemaker to the door to act as the click of the camera. Place the long hare inside the camera. You place the monkey picture alongside the rabbit picture board, which acts as film.

Nearby, but outside audience view, Bill places the comb, puff, glasses, tooth brush, rabbit wand, chicken, and squirt camera.

Now for the fun.

snake can lens

bunny slide pulled up as film

horn on door

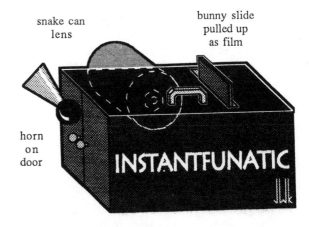

Figure 126

Instantfunatic Routine

"As clowns, we are always having our pictures taken," explains Bill, in character as Fumbles, to his audiences. "So I thought it was about time I got a camera to take pictures myself. So I've brought my own INSTANTFUNATIC with the emphasis on FUN. I want a funny picture . . . so my model will be my partner, Cinnamon!"

Fumbles brings forward a stool at this point.

"Here, Cinnamon, sit right here on my electric stool. That's a CURRENT joke!" Bill usually gets little response to this, so he says, "By your reaction, not CURRENT enough!" That brings a mild laugh. "Now look here, Cinnamon. You just sit on the stool and smile pretty."

Jean takes her place on the stool.

Fumbles now gets behind the camera, looks through it, and decides that Cinnamon has too much shine on her face.

"We'll have to fix that!" he says. Quickly, he brings out the big powder puff and gives Cinnamon a smack in the face with it. Cinnamon reels back and forth as though dazed, choking and coughing, as Fumbles goes back to the camera.

He clicks a picture, but pulls out blank film.

"Oh, I see the problem," he explains. "I forgot to remove the LENS CAP." Fumbles unscrews the lens cap, and out pop the spring snakes from the can. Both he and Cinnamon yell and react to the snakes, along with the audience kids. Bill throws the snakes aside and continues.

"Okay, Cinnamon. Now SMILE!"

Fumbles clicks another picture, honking the horn each time. He checks the film again, and it's still blank.

"I wonder what happened?" he asks, scratching his head.

This time he looks inside the camera.

"Ah, yes, I see the problem! There was a HAIR on the lens!" Bill pulls out the long hare bunny cloth now for a groan/laugh. He puts it aside and continues.

"Now smile pretty, Cinnamon. Oh, wait—your hair needs combing!"

Fumbles takes out the big comb, gives it to Cinnamon, and she combs her hair.

He remarks, "I like to TEASE girls anyway!"

Just before he starts to take another picture, Fumbles decides that Cinnamon's teeth need SHINING. He takes out the big toothbrush and pretends to clean her teeth.

"Cinnamon, you look lonely. Why don't you choose someone to have your picture taken with? Who will it be?" Cinnamon picks a boy in the audience, who comes forward to help.

"You don't look funny enough to have your picture taken with a clown," says Fumbles. So he puts the big sunglasses on the boy. "That's much better. But maybe we should turn this boy into a rabbit. What do you think?" he asks, addressing the audience. "Should we turn him into a rabbit?"

The crowd usually shouts their approval.

"Boy, with friends like that, who needs enemies!" quips Fumbles. Then he brings out the rabbit wand and waves it over the boy's head, letting the banner roll down in front of the boy. Instantly the rabbit picture appears with the boy's face showing through.

"Now, at last, we are ready to take this picture," says Fumbles. He has the boy stand beside Cinnamon. She holds the rabbit banner in front of him.

"Okay, are you two ready? Good! Now watch the BIRDIE!"

Fumbles quickly brings out the rubber chicken and holds it up while looking into the camera.

"Ready? One, two, three! SMILE!"

He clicks the camera (honks the horn). Then he brings out the monkey picture without letting the audience see it.

"Oh, no, I goofed! I only got a picture of Cinnamon," he says, turning the monkey picture around to show the audience.

A moment later, he lets Cinnamon see the picture. She jumps off the stool and chases Fumbles around, giving him a few funny clown whacks to teach him a lesson. Finally, the excitement settles down. Fumbles and Cinnamon give the boy helper an actual picture of themselves and send him back to his seat with a round of applause.

It's a fun routine and open to adaptation to your clown character. As a magician, I wouldn't pass up the "hair on the lens" bit without producing a real live rabbit instead of using the long hare. In fact, I might let the "hair on lens" concept be the blow-off of the entire routine, using the rabbit's appearance to conclude. But that's just me. What about you?

CARD, SILK, PIE

At first, this routine was titled and performed as the "Card, Silk, and Ax on the Back." However, due to the violent aspect surrounding the third element, namely the ax, and not wishing to negatively influence children or young performers, Frederick the Great has felt the necessity to change the routine from using an ax to using a cream pie of some sort. Chilled coconut cream pie is Frederick's favorite, and he has asked me to write up the routine with that in mind.

Frederick always uses three clowns for this magic theme skit: himself (an aristocratic whiteface clown); a tall, big buffoon (like Leon "Buttons" McBryde); and a short mischievous clown (like Earl "Mr. Clown" Chaney). You may adapt the skit to suit your needs and availabilities.

With Frederick at center stage and Buttons to his right, I describe the action.

The Show

Frederick begins: "Tonight I would like to perform a trio of superb magical effects that I think will thoroughly and totally baffle not only the entire audience, but you as well, Buttons!"

"Say, what?" Buttons replies. He's the big stupid-acting guy, of course. I can call him *stupid,* because I read Leon's lecture notes!

"I am going to perform THREE TRICKS," Frederick quickly states.

"Oh, great. What are you going to do?" asks Buttons.

"First, my big, tall friend . . . I will have you select a card from this deck. Here . . . take any card you want."

Buttons takes a card and looks at it. Unknown to Buttons and the audience, Frederick offered him a deck with 51 cards that are all the same, with only the bottom card (faceup card) being something different. Let's say the selected (forced) card is the five of hearts.

"And show it to everyone in the audience," Frederick instructs him.

Buttons starts to walk off the stage to his right.

"Hey, where are you going?" asks Frederick.

"I'm going to show my card to everyone in the audience. First, I'm going to show my card to him . . ." Buttons points to a man, "and then to her . . . and then to that little girl . . . and everybody else including all those people way back there in the back."

Frederick crosses his arms, fumes in place for a moment, then says, "You idi . . . I mean, Buttons, why don't you just stand here on the stage and hold the card up so everyone can look at it here in the spotlight?"

"Hey," says Buttons, "I didn't think of that! That's a good idea! Say, Frederick, did you go to college?"

"What does college have to do with this?" asks Frederick.

"Well, you must have gone to college to learn something that smart, I think."

"Never mind! Just show them the card!"

So Buttons holds up the card, showing it to the audience, and now everyone knows it's the five of hearts. Then Frederick has Buttons put the card back into the deck.

"Slide it back into the deck WITHOUT letting me see the card," Frederick instructs him. And that's when it happens—Mr. Clown (Earl Chaney, the short mischievous clown) quietly runs from the wings at stage right with a jumbo five of hearts card (it's back covered with a half dozen O-rings of masking tape) and sticks the card on the middle of Button's back. Then Mr. Clown runs back out of sight.

"And now," Frederick continues, "I will magically make your card vanish from the deck and reappear . . . ON YOUR BACK. Watch!"

Frederick pulls out a magic wand, waves it over the card box, and says these words. "Little card . . . fly from the pack . . . find yourself on Buttons' back!"

Frederick immediately extends his right hand to Buttons. "Here, Buttons, let me shake your hand." The moment he takes Buttons' hand, he pulls Buttons gently so he turns his back to the audience. Then Frederick lets go of Buttons and reaches to the card on Buttons' back.

"And you see, here is your card . . . it has magically appeared on your back." With that, Frederick pulls the card off with a rip and hands it to Buttons, who now turns back around.

"Gee," says Buttons, scratching his head, "I think it GREW after it vanished!"

Frederick puts the card, deck, and wand aside during the audience reaction, then starts the second phase.

"Now, Buttons, for my second fantastical illusionary feat."

Buttons looks down at his shoes as he hears the word "feat."

"Is it going to be as big as my FEET?" he asks Frederick.

"Your what?" Frederick acts confused.

"My feet. You said something about a LOSEN-ARY FEET. Does that mean my feet smell bad?"

"I'm talking about my second trick, you . . . you nice young man! In this second of my three greatest feat . . . I mean, TRICK, I will use a silk handkerchief . . . woven of the purest silk imported all the way from China." Frederick removes a yellow silk handkerchief from his pocket.

"I know all about China," says Buttons. "I knew a Chinese guy who got thrown into jail. His name was Hung Won. His brother was Hung Too!"

Frederick stares at Buttons, then slowly turns his head to stare at the audience, mugging like Jack Benny.

"I can't believe you said that," Frederick remarks. "Don't you know VAUDEVILLE is dead?"

Buttons replies, "I didn't even know he was sick!"

"But nevertheless . . . just never mind. On the count of three, I am going to make this yellow silk scarf vanish into thin air—"

Buttons interrupts, "Did you say thin HAIR?"

"No, thin AIR!" retorts Frederick.

"Well, if the air is so THIN," asks Buttons, "where will the scarf go? Maybe you should use THICK air so it will have someplace to hide."

Frederick fumes some more, then says, "Will you let me continue?"

"Go right ahead," says Buttons good-naturedly.

"As I started to say," Frederick goes on, "the scarf will vanish . . ." He starts pushing it into his fist (actually into a thumb tip) as he talks. "and when it is gone, it will reappear ON YOUR BACK."

"Oh, yeah?" says Buttons. He reaches behind his back, turning so the audience can see it momentarily, and feels nothing. "Well, it's not there now."

"Of course it's not there now!" says Frederick. "I'm still pushing it into my hand."

"Hey, I see that now," Buttons remarks, turning his back to stage right and intently watching as Frederick finishes tucking the silk into his fist. This time, Mr. Clown again runs from the wings and sticks a duplicate yellow silk on Buttons' back, again using an O-ring of masking tape. Then Mr. Clown runs out of sight once more.

Children in the audience will often try to tell Buttons what is happening at this point, but Buttons and Frederick completely ignore their warnings. Mr. Clown, on the other hand, may gesture with a finger to his lips for them to keep quiet. It really doesn't matter because it's all in fun.

Frederick now picks up his magic wand again, waves it over his fist (having already stolen the silk-loaded thumb tip away), and says the magic words. "Little silk scarf . . . clackity-clack! Make your way to Buttons' back!"

Frederick opens his hand to show the silk is gone, ditches the wand (and the thumb tip), then shakes Buttons' hand again and pulls him around. The audience immediately sees the silk on Buttons' back, and Frederick pulls it off at the tape point, then shows it to Buttons.

"Wow, wee! I can't believe that! You did it again! Frederick, that's wonderful."

"Yes, I know," says Frederick, smiling.

"First you vanished my card, and then you magicked it around onto my back. Then you disappeared that yellow silk scarf, and you magicked that onto my back."

"Absolutely correct, Buttons," Frederick continues, "which brings me to my third and final illu . . . TRICK of the evening."

From his left, Frederick picks up a cardboard pie box. (In reality, there is no pie in it, but Frederick pretends that it contains a pie.)

"In this box, Buttons, I have a very nice cream pie . . . in fact, a coconut cream pie made fresh this morning and refrigerated all day long."

"Well, yum-yum," says Buttons, "let's eat it all up!"

"No, no," says Frederick. "This pie is not for eating."

"It's not?" Buttons asks quizzically. "What's it for?"

"Why, it's for my third and final magic trick," Frederick explains. "First, I vanished the card, and it landed on your back. Second, I vanished the scarf, and it landed on your back. Third, I am going to vanish this coconut cream pie, and . . ."

During this short speech, Mr. Clown has rushed from the wings a third time, this time with a cream pie in his hand. At this point in Frederick's speech, Mr. Clown is just a step behind Buttons with the pie raised to back level.

"Oh, no!" says Buttons as the realization hits him. "You're not gonna make that coconut cream pie vanish and reappear on MY BACK! I'm gittin' out of here RIGHT NOW!"

Just as Buttons says that, he swings around to his right in order to leave the stage. As he does, his right arm goes up from under the pie and "accidentally" knocks it into Mr. Clown's face.

Buttons storms off the stage, leaving Mr. Clown covered with cream pie.

Frederick grabs his prop bag and, in leaving, announces: "I think it's time we all disappeared!"

THE BIG NEWSPAPER

The concept of something ordinary growing from its normal size to many times larger has always intrigued me. One day while on an airplane, my thoughts on this concept centered around an ordinary newspaper.

In my vision, I saw a clown, a park bench, and a newspaper. I saw the clown sit on the bench, open the paper, and read it. Then he opened it again, and the paper grew to twice the normal size. He opened it again and again until the newspaper was larger than the park bench, covering the clown entirely. Then I saw the newspaper fall to the stage, and the clown was gone.

"You're thinking like a magician," Leon McBryde

told me, and I admitted he was right. "A clown wouldn't do it that way."

"How would a clown do it?" I asked. "With more clowns?"

"Well . . ."

"Because I have another version," I continued. "Picture this: The one clown comes onto the stage and opens the paper so big it covers the bench and him. Then all kinds of clown hands appear around the edges of the paper, which is now maybe 12 feet wide. Then different clown heads stick out around the ends and top of the paper. Then their heads go back behind the giant newspaper, which is maybe 8 x 12 feet. Finally, the one clown folds it back up, tucks it under his arm, and walks away. How about that?"

Leon admitted that was better clowning as opposed to magic. But my idea was to make the two work together.

Opening the newspaper from normal size to 8 x 12 feet was funny, especially if the clown played it right. Using its size to make him vanish was too magical, especially if he didn't come back.

Producing other clowns from the paper was fine magic. But what we did with them was another matter—and I wanted it to be clowning.

You'll read the final skit idea in a few moments. But first, let's look at the logistics.

Behind the Scene

The park bench pictured in Figure 127 has its back covered with the same material as the curtain behind it. It is set just a few feet from the curtain, and the curtain below the bench back is pinned open as in Figure 128. This creates a black art setup (see Appendix A) in which the viewers think they are seeing through the bench but are not, thus allowing people to enter and exit the stage unnoticed. This allows a clown to magically vanish (though he could simply go behind the bench) or a lot of clowns to appear.

The big newspaper is a lot of newspapers glued together so that it may start small, but be opened up to arrive at a size large enough to cover the bench and more.

Leon suggested using a stiff, but flexible, wire glued into parts of the newspaper so it would stand up on its own. That's an option. However, I felt that once the paper was opened to about six feet wide, especially if the clown sat on the end of the bench, a second clown hiding behind the bench could slip out as in Figure 129 and start helping the first clown hold up the paper. If both were wearing white gloves, the second clown's right hand could substitute for the first clown's right hand as in Figure 130.

Using this technique the paper could be opened larger and larger, with more clowns feeding out through the curtain, behind the bench, then behind the paper, at least in my second scenario.

lower curtain pinned open behind bench

back covered with cloth to match curtain

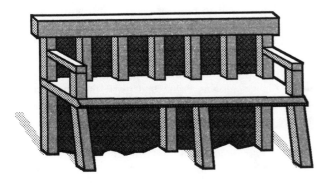

Figure 127

Figure 128

Figure 129

Figure 130

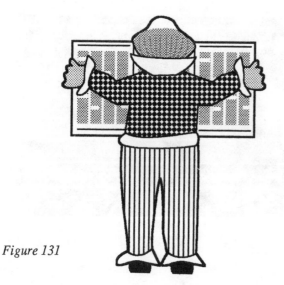

Figure 131

Figure 132

Now, you have the basic behind the scene secrets. Try this for a final scene.

The Show

A clown walks onto the stage, on which sits a park bench. The clown picks up a newspaper from the bench and starts to read it. He opens the paper, and it gets bigger. As this happens, the clown turns his back to the audience as in Figure 131.

As the clown opens the paper it gets larger and larger. Now it's at least 6 x 8 feet in size, and the clown is still trying to read it, holding it up as in Figure 132.

Finally, the clown folds down the paper, bit by bit, only to find a half dozen other clowns standing on the other side of the paper reading various sections of it. The first clown finishes folding the paper, then walks off with it, while the six clowns argue and gripe that they were reading it too. Where they came from is left in the world of magic, but the clowning element actually overrides it.

That's where Leon and I left it. I like it. But what about you? How would you do this skit? How would you add your creative clowning touches to this simple scene? We don't have all the answers. A part of the answer is you.

CHAPTER 13

CLOWN TRICKS FOR TWO OR MORE PERFORMERS

Clowns have been divided into three major categories: whiteface, auguste (pronounced "aw-goost"), and tramp or character. Traditionally, each type of clown possesses similar character traits and makeup designs. The whiteface, who is characterized by having primarily a white face, is the smartest and most skillful of the clowns. When working with other clowns he plays the roll of the straight man. The auguste's face color is pink with white trim. When working with the whiteface, he is the buffoon. It's the auguste who gets squirted, falls down, and receives the pie in the face. He is the victim of the whiteface's pranks. The tramp character is distinguished by a stubbly beard with tan or pink cheeks and white mouth. When working with other clowns the tramp is the least skilled and intelligent. He is the victim of pranks by both the whiteface and the auguste.

Although I have identified the general character traits of the three types of clowns, these traits are usually only evident when two or more clowns are working together.

Virtually everything in this chapter takes two or more clowns to accomplish. So if you're working with a partner, or a whole clown troupe, I sincerely hope you'll find a skit, trick, gag, or routine that you can use as it is or adapt to your situation. At the same time, I hope I'll make you think in terms of more than just yourself. Sometimes, working with more than a one-man or one-woman show can be fun. Let's see what happens!

SPIKE OUT OF NOAH'S ARK

While a whiteface clown starts talking onto the stage, an auguste hurries across the stage carrying a wooden box about a foot square.

"I'm in a hurry . . . a real hurry . . . out of my way!" says the auguste.

"Wait a minute, you!" exclaims the whiteface. "I'm trying to do a show here!"

"That's your opinion, bud!" wisecracks the auguste.

"Say, now that you've interrupted me . . . what do you have in that box?"

The auguste looks left and right, as though he's being followed. Then he says, "It's a big secret. Can you keep a secret?"

"Of course I can keep a secret!"

"Well, I don't know. Oh, all right. In this box . . . I have a valuable antique . . . you know, an expensive piece of junk! It's worth a million dollars!"

"A million dollars? You've got to be kidding!"

"No, no I'm not!" answers the auguste seriously.

"Well," asks the whiteface, "what do you have in the box?"

The auguste looks around again to make sure no one is watching him. Then he opens the box and removes a large metal spike, like a thick nail or railroad spike.

"This SPIKE is what I have," he tells the other clown, using a grave tone. *"And this spike is worth a million dollars!"*

The whiteface laughs. "A million dollars? Why, what makes you think that spike is worth a million dollars?"

Opening his eyes wide as he explains, the auguste states, "Because this spike is OUT OF NOAH'S ARK!"

He waits for the whiteface to reply.

The whiteface stares at him, then turns his head slowly toward the audience, shakes his head "no," then looks back at the auguste.

"What . . ." says the whiteface slowly "makes you think that this spike is OUT of Noah's Ark?"

"Hey, not only do I THINK that this spike is OUT of Noah's Ark," replies the auguste, "but I can PROVE IT!"

"You can prove it?"

"I can PROVE it!"

"Then let me see you prove it!" demands the whiteface.

The auguste starts to speak, then stops and holds up one finger to indicate a pause. Then he says, "Just a moment. If I can PROVE . . . that this spike is OUT of Noah's Ark . . . will you give me a FIVE DOLLAR BILL?"

The whiteface hesitates, then says, "All right. You prove that this spike is OUT of Noah's Ark, and I'll give you five dollars."

"In cash?"

"Yes, in cash."

"Right now? Today?"

"Oh, all right. Yes."

"Could I SEE the five dollars?"

"You are trying my patience!" says the whiteface. Yet grumbling, he pulls out a five dollar bill and says, "All right, here it is, right here in plain sight. Now, you'd better prove that this spike is OUT of Noah's Ark!"

"Oh, I will," says the auguste. "I told you this spike is OUT of Noah's Ark, and I can prove it!" He drops the spike back into the box, freeing one hand. "After all, it's not IN Noah's Ark, is it?" He stresses the word *in.*

"Well, no, it's not *IN* Noah's Ark," admits the whiteface.

"Then if it's not *IN* Noah's Ark . . ." states the auguste dramatically, "the spike has to be OUT OF NOAH'S ARK! That proves it—and thanks for the five dollars!" Immediately, he snatches the five dollar bill from the other clown's hand, shoves it into the box, snaps the box lid shut, and hurries off.

The whiteface stands his ground amid the audience laughter, muttering something like, "I know he did it, but I DON'T KNOW HOW!"

VANISHING RUBBER CHICKEN

This magic is so-o-o simple you're sure to have lots of fun doing it. All you need is a rubber chicken with a pin attached to it, hook fashion, as shown in Figure 133, and a large scarf about 36 inches square.

I'll describe the routine with two of my clown friends in mind: Vickie "Ruffles" Miller (a whiteface) and Joyce "Bubbles" Quisenberry (auguste), sometimes known as the California Girls, because they started clowning in their hometown of Riverside, California.

"Ruffles! Ruffles! I just learned this fantastic new magic trick from that magical magician man, David Ginn!" Bubbles exclaims as she comes out onto the stage with a small prop case.

Ruffles responds, "A new magic trick? What is it?"

"Oh, it's great. It's called the Vanishing Chicken!"

"Aw, come on, Bubbles!" laughs Ruffles. "Anybody can make a chicken vanish—you just go to Kentucky Fried and eat dinner!"

Bubbles shakes her head. "No, no, I'm not talking about eating a chicken for dinner! I'm going to make a RUBBER CHICKEN dish-appear!"

"I can't wait to see this," says Ruffles, directly to the audience. "Okay, what do I do?"

Bubbles pulls a three-foot scarf out of her bag.

"Glad you asked. Here, hold this big KER-CHANK."

"Don't you mean . . . handkerchief?" asks Ruffles.

"That's what I said. Now hold this KER-CHANK," says Bubbles.

So Ruffles takes the 36-inch silk and holds it under her chin.

"Now, here is the chicken," says Bubbles as she pulls a rubber chicken from her prop bag. "Isn't he nice?"

Figure 133

Ruffles pipes up, "I thought chickens were all SHE'S. Roosters are HE'S."

"You're certainly right, my dear," nods Bubbles. "Now I'm going to make HER dish-appear."

"How are you going to do that?" asks Ruffles.

"Easy! First, I put the chicken up under the big scarf. Like this." Bubbles lifts the silk which Ruffles is holding, and puts the rubber chicken under it, immediately hooking the pin to the center of Ruffles' costume. Partners working together can determine through rehearsal where best to hook the chicken in terms of looks and of not getting stuck by the pin.

"Next, I pull one hand out like this . . ." says Bubbles, leaving one hand under the silk, as if she's holding the chicken. "And then I wiggle my fingers magically like this." She wiggles her fingers. "And last I pull the cloth and chicken away like this . . ."

Bubbles grabs the silk with her outside hand and pulls it away with both hands as if the chicken was still inside it. It is important here that Ruffles keeps her eyes on the cloth and her partner clown. Suddenly, Bubbles tosses the silk into the air and whips it open to reveal that the chicken is gone.

"VOY-LA!" exclaims Bubbles. "LE CHICKEN has DISH-APPEARED!"

Of course, the audience is laughing now because they see the rubber chicken hanging on the front of Ruffles' costume.

"Bubbles! You did it! You really made that rubber chicken vanish into thin air!" Ruffles says excitedly, completely ignorant of the chicken hanging on her front. "I can't imagine where it went!" Of course, audience kids are trying to tell her, but she purposely ignores them.

"It's just amazing! I'm so proud of you," Ruffles says, patting Bubbles on the back. You finally did a magic trick that worked! Hey, everybody, let's all give Bubbles a really big round of applause!" Ruffles leads the applause.

All this time Bubbles is smiling, laughing, and waving the silk around as if she's really done something great.

"Thank you! Thank you! Thank you!" says Bubbles, waving her scarf.

"Well," says Ruffles, "you certainly fooled me! I think I'll take a break and go try to figure this one out." Ruffles then exits with the rubber chicken still hanging on her front.

This is where the bit with the vanishing chicken ends. But it's not a good place for the routine to end, so I'll offer you three possible endings.

Running Gag

What you've already read could be the setup for a running gag throughout a show, especially with other performers and acts. Ruffles could come out several other times during the show, chicken still hanging on her, saying, "I just don't know how she did that!" Never finding the chicken which is right there in plain sight.

KFC Ending

Ruffles could come back onto the stage with a Kentucky Fried Chicken bucket (or any recognizable local brand). The rubber chicken is still hanging on her, but unknown to the audience, the bottom is cut out of the bucket.

Ruffles says, "All right, Bubbles. I know where you made that rubber chicken disappear to."

Bubbles says, "You do?"

"Yes, I do," says Ruffles. "It went right into this Kentucky Fried Chicken bucket. You can't fool me!"

Of course, this makes the audience laugh, since everyone can see the chicken hanging on Ruffles' front.

"Into the KFC bucket?" asks Bubbles.

"Yes, that's right," says Ruffles. "And I'm going to reach in and pull it out."

Bubbles starts laughing. "You are?" Bubbles turns to the audience. "How is she going to do that?"

"Yes, I are—I mean, I am. Just like this!" says Ruffles. She reaches into the bucket, puts her hand through the open bottom, grabs the chicken off the front of her costume, and pulls it through the bucket. "Here it is! And here's something else for showing me such a DUMB MAGIC TRICK!"

At this point she starts beating Bubbles on the head or back with the rubber chicken and thus chases her off the stage. End of skit.

Chicken on the Back

Ruffles comes back onto the stage after Bubbles has done something. Secretly, she has the chicken hanging on her own back now.

Ruffles says, "Bubbles, I figured out the chicken trick. But you really fooled me."

"I did?" says Bubbles.

"Yes, you did. And I bet I looked pretty silly standing out here with that rubber chicken hanging on me, not even seeing it myself."

Bubbles nods her head. "Well, yes, you did look pretty funny."

Ruffles, standing immediately beside her friend, sneaks the rubber chicken off her back and pins it to Bubbles' back.

"Yes," says Ruffles, "I'm sure I did. And that doesn't bother me, Bubbles."

"It doesn't?"

"No, because I know you did it all in fun," Ruffles explains. Now she reaches out to shake Bubbles' right hand. "And I just want to congratulate you for that."

"Gee, thanks, Ruffles!"

As Ruffles shakes Bubbles' hand, she pulls her partner around so that Bubbles' back is directly to the audience, letting everyone see the rubber chicken hanging there. Naturally, the kids start laughing again, telling about the chicken, but the two ignore them.

"See you later, Bubbles!" Ruffles hurries off the stage.

Bubbles now addresses the audience. "Isn't that nice? I played a trick on her, and she took it so well."

Personally, I like ending it there. But what about you?

BALLOON POP

In one of his many convention lectures, magician Karrell Fox demonstrated what I consider the easiest way in the world to magically pop a balloon. With Karrell's permission, I'd like to share it with you here.

Insert a thumbtack in the tip of a thumb tip or rubber thumb tip counter. By holding a balloon as in Figure 134, then hitting the balloon with the thumbtack-thumb, you

Figure 134

can pop a balloon using one hand, unknown to the audience. To make sure the balloon pops, blow it up full until it's tight.

Now, with this method of working in mind, let's see how two clowns can have fun with the "Balloon Pop."

Homer the Clown, a tramp clown who in real life is Don Burda of California, starts off this routine at center stage.

"I have just completed a class in IMAGINARY SHARP-SHOOTING, and I would like to give all of you fine people a practical demonstration of my art. Since real firearms . . . that is, GUNS . . . are rather dangerous, I have learned to shoot with my imagination. If I may have an assistant to demonstrate. You there . . . in the wings."

Out comes Don's wife, Dee, carrying a balloon. He places her to one side of the stage, draws his imaginary finger gun, counts to three and fires. Nothing happens.

"Well, how do you like that! It worked!"

The audience expresses dissatisfaction.

"Oh, you're wondering about the balloon Dee is still holding. Well, that's another balloon. The first one popped . . . in my imagination. Did you know I could do IMAGINARY JUGGLING too? Watch this!" Homer quickly closes his eyes. He pauses a moment, then says out loud, "OOOPS!" He waits for the laugh.

"Oh, I get it. You wanted to SEE the balloon pop! Hold it up, Dee, I'll try once again. Ready . . . aim . . . FIRE!"

Homer points his finger gun and pretends to shoot.

Unknown to the audience, Dee pops the balloon with her thumb tip gimmick.

"Did I not tell you?" says Homer, bowing to applause.

"Next, I will repeat the feat . . . but this time I will be blindfolded." Homer proceeds to blow up another balloon, hand it to Dee, then blindfold himself with a bandana. He draws again, points in the wrong direction, shoots, and pops the balloon anyway.

Pulling off the bandana from his eyes, Homer again accepts the applause. "Thank you! Thank you! And now, for my final display of shootmanship . . . Did I say that? . . . Anyway, I will blow up not one, but two balloons, and pop them with a single imaginary bullet."

He proceeds to blow up the balloons, having Dee hold one in each hand.

"On the count of three, I will fire into the first balloon, popping it, and the imaginary bullet will be thrown into space by the popped balloon. That bullet will be hurled all the way to a satellite a thousand miles away, where it will bounce off the satellite and fire itself back down here to pop the second balloon. Believe it or not, here it goes!"

Homer takes careful aim, counts to three and yells, "BANG!"

The first balloon pops. Homer immediately looks upward toward space. Dee transfers the still-inflated balloon to her other hand (where she has the thumb tip). Homer pretends to see the bullet coming. He realizes it won't hit the balloon. He runs over to Dee and moves her position, then gets the balloon in the right position. Then he steps back and holds his fingers to his ears.

He looks up, then shouts, "Five, four, three, two, one!"

Nothing happens. Homer waits a moment. Still nothing. He takes his fingers out of his ears. He looks at the balloon. Then he looks at the audience and shrugs his shoulders, gesturing with his hands at the same time. That's when the balloon pops, and Homer jumps.

"Sorry," he says. "BAD TIMING!"

MIND READER CLOWNS

You can have plenty of fun with these two clown mind-reading routines, just engineered for laughs.

Buttons and Homer

Here I'll share a bit of live action I witnessed a year ago at the Brad Brothers' Carolina Clown Cavalcade in Raleigh, North Carolina. Don "Homer" Burda and Leon "Buttons" McBryde were on stage for the Saturday night show, and here is part of what happened.

Buttons announced that he could do a magic trick, a "mind-reading card trick."

"I'd like to see that," said Homer.

Buttons said, "You do not understand. I have magical and super powers of the mind!"

"You don't have any such thing," Homer replied.

"Oh, yes I do!" exclaimed Buttons.

"Well, Buttons," Homer continued, "if you did, you would be able to tell me whatever card I picked out of a deck."

"I just happen to have a deck of cards," said Buttons, and he pulled out a deck of jumbo playing cards, seven inches tall.

Buttons proceeded to spread the jumbo cards out in a fan.

"Here, Homer, just pick one of these cards."

As Homer reached for a card, Buttons handed Homer the top card.

"I bet I can tell you what card you picked!" shouted Buttons.

"No, no, wait a minute," said Homer. "That's not the card I wanted." Homer then put the card back. "Now, let me pick a card."

Buttons spread the cards again. "All right, just take a card, pick a card, any one of these cards."

As he did, Buttons pushed one card up about four inches higher than the deck, making that card clearly stand out. No matter which card Homer tried to pick, Buttons turned the extended card toward Homer's hand. Finally, Homer managed to avoid the protruding card and picked another one.

"That's the one you want?" asked Buttons, in a disappointed tone.

"That's the one," said Homer.

"Well, then, show it around to all the people out there," said Buttons.

"But you might see it," replied Homer.

"No, I won't. Look—I'll go to the back of the stage while you show everybody." And back he went.

Homer waved the card around. It was the nine of spades.

Meanwhile, Buttons switched the jumbo deck for a regular size deck with assistant Dee Burda. When no assistant is available, Buttons switches the decks in his pocket.

"Are you ready?" asked Buttons.

"Yes, I am ready," said Homer.

Buttons came forward, extended the regular size deck, and said, "Put your card back into the deck."

Homer pushed his face-down jumbo card into the regular size deck held in Buttons' hands. Then he turned away and immediately turned back, doing a classic double-take.

"I will now shuffle the cards," said Buttons, and he proceeded to perform a comedy clown shuffle of 51 regular size cards and one jumbo card, which looked very funny.

"Wait!" said Homer. "Wait a minute! That's not fair! Hold on just a cotton-pickin' minute, Buttons!"

By this time Buttons was laughing and talking away, happily shuffling the cards back and forth, up and down, off in his own world. Finally, he stopped, totally ignoring Homer's protests.

"I am now ready to find your card!" Buttons announced. He reached into the deck and pulled out one regular size card.

"Is this it?" he asked, holding up the six of hearts.

"No, that's not it!" said Homer.

Buttons acted muffed but returned the card to the deck. Then he pulled out another regular size card.

"Well, is this it?" he asked.

"No—that's not it either!" replied Homer, laughing at Buttons. Aside to the audience: "He can't even find my BIG card in that LITTLE deck!"

"Hmm," said Buttons, putting the card back. "I'll try one more time." He quickly turned to the audience for help. "Which one is it?" Some of the kids, of course, helped him by telling him it was the big card. "Oh, yes, that's right." Hearing this, Buttons pulled out the jumbo card and held it up.

"IS THIS IT?" he asked.

"Of course that's it!" said Homer. "But you're no mind-reader magical man, Buttons—you tried to TRICK ME! Now get outta here!"

This was only a part of the Buttons and Homer act that night, and there was lots more to it than that. But maybe this piece will give you a few ideas . . . for the fun of it.

Holey Hat

Here is another two-clown routine that's easy to perform. All you need to do is personalize, customize, and maximize the entertainment of it.

Get a tall felt flown hat, in fact, a Mad Hatter type hat and cut a hole in one side large enough to see through. This hat must be big enough to slide down over one clown's head, preferably the auguste clown of the pair.

The whiteface clown invites the auguste to help, perhaps placing him under a magic spell so he can "read minds." The whiteface has the auguste turn his back on the audience and places the hat completely over the other's head. This is the basis for the comedy.

Once the auguste is covered, the whiteface proceeds to pick up objects, which he holds up and asks his helper to name. To the amazement of the crowd, the auguste names each object correctly.

Of course, the hat-covered clown is standing with his back to the audience near the front of the stage and can see every object held up by the whiteface near center stage.

When the whiteface finally asks the audience to acknowledge his friend with a big round of applause, the auguste turns to face the spectators, revealing his face through the hat as he styles for applause. In character, the whiteface gets angry because his partner has revealed the secret and tosses him or chases him off the stage.

That's your framework and method for a good mind-reading comedy skit. Now get busy and flesh it out!

FLOATING VIOLIN

At a convention of the International Brotherhood of Magicians in New Orleans, comedy magicians Duke Stern and Karrell Fox performed a spoof I've always thought perfect for clowning.

Karrell Fox announced that he would perform a new version of magician Norm Nielsen's masterpiece, the "Floating Violin." He picked up a white bedsheet, held it stretched between his arms, and suddenly the audience heard violin music. Then, to the spectators' amazement, a violin and bow magically appeared at the top of the cloth, floating on its edge.

This mysterious "floating" of the violin, plus the music, went on for about 30 seconds. Then Karrell let go of the cloth in order to take his bow, dropping the sheet to the floor. And there sat hilarious Duke Stern on his knees, holding up the violin and playing it with the bow. To all the magicians, it was a very funny sight.

Basically, I'm suggesting that two clowns could do the same gag. It's simply a matter of announcing what you're going to float, then picking up the sheet and spreading it wide open, near the edge of the stage so your buddy with the floating object can sneak behind it (Figure 135). You could also do this at center stage if your friend had a way of coming through the back center stage without shaking the curtains and without being seen.

Aside from the floating violin, you might consider these other variations:

FLOATING CARROT. Have your hidden friend hold up the carrot, making it float above the cloth. Then the carrot disappears. When you drop the cloth, there he sits—eating the carrot!

Figure 135

FLOATING SQUIRT BOTTLE. Let your friend cause a squirting bottle to float. Then, when you reveal it, he squirts you with the water, or you grab the bottle and squirt him.

FLOATING FLOWER. A wilting flower floats back and forth across the sheet you're holding. When you "accidentally" drop the sheet, your clown friend acts embarrassed and the flower visibly wilts. Use a trick wilting flower for this bit.

Now it's your turn to think up your own version.

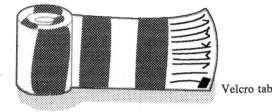

Figure 137   Velcro tab

ENDLESS SCARVES

Tie 15-20 silks together, using at least 18-inch squares, end to end as in Figure 136. Sew a one-inch Velcro square onto the end corner of two of the silks.

Cut the bottom and top off a large juice can, and spray paint the can some nice color to suit yourself. Tape a smaller juice can, with bottom intact, inside of it as shown using duct tape. Spray paint the insides black. This smaller can must comfortably hold one clown sock, say red and white striped, which can easily come out.

Sew a one-inch square of Velcro to the top of a clown sock, then roll the sock as in Figure 137, and ease it into the inner juice can as in Figure 138, with the Velcro easily accessible at the top. Then run one end of the silk chain through the can, and secure it to the other end with the Velcro tabs as in Figure 139. Now, place the can on a table, and stuff the silk chain into the can loosely silk by silk. One silk will remain partly outside the can as in Figure 140; I suggest you make that silk similar to the color of the can.

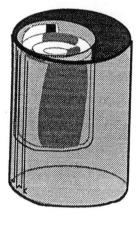

Figure 138

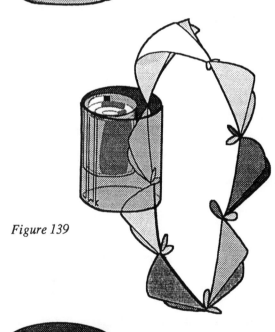

Figure 139

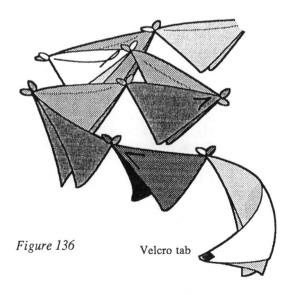

Figure 136   Velcro tab

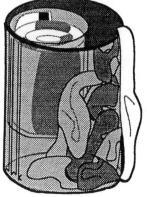

Figure 140

The Show

This routine starts with one clown, a female, entering the stage, carrying the can with one hand under its open bottom to hold the load inside.

"Ladies and JELLYFISH!" She stops, looks around. "Oh, sorry, I mean gentlemen! Today I will perform one of the great feats of magic." She stops and looks down, holding up one clown shoe. "Actually, I have two of the great *feets* of magic, but never mind! I am going to produce from this small canister *one thousand* scarf handkerchiefs right before your very eyes and if you don't have *very eyes,* any kind of eyes you've got!"

The clown waves her free hand over the can, then shouts. *"Mumbo, jumbo, dumbo, columbo! Ah, hah! Here . . . they . . . come!"*

She reaches into the can and starts pulling out the silks, singing some monotonous tune with a "LA-DA-DA-DA" vocal, not real words, in lieu of a live orchestra. A march or chase type song would be good here, and you could have it played on tape if you like. But the clown doing it herself would be funnier. An alternate plan is for the clown to count the silks out loud as they come out. Again, it depends on you!

After she pulls out about ten silks, the second clown enters.

"Hey, what are you doing?" the new clown asks. Let's assume this clown is a male.

"Why, I'm pulling *one thousand* scarf-kerchiefs out of this wee little canister."

"Scarf-kerchiefs?" says the second clown. "Why do you call them that?"

"Because I can't decide whether to call them scarves or handkerchiefs," replies the first clown, "so I just call them both!"

Second clown says, "Well, you can't even get 1000 *scarf-kerchiefs* in that can! How could you pull them out?"

First clown replies, "Of course I can! Just you watch!"

At this point in the routine, no one knows the big can is bottomless. So the first clown now lets go of her grip on the can and starts pulling the silks out faster and faster, "La-da-da-ing" the song or counting the silks again. The second clown stares at the can, shakes his head in wonder, and can't seem to figure out where all the silks are coming from . . . *because* he is watching the *top* of the can.

After a few moments, however, he happens to look down at the silks on the floor. He sees them moving. With his finger, he follows them up as they are pulled

through the can. When he realizes they are the same silks coming out of the can and going back into the can, his finger points at his own head as if to say, "I've got this one figured out!"

Now he stops the action.

"Wait a minute! Wait a minute!" he says. "I can do that. I can pull 1000 scarf-kerchiefs out of a can too!"

"Oh, yeah?" replies the first clown. "I don't think you can!"

"I certainly can," boasts the second clown. "Just give me that can, and I'll show you."

Unknown to the audience, when the second clown says "Wait a minute," she separates the silks, which are held together with Velcro, leaving one silk hanging out the top. The rest of the silk chain then drops to the floor.

"Just watch this," says the second clown. "One thousand scarf handkerchiefs out of this little can!" And he starts pulling with the silk the first clown left dangling out.

"LA-DA-DA" or "ONE, TWO, THREE!" as the second clown pulls silks out rapidly, finally pulling out the last silk, when he stops singing or counting.

"Huh? What happened?" he exclaims.

"See! I told you! You have to know REAL MAGIC to do this stuff," says the first clown. "Here, give me that can and I'll show you! I'll do magic that will knock your SOCKS off!"

She takes back the can and the string of silks, being sure to grasp the end of the Velcro which will hook to the hidden clown sock.

"Now, watch this: First, you stuff these scarf handkerchiefs down into the can, like this."

She sticks the Velcro silk to the sock, then stuffs the silks into the can, one after the other, holding her hand on the bottom.

"Then you say the magic words: *Rocko, blocko, gitta his SOCKO!"*

The second clown scratches his head and looks on seriously.

The first clown says, "And then you start pulling like this."

She starts pulling out the silks again, counting or singing, but making some noise. As the silk string comes to its end, out comes the single clown sock, dangling from the final silk. Make sure the color of the sock contrasts with the silks so it is easy to see.

"What!" shouts the second clown. "What is that?" He looks around, then looks down and pulls up his pants leg to show one matching sock. Then he pulls up his other pants leg and shows his other sock is *missing* (he actually never had it on). "Hey, you got my SOCK!"

The first clown laughs.

"I told you this trick would knock your socks off— but I only got ONE of them! See you later!" she shouts, and off she runs with the second clown right behind her.

"Give me my sock back!" he shouts, as the audience laughs and applauds.

ALMOST GONE CANDLE VANISH

Here's a comedy vanish that Abb Dickson thought up and that he and I used in our first full evening magic stage show way back in 1968 at the University of Georgia.

Abb had a single leg table into which he had drilled a hole, a hole slightly larger than a one-inch wooden candle he fashioned from a piece of wooden dowel. The candle was 15 inches tall, and Abb wedged it into the hole as shown in Figure 141. I think he used a folded piece of paper to create the wedge; otherwise, the candle would fall right through the hole.

Attached to the upper end of the candle was a piece of string, which was also attached to the table.

Here's how two clowns would handle the "Almost Gone Candle Vanish."

As the first clown starts to make an announcement, a second clown hurries onto the stage carrying the table described above.

Comic magician Abb Dickson.

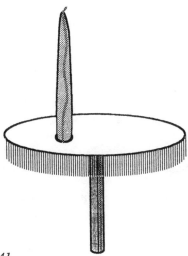

Figure 141

"Hold it! Hold it! It's magic time, and I can do great, wonderful, stupendous MAGIC!"

"Oh, you can?"

"That's right," says the second clown. "I can do better magic than you! I can make a candle VANISH from on top of this table right before your VERY EYES, and you'd better believe it too."

Think of Abbott and Costello here.

The first clown says, "Is that the candle you are referring to?"

"Yes, absolutely," says the second clown, secretly holding one hand behind his back.

"Are you going to make it vanish?" asks the first clown.

"Right, absolutely right," says the second clown enthusiastically. "But before I do, let me ask you three questions. First, if I can make this candle vanish from the top of this table in less than ten seconds, would you say that was a good trick and buy me a Coca-Cola?"

"Yes, I suppose so," replies the first clown.

"And second, if I could make the candle vanish from the top of this table in less than five seconds, would you say that was a very good trick and maybe buy me a cheeseburger too?"

Patiently, the first clown agrees. "I suppose so, being the nice person that I am."

"And third," continues the second clown, "if I could make THIS CANDLE completely and TOTALLY disappear from the TOP of THIS TABLE . . . in less than ONE SECOND, would you say I was a SUPER GREAT MAGICAN and buy me a STEAK DINNER after the show?"

"Did you say ONE second?"

"Yes, absolutely."

"For a steak dinner?"

"Right, absolutely."

"Oh, all right. But you have to do it in ONE second. When are you going to do it?"

"When you start counting," says the second clown.

The first clown puffs himself or herself up. "Ready? ONE—"

Immediately the second clown pulls a wooden mallet or hammer from behind his back and slams it down on the candle. Immediately the candle goes down through the table and dangles on the string below it as in Figure 142.

"HEY, IT'S GONE!" shouts the second clown with zest. "And you owe ME a steak dinner after the show!"

The second clown picks up the table and boldly stalks off the stage. The first clown simply stands there a moment and mugs his anger/disgust at his friend's stupid trick. Then, it's on with the show.

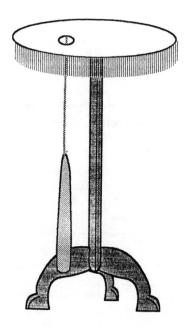

Figure 142

THE GREAT HOUDINI ESCAPE

Ask anyone on the street, at school or work, to name the greatest magician of all time, and most will answer "Houdini." Sure, sure, David Copperfield, Doug Henning, and Harry Blackstone, Jr., have had lots of TV exposure and have advanced magic to a great degree, but Houdini has become somewhat of a legend. National Magic Day in the United States, which is October 31 (and also Halloween), actually commemorates Houdini's death in 1926.

In this magic escape skit involving two clowns, we'll pay a comedy tribute of sorts to the Great Houdini. In fact, I'll offer you two versions of this skit. See which one suits you.

To perform this, your main prop will be a large, human-size paper bag. Get some brown paper for this, the kind that comes in long rolls, and glue or staple a bag together, large enough for a clown to get inside. In one side of the bag, cut a circular hole so the clown can see out. On the back side of the bag, cut a slit the length of the bag so the clown can step out. You will also need a four to six-foot length of rope.

Here's the first version.

The Great Houdini Escape One

The auguste clown enters the stage and tells his friend, the whiteface, as well as the audience, "I have been reading a book all about the Great Houdini. Do you know he could escape from anything? I mean, he could get out of ropes, chains, boxes, straitjackets, everything!"

"Is that right?" says the whiteface. "Did he ever figure out how to get out of yard work?"

The auguste stares at his friend. "I AM SERIOUS!"

"Sorry," the whiteface replies. "So you've been studying Houdini. And I suppose you can escape just like Houdini?"

"How DID you guess?" remarks the auguste. "In fact, I just happen to have brought along my newest Houdini escape trick. And I will be ever so happy to show it to you."

"Oh, what do you intend to escape from?"

The auguste smiles big and proudly announces, "A PAPER BAG!"

The audience laughs. So does the whiteface.

"From a *paper bag?*" says the whiteface. "Are you crazy? Anybody could get out of a paper bag. You just tear your way out, that's all."

"I'm not going to tear it," says the auguste. "That's the challenge—to escape from a human-size paper bag

WITHOUT TEARING the bag! Now, look, here's the paper bag." He brings out the bag from offstage or nearby. "Just look at this tough, brown paper! It's so strong, it'll even hold GROCERIES!"

"Or GARBAGE!" quips the whiteface.

"I will ignore that," says the auguste. "Now, I'll get into the paper bag . . . and once I do, you tie it up at the top with this rope." He hands his whiteface friend a piece of rope. Pulling up a nearby chair, he sits down in the chair and extends his feet forward. "Now, slide the bag onto my legs."

The whiteface complies. The auguste helps pull the paper bag over his legs, pulls more bag up his legs, then hops to his feet. He jumps up and down a couple of times, as the whiteface assists in getting him fully into the bag.

NOTE: If you make it a point to get your feet or shoes all the way to the bag's bottom at the start, while sitting, you can put the bag on without tearing it. Another thought: Perhaps the bag could be made from heavy cloth or upholstery material.

Now the auguste is standing inside the bag, as the whiteface ties the top with the rope. The auguste talks through the face hole in the bag.

"Now, just tie up the top real good."

The whiteface pretends not to notice the hole. "Huh? Where is that voice coming from?" Then he sees the hole and his friend's face. "Hey, now, all right! What is this? There's a HOLE in this bag!"

"Of course, there's a hole," replies the auguste. "You want me to breathe, don't you?"

rope

face
through
hole

Figure 143

"Well, I suppose so. But it's not fair escaping through that hole. Just remember that!"

The auguste says, "Of course not. Anyway, I can only get my face through this hole. It's just enough to see you."

"All right. When are you going to escape?" asks the whiteface.

"When you count to ten," says the auguste. "Now start counting . . . and do it SLOWLY!"

The whiteface stands directly facing the audience, holding one hand on the rope at the top of the bag. He commences the count: "One, two, three, four . . ." The moment he starts counting, the auguste slips out of the bag through the large slit in the back of the bag and runs around behind his friend.

"Four, five, six . . ." says the whiteface.

The auguste taps him on the shoulder. "Excuse me, sir. What are you doing?"

"I'm holding this bag while my friend here makes his Great Houdini escape," says the whiteface, not looking at the auguste. "Now don't interrupt my counting. I'll have to start over. One, two, three, four . . ."

The auguste taps his friend's shoulder again.

"Excuse me, sir. Has he escaped yet?" asks the auguste.

"For heaven's sake," remarks the whiteface, stopping his count again. "No, he has not escaped yet . . . and he'll never get out if you don't stop interrupting me!"

"Sorry."

"Now, I will continue my count: four, five, six, seven . . ."

The auguste taps his friend's shoulder once more, interrupting: "Excuse me, sir. Would you give him a message for me?"

"Seven, eight, nine—what? A message? For crying out loud!" says the whiteface. "What kind of message?"

"Tell him," says the auguste, "when he gets out of that silly bag you're holding, to meet me at Burger Doodle for dinner. And he can even bring you along with him. That's all."

"Well, that's very nice of you," says the whiteface. Then he turns to look at the auguste, for the first time seeing that it's his friend.

The auguste smiles.

The whiteface fumes in mock anger, dropping the bag.

"I'm going to DISCOMBOBULATE YOU!"

The auguste runs off the stage, followed rapidly by the whiteface.

End of version one.

The Great Houdini Escape Two

This version uses the same two clown characters and props, only this time the auguste announces that his objective is to escape, but not until he makes a real ice cold Coca-Cola appear with him inside the bag.

"You see, when I do escapes, I get thirsty!"

The whiteface ties the auguste up in the bag, then holds the top as described earlier. Then the auguste sneaks out the back of the bag and starts tiptoeing away.

"Pssst!" says the whiteface, seeing his friend sneaking off. "What are you doing?"

The auguste answers in a loud whisper, "I'm going to get the Coke."

"But they can see you," replies the whiteface.

"No, they can't!" says the auguste. "There's an invisible wall right here, and I'm behind it. So they can't see me at all."

The whiteface scratches his head quizzically. "Oh, I see. But wait a minute—I can see YOU."

"That's because YOU have X-ray vision," says the auguste.

"Oh, you mean like Superman?"

"That's right. Now, I'll be right back with the Coke."

The whiteface whistles while he waits. Then the auguste returns with a Coke in his hand, re-entering the bag from the back.

"Now I've done it!" the auguste announces through the hole in the bag. "See—here!" He hands the Coke can out through the hole to his friend.

"Well, well, very good!" says the whiteface. "But listen, I'd like to try this too. Do you think it would be all right—psst, with the invisible wall and all?"

"Sure," says the auguste. "Tell you what: I'll hold the Coke while you give it a try." He takes the Coke through the hole.

The whiteface faces the audience, announcing, "And now, ladies and gentlemen, I will walk behind the bag and completely VANISH."

Immediately he walks behind the bag to the other side.

"Psst!" says the whiteface. "Am I gone?"

The auguste looks at him. "No, you're not gone."

"What? Why not?"

"Because you're standing IN FRONT of the invisible wall!"

"Oh, how silly of me!" says the whiteface. "How do I get behind it?"

"You have to open the door."

"Where is the door?"

"Right behind you."

The whiteface turns his back on the audience and starts looking for the door. Meanwhile, the auguste takes a swallow of Coke, waves good-bye to the audience, and hops offstage inside the bag.

"I can't find any door!" says the whiteface. Finally, he turns around. He looks left and right, doesn't see his auguste friend, then shouts, "HE'S ESCAPED!"

And hurries offstage.

Now it's your turn to think. Or perhaps this would be a fun subject for brainstorming between two or more clowns. Where else could this skit go? What else could be in the bag? Could the auguste pull all sorts of production items out of the bag, handing them to his whiteface pal through the face hole? Rubber chickens? Pigs? Could he complain that he cannot escape until he gets the bag cleaned out? Could another clown somehow sneak into the bag (if it were large enough) from the back curtain? Could the clown inside the bag operate one or two hand puppets from inside the bag, using the face hole like a puppet theater stage? Could ventriloquism work here?

Be creative, clowny, and magical. After all, when you're in front of people performing, I won't be there with you. How will you do this? Think it out first, then try it in practice, then for a small group, and finally before full-fleged audiences. Have fun yourself while amazing the audience with magic and laughter.

ONE LAST THING

Leon McBryde often quotes Ray Kroc, former president of McDonald's Restaurants, as having said: "When you're green you grow. When you're ripe, you rot." I believe that. I don't have all the answers. I'm still learning—and enjoying the experience.

So, what is my advice to you as you continue in clowning and magic?

Read, study, absorb books on magic, comedy, clowning. Listen to tapes and watch videos. See every clown and magician and comedian you can, both live and on TV.

Then ask yourself three questions: What did I like? What did I not like? And how would that idea fit my character?

Use what you learn to stimulate your thinking and fire you up or tell you what not to do, but don't copy.

Absorb, adapt, practice, and keep thinking creatively. Find the real clown in you, and have fun doing it. Build your act on personality.

Love your audiences and *never* stop learning.

APPENDIX A

STANDARD MAGIC PROPS

Any craftsman must have a proper set of tools. In addition, the craftsman must also understand the tools used in his profession or hobby, whether he owns them or not. That is what this section is all about, understanding 58, more or less, standard magic tools of the trade, all of which apply to clowning in various ways. This list is by no means inclusive of all the possible magic props you will encounter in clowning and magic, but it's a start.

You do not need to run out and purchase every one of these props. But if you continue in clowning and magic, having knowledge of these items now will be a great help to you.

APPEARING CANE A metal or plastic coil under tension, which, when released, expands instantly from two to 36 inches in length. Adapted for magic purposes by magician Russ Walsh in the 1940s (in metal); later perfected in plastic by Fantasio in 1977. The plastic version has advantages: It needs no oiling, will not rust, does not cut your hands, comes in various colors, and costs about half the price of metal. With this prop, you can reach out and magically produce a cane from "thin" air, or change a silk handkerchief into a cane.

BANANA TRICK A single sponge or foam banana multiplies to two in your bare hands, then three, four, and more. Bananas finally vanish from the bag or hat you're putting them into, or you can change them into something else. Sleight-of-hand trick almost any clown can learn with a few hours practice, and well worth the time it takes. Inexpensive.

BLACK ART PRINCIPLE Black objects cannot be seen against a black background, provided the lighting is not too bright. If the background is black cloth or felt, and the object to be concealed is felt-covered or has black felt coating (called flocking), the principle works at its best.

BLACK HAND GAG Comedy item. A gimmicked towel you hand to a volunteer helper to "wipe his hands off before you help with this trick." When you retrieve the towel, you find black hand prints all over it.

BLENDO Effect in which a number of silks visibly change into a large, multicolored scarf or even a flag. The trick is accomplished in many ways, some mechanical and some with sleight-of-hand.

BLOOMING BOUQUET Feather flower bouquet you show without blooms (or you pluck off the blooms). Through a series of magic and comedy gestures, you make the flowers bloom. The cheap mechanical version from India works great for clowns and magicians doing kidshows.

BONGO HAT A comedy paper-folding novelty which starts as a small triangle, then unfolds to reveal larger hats in different colors.

BOTANIA Gimmicked metal can or tube which houses a collapsed feather flower bush. When released, the bush opens up many times larger than its container. See the "Tree of India" in Chapter 10.

BREAKAWAY FAN A folding cloth fan that looks solid when opened, but when handed to a spectator to reopen, falls apart as in Figure 144. Easy to operate. Can be repeated many times. Since it always works in the performer's hands and fails in the spectator's hands, it is best if the performer finally lets the fan fall apart on himself, followed by the helper opening it correctly.

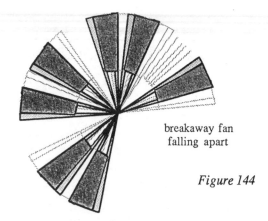

breakaway fan
falling apart

Figure 144

BREAKAWAY WAND A magic wand that appears solid, but when handed to an audience helper, falls apart into a half dozen pieces all strung together by a strong cord. Inferior versions show obvious pieces of wand strung together before the wand falls apart. At this writing, Supreme Magic of England makes the best version because it looks solid when you use it. It collapses from pressure of the thumb and first finger upward on the wand while the other fingers pull down, similar to the wilting flower.

CHANGE BAG A bag with two compartments, usually mounted on a circular frame of metal or wood and supported by a handle. (See Figure 145.) You place an object in one side, then switch bag sides by either twisting the handle or flicking a little wire switch beneath the handle. Can be used to produce, vanish, or change one object for another, thus its name. A newer version, known as a *tote bag*, appeared in the 1970s using a drawstring top closure and no ring or handle.

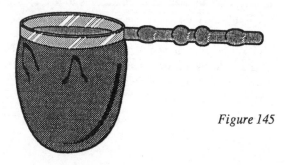

Figure 145

CLATTER BOX As an audience helper opens this wooden box to find a vanished silk, the box falls apart into seven pieces, smashing to the floor. Box is easily reset for next show. Comedy item.

COLOR CHANGING SHOELACES Pull a yellow shoelace through your hand and it changes to green. Open your hand to reveal a hidden red lace. Then you reproduce the yellow shoelace from a pocket.

COSTUME BAG Cloth bag vanishes a silk, then turns inside out to reveal a kid-size costume you have your audience helper don. Examples include Santa, Merlin, prisoner, chef, Chinese. Good for "dressing up" your show and causing laughs.

DANGER TRICK Any trick which makes the audience think that something terrible is going to happen to an audience volunteer, but which is most often played for comedy. Examples include arm choppers, guillotines, sword through neck, spikes through arm. Most of these tricks are controlled completely by the performer and offer no real danger. *As a clown, you must decide whether your character would use such a trick and why.*

fake hand   real hand

Figure 146

DAYLIGHT SEANCE CLOTH A wooden rod holding a dark, opaque cloth with a fake hand attached to the rod as in Figure 146. This allows the performer to cause magical things to happen using his free hand. Effectiveness in magic depends on how real the fake hand looks. Clowns who wear gloves have the advantage of covering the fake hand with a matching glove, which duplicates the clown's hand better.

DOVE A gentle bird, smaller than a pigeon, often used by magicians and clowns as a magical production item. Easy to tame and finger train when very young, these birds may be hidden in small places, producing a convincing magical effect when they appear.

DOVE PAN A metal pan that is shown empty and capped with a lid cover. When the cover is removed, something magically appears (originally one or two doves). Can be used to produce doves, a rabbit, a cake, candy, and other things. Made in sizes ranging from cupcake to a very large duck pan. Completely mechanical in operation. Easy to use.

DRAWER BOX Production device, a drawer which slides in and out of a box. Show drawer empty, slide into box, and pull out again to make production appear. Very small sizes hold a fake mouse or small spring snake, whereas larger models can contain a live rabbit.

DYE BOX Sometimes called a popcorn dye box. Invented by magician Tommy Windsor in the 1940s. You stuff handkerchiefs into the popcorn box and close it, then reopen it to reveal something else, such as rice or oranges or different colored silks. Works with a back double wall; very cleverly made. A simple but very effective prop; inexpensive. You can buy the *Dye Box Book,* which teaches you how to use and make your own dye box.

EGG BAG Place a wooden egg into this gimmicked pocket bag and the egg vanishes. Many variations. My own bag finally turns inside out to reveal a chicken that supposedly laid the egg. Easy to use.

FOO CAN Metal can you can pour water into, yet when you turn it over, no water pours out. Easier to buy from a magic shop than to make! Many versions available.

FRAIDY CAT RABBIT A kidshow sucker trick invented by Bill Paul and manufactured by Gene Gordon in the 1960s. Now made by Abbott's Magic in Colon, Michigan. You show a black face rabbit, put him in a little "house," then change him to a white face by turning him around. You change him back to black, but the kids realize right away that you "turned him around." Finally, you show that he's not white on the back—but just the back side of the black rabbit.

GAG BAG Cloth bag which changes colors five times or more as you turn it inside out. Easy mechanical item; just needs a good line of patter from the performer.

HIPPITY HOP RABBITS Another color changing rabbit sucker trick for kids. Two rabbit cutouts (see Figure 147), one black and one white, supposedly change places under two houses. It's the good old "you turned it around" theme again, and finally you do turn the rabbits around to reveal a red and a yellow rabbit. Easy mechanical trick.

Figure 147

HOT BOOK When you open this book, flames leap forth, often to the shock and amusement of the audience. Hot books or flame books operate with either a flint/steel striker or an electronic ignition system, which in turn sets a thick wick saturated with lighter fluid on fire. The flames are extinguished by closing the book cover. Not to be used near children or too close to your wig!

LINKING RINGS This trick is over 500 years old and was probably seen by Marco Polo in his travels through Asia. The performer links and unlinks what appears to be solid steel rings. Beginner's sets range in size from three to five inches, though professionals use 8, 10, or 12 inch rings for stage shows. Learning the trick is easy; entertaining with a good routine is what takes the work.

LOTA BOWL OR VASE Metal or plastic water container, gimmicked with a double wall. When you pour water out of the inner chamber, more water flows from the outer chamber to the inner, thus refilling the vase. Pouring may be repeated seven to ten times, depending on the size of your vase. A comedy magic prop.

MAGIC COLORING BOOK Gimmicked child's coloring book which starts out with blank pages. Then the pages become lined pictures, and finally the pictures become magically colored in. You can also reverse the process. Based on the Svengali principle invented by Burling Hull in 1909. Easy item for clowns or magicians, and by embellishing your routine with costumes, magic wands, and magic words, you can entertain with such an item for five to ten minutes at a children's show.

MAGICIAN'S ROPE A soft, white cotton rope with a cotton core, usually $1/4$ or $3/16$ inch in diameter, which is ideal for all types of magic tricks. It is highly visible on the stage and cuts easily. Obtainable through magic shops.

MILK PITCHER Most kids involved in magic get one of these early in the game, but don't feel bad if you don't have one yet. The effect is that you pour about half a pitcher of milk into a paper bag or cone, and the milk vanishes when you tear up the paper. Completely mechanical. Works with a double wall so pitcher appears full, but when you pour, the milk between the walls goes inside the main pitcher. Best to use "OOM," a chemical "milk" instead of the real thing. Milk pitchers range in price from $10 to $50, depending on quality, some pitchers even have "milk" sealed in so you never empty or clean the pitcher. Available at most magic shops.

MISMADE FLAG Patriotic trick in which you attempt to make an American flag (or that of your country), but accidentally drop one of the silks, which makes the flag come out with a color missing. You finally do get the flag made by magic. Different versions available.

MOUTH COILS Tear up a piece of paper, stuff it into your mouth or hand, and pull out a long, multicolored paper streamer, ranging from 12 to 50 feet. Personally, I never do "mouth tricks" because someone might be offended; thus, I always work this trick out of my fist. Buy a dozen or so because they are not reusable.

MULTIPLYING RABBITS A small sponge bunny is placed in a spectator's hand and his hand is closed. When the spectator is told to open his hand, two bunnies appear. Repeat this again, and finally a whole bunch of baby bunnies appear. Neat close-up trick for kids or adults, and relatively easy to learn.

MUTILATED PARASOL Show an umbrella open, close it, and wrap it in a mat or newspaper. Vanish six silks in a change bag. When you pull out the umbrella, the cover is gone and the six silks take its place. You now find the cover in the change bag. Then you reverse the process and make things right again. Entirely mechanical and very easy. Made by Abbott's Magic and others.

PAPER HAT TEAR Gimmicked paper which allows you to tear it up, then open out pieces to make a hat for a volunteer's head. Examples: wizard hat, clown hat, Santa hat, lady's hat, mouse or rabbit ears. Not reusable. Usually sold in boxes of 10-12.

PHANTOM TUBE Metal tube you show empty, then make a large silk production from one end. This is a double-walled tube available from magic shops. Looks impossible to the audience.

PHONEY RING A ringing device mounted inside a box, typically worn somewhere inside your clothing and operated by a push button. Also comes with a telephone receiver and cord, which you attach inside you coat. Press the button, cause a ringing, then reach into your coat and pull out the receiver to answer a call. Turn to someone and say, "It's for you!" Many other possibilities.

PICTURE SILKS Various size silk scarves with printed pictures or messages on them. Pictures include a butterfly, rabbit in a hat, "Good-bye," "The End," "Thank You," "Happy Birthday," various card faces, and more. Due to the price of silk, these are now on the expensive side, but well worth the investment if you use one in a lot of shows.

RABBIT Ideal magic production item, whether live or imitation, because virtually all children and adults like rabbits. Magicians often use dwarf rabbits so they don't outgrow their production or vanish boxes. Of course, if you use a spring rabbit (fur-covered imitation rabbit with metal spring inside), you can fit what appears to be a large rabbit into a small space.

RABBIT WAND Large magic wand that contains a roll down banner showing a rabbit in a top hat. A hole is cut at the rabbit's face so you can hold it in front of a child's face to make him or her look like a rabbit. Great for birthday parties and birthday child photos.

ROLL-ON TABLE Also called a suitcase table at times. A table which carries your props in its folded-down state, yet opens up to use on the stage.

RUBBER PRODUCTION GOODS Items made of latex rubber to imitate the real thing, but allowing you to collapse the product into a small space. Examples include a rubber chicken, rooster, duck, pig, and a whole line of fruits and vegetables.

RUN, RABBIT, RUN Great sucker trick in which a cutout bunny vanishes from one door and is seen running across a brick wall to another door on a platform held in your hands. Kids love this one. Bunny finally disappears completely, only to be found in your back pocket or elsewhere. Magic dealer item.

SILKS Thin cloth scarves or squares used in hundreds of magic tricks. The best ones are 100 percent pure silk, thus the name used by magicians and clowns. However, it is better to call them *scarves* or *handkerchiefs* in front of an audience and not *silks*. The psychology is that scarves and hanks seem thick (making tricks more impossible to figure out), whereas silk is thin. Some silks are made of a silk and rayon blend, making them somewhat thicker, meaning they are harder to hide and come out more wrinkled than pure silk, though the silk/rayon blends cost less and are just as good for certain tricks.

SIX FOOT RULER Gag ruler used to measure child's height. It has six footprints on it, making the child six feet tall.

SPONGE BALL TO BUNNY A red sponge ball which changes to a red sponge bunny rabbit when turned inside out as it is pushed through your hand. Made by Goshman under the name "Miracle Rabbit."

SPRING FLOWERS Tissue paper flowers, often with heavy paper or plastic outside petals and with metal springs inside. These can be compressed flat, and they pop open on release.

SQUARE CIRCLE A magic production device consisting of a square box with no top or bottom and a circular tube inside it. You show both parts empty, then produce a large load of items. The gimmick, or load chamber, is a black tube slightly smaller than the visible one, usually with a bottom. When you remove the visible outer tube, the black tube remains inside the box and is not seen due to the black art principle.

SQUEAKER Hand-held plastic bulb, not visible to the audience, which you squeeze to make a squeaking sound. Many effects possible, mainly based on the idea that anything you touch magically squeaks. Clowns can hide a squeaker inside a glove, working it with one or two fingers.

SUCKER DIE BOX A hundred year old trick in which you place a large wooden die in a two-sided box. The die appears to slide back and forth inside the box as you show one door open at a time. Finally, the die vanishes and reappears in a previously empty hat. Many variations available in all price ranges.

TEMPLE SCREEN Easy cardboard production device invented by U. F. Grant in the 1930s and now made by MAK Magic of Columbus, Ohio. You can show both sides of a three-fold screen (each panel about 8 x 18 inches), then produce a large load of silks, doves, and more.

THUMB TIP A metal, plastic, or rubber imitation thumb tip, slightly larger and longer than your natural thumb tip, used for vanishing and producing small objects or thin silks. Gloved clowns can use a thumb tip by painting it white or covering it with white cloth to match the gloves. A thumb tip should not be worn past the first knuckle, so the knuckle can bend, but it should fit snug at that point.

TWENTIETH CENTURY SILKS Trick in which you tie two silks together and vanish a third (say, multicolored silk). When you pull the tied pair apart, the multicolored silk has returned tied between them. Many variations on this.

VANISHING CANE What appears to be a solid three-foot wooden cane suddenly changes to silks or vanishes completely from a rolled up tube of newspaper. Adapted from the collapsing French opera cane of the 1800s by American magician Russ Walsh in the 1930s, using spring steel. In the late 1960s Fantasio began making the vanishing cane in space-age plastic, adding colors and thus inventing the color-changing cane and triple color-changing cane, used by magicians worldwide. I personally advocate the plastic Fantasio models because they are colorful, don't need maintenance, and will not cut your hands as the metal canes can, and will.

VISIBLE COLOR PAINTING A frame holds a black and white picture, that when pulled out the top, changes to full color. Looks great and impossible, but easy to do. Made by Hank Lee in Boston, Ickle Pickle in St. Louis, and Repro 71 in England. Many inserts are available, so it's not always the same picture changing from black and white to full color. Inserts include: clown, Santa Claus, boy scout, Frankenstein monster, "Happy Birthday," Christmas tree, Easter Bunny, and more.

WHAT'S NEXT The old spot card trick where you show four spots on one side, one spot on the next side, six spots on the next side, and three spots on the other side, all done with a two-sided card. Finally, you reveal eight spots on the back. Mechanical trick, easy to do. Just add personality.

WILTING FLOWER This is a comedy item consisting of a single stem, single bloom feather flower which you hold in one hand. At any time you wish, the flower wilts or droops over, causing much laughter. The flower contains a spring/cord arrangement inside, which you operate by a ring at the bottom of the stem.

APPENDIX B

RESOURCES

Where do I learn? If you continue in clowning and magic, that's a question you'll want answered. And since I want you to succeed in clowning, in comedy, and magic, and in any other kindred arts that interest you, I'll spend this section offering you a variety of sources for clown and magic clubs, books, magic and clown props, makeup, and costuming.

One important note: If you write to any of these folks, do me and them the courtesy of sending a *self-addressed, stamped envelope* for their reply. You can't imagine how many inquiries mail order companies get with absolutely no postage. If the company sends those customers *anything* by return mail, it spends hundreds of dollars yearly on such replies. So let's do the courteous thing, and pay our own way!

MAGIC AND CLOWN PROPS

Your first step in finding magic and clown props should be to check the local telephone book yellow pages to see if there are magic, clown, or novelty shops in your city. If so, you can visit them and check out books and props personally. After that, mail order is the next step. Here are some reputable companies that might be of help.

Abbotts Magic Company
Colon, MI 49040

Al's Magic Shop
1012 Vermont Avenue N.W.
Washington, DC 20005

Axtell Expressions
230 Glencrest Circle
Ventura, CA 93003

Balloon Box
St. James Park
2416 Ravendale Court
Kissimmee, FL 34758

Books by Mail
P. O. Box 1444
Corona, CA 91718

Bumper and Company
3468 Citrus Street "B"
Lemon Grove, CA 92045

Daytona Beach Magic
136 S. Beach Street
Daytona Beach, FL 32114

David Ginn
4387 St Michaels Drive
Lilburn, GA 30247

Dewey's Good News Balloons
1202 Wildwood Drive
Deer Park, TX 77536

Eddie's Trick Shop
2860 Washington Street
Avondale Estates, GA 30002

Freckles Clown Supplies
5509 Roosevelt Blvd.
Jacksonville, FL 32244

Funhouse Magic Shop
3535 Belair Road
Baltimore, MD 21213

Fun Technicians Inc.
4782 Streets Drive
Syracuse, NY 13215

Hades Publications
Box 1414, Station M
Calgary, Alberta
Canada T2P 2L6

Hades Seattle Magic Sentre
89 S. Washington St.
Seattle, WA 68144

Haines House of Cards
2514 Leslie Avenue
Norwood, OH 45212

Haley House Publications
1705 Barbara Lane
Connersville, IN 47331

Hank Lee's Magic Factory
125 Lincoln St (P.O.Box 1359)
Boston, MA 02205

Ickle Pickle Products
883 Somerton Ridge Dr.
St Louis, MO 63141

Ken's Illusionarium
R. R. 3, Site 11, Comp. 202
Kamloops, BC
Canada V2C 5K1

LaRock's Fun & Magic Outlet
2123 Central Avenue
Charlotte, NC 28205

Leon McBryde
Pro-Knows Props
P. O. Box 12
Buchanan, VA 24066

Magic Art Studio
137 Spring Street
Watertown, MA 02172

Magic Books by Post
29 Hill Avenue
Bedminster, Bristol
U.K. BS3 4SN

Magic Inc.
5082 N. Lincoln Ave.
Chicago, IL 60625

Magic Touch
144 N. Milpitas Blvd
Milpitas, CA 95035

Magicland
3767 Forest Lane
Dallas, TX 75244

Maher Studios
800 W. Littleton Blvd
Littleton, CO 80120

Mark Wade's Kidshow Creations
101 Dorchester Drive
Baltimore, OH 43105

Mecca Magic
49 Dodd Street
Bloomfield, NJ 07003

Morris Costumes
3108 Monroe Road
Charlotte, NC 28205

Morrissey Magic Ltd.
2882 Dufferin Street
Toronto, Ontario
Canada M6B 3S6

Norm Nielsen Magic
P. O. Box 34300
Las Vegas, NV 89133

Paul Diamond Magic
4811 N. E. 27th Avenue
Ft. Lauderdale, FL 33308

Piccadilly Books
P.O. Box 25203
Colorado Springs, CO 80936

Potsy and Blimpo
Make-Up and Clown Supplies
14371 Spa Drive
Huntington Beach, CA 92647

Samuel Patrick Smith
Books and Tapes
P. O. Box 769
Tavares, FL 32778

Stevens Magic Emporium
3238 E. Douglas
Wichita, KS 67208

Sun Magic Company
716 E. Camelback Rd
Phoenix, AZ 85014

Supreme Magic Company
64 High Street
Bideford, Devon
U.K. EX39 2AN

Tannen Magic Inc.
6 West 32nd St. 4th Floor
New York, NY 10001

T. Myers Magic
1509 Parker Bend
Austin, TX 78734

Up, Up and Away
(Peachey Keene Props)
Box 147 Main Street
Beallsville, PA 15313

Under the Big Top
1525-A N. Placentia Avenue
Placentia, CA 92670

U. S. Toy Co. (Magic Dept.)
2008 West 103 Terrace
Leawood, KS 66206

CLOWN AND MAGIC ORGANIZATIONS

The more clowns and magicians you are around, the better opportunities you will have to learn. Write to any or all of these organizations for information, sending them return postage for their applications and/or brochures.

Clown Camp
University of Wisconsin
LaCrosse, WI 54601

Clown Hall of Fame
212 East Walworth Avenue
Delavan, WI 53115

Clowns International
174 Stockbridge Road
Winchester, Hants.
U.K. SO22 6RW

Clowns of America International
P. O. Box 570
Lake Jackson, TX 77566

Fellowship of Christian Magicians
Mail Center   P. O. Box 232
Sterling, CO 80751

International Brotherhood of Magicians
P. O. Box 89
Bluffton, OH 45817

International Shrine Clown Association
1122 Third Avenue
Rockford, IL 61108

Secret Six Organization
(so secret I don't know the address
OR the other five members! —DG)

Society of American Magicians
1333 Corry Street
Yellow Springs, OH 73120

Society of Young Magicians
P.O. Box 290068
St. Louis, MO 63129

World Clown Association
P. O. Box 1893
Huntington Beach, CA 92647

MAGAZINES AND NEWSLETTERS

Many of the magazines in this list are publications of the organizations listed along with them. For a subscription, you'll need to join the organization, so send them an inquiry for details. Other magazines are independent and simply require a yearly subscription fee.

The Christian Conjurer
FCM Mail Center
P. O. Box 232
Sterling, CO 80751

Clowning Around
World Clown Association
P. O. Box 1905
Allentown, PA 18105

The Joey
Clowns International
174 Stockbridge Road
Winchester, Hants.
U.K. SO22 6RW

Genii
P. O. Box 36068
Los Angeles, CA 90036

Laugh-Makers
P. O. Box 160
Syracuse, NY 13215

The Linking Ring
International Brotherhood of Magicians
P. O. Box 89
Kenton, OH 45817

Magic Manuscript
6 West 32nd Stree, 4th floor
New York, NY 10001

Magigram
Supreme Magic Company
64 High Street
Bideford, Devon
U.K. EX39 2AN

MUM
Society of American Magicians
P. O. Box 368
Mango, FL 33550

New Calliope
Clowns of America International
P. O. 570
Lake Jackson, TX 77566-0570

New Tops Magazine
Abbott's Magic Co.
Colon, MI 49040

SYMbol
Society of Young Magicians
P.O. Box 290068
St. Louis, MO 63129

MAKEUP AND COSTUMES

Magic and clown shops carry the makeup you'll need, or you can get supplies via mail order. You can also check with theatre, costume, and novelty shops. Here are some makeup suppliers who can either sell to you direct or steer you in the right direction.

Ben Nye Company, Inc.
5935 Bowcroft Street
Los Angeles, CA 90016

Bob Kelly Cosmetics Inc.
151 West 46 Street
New York, NY 10036

The Circus Clowns
3556 Nicollet Ave.
Minneapolis, MN 55408

Clowns 'N Kids
P. O. Box 80279
Indianapolis, IN 46280

Costumes by Betty
(Betty Cash, Shirley Muller)
2181 Edgerton Street
St. Paul, MN 55117

Kryolan Corporation
132 Ninth Street
San Francisco, CA 94103

Mehron, Inc.
45 E. Route 203
Valley Cottage, NY 10989

Morris Costumes
3108 Monroe Road
Charlotte, NC 28205

M. Stein Cosmetic Company
10 Henery Street
Freeport, NY 11520

Playbill/Ideal Wigs
37-11 35th Avenue
Astoria, NY 11101

Pricilla Mooseburger Originals
(Trish Manuel Bothun)
P. O. Box 529
Maple Lake, MN 55358

Potsy and Blimpo
14371 Spa Drive
Huntington Beach, CA 92647

Pro-Knows
P. O. Box 12
Buchanan, VA 24066

Wig Creations Ltd.
12 Old Burlington Street
London
U.K. W1X 2PX

BOOKS, TAPES, AND VIDEOS

We all have opinions of what is good and bad, helpful and not. I am no different. Therefore, I will purposely confine this recommended list to books, audio tapes, and videos of which I have personal knowledge. Most of these are available in magic shops and through mail order, not in libraries. If I don't mention a particular book or tape that you like in this list, simply assume I an not familiar with that particular title.

Abbott's Encyclopedia of Rope Tricks, 3 volumes. All the rope magic you'll ever need to know . . . and more!

Almost Unpublished (David Ginn). Stage, kidshow and family-oriented tricks, routines and philosophy from my shows, including the "Blooming Bouquet" and "Farmyard Frolics."

Another Book (Karrell Fox). One of Karrell's Supreme Magic hardbacks filled with simple, yet effective, magic.

Balloonasaurs and Dinobubbles (Stan McGahey). Nice little paperback teaching about a dozen dinosaur balloon sculptures, which children love.

Balloon Sculpturing for Beginners (Dr. Dropo/Bruce Fife). A nice little book to get you started doing balloon animals.

Balloons on the Mailbox (Greg McMahan). Tricks and routines for children's birthday parties (thus the title), gained from practical experience.

The Balloon Video (Brian Flora). Very practical lessons on basic balloon blowing and tying techniques for making one-balloon animals. Brian also teaches one elaborate sculpture, a hot air balloon, to show how far you can go with this kind of fun.

Be a Clown (Mark Stolzenberg). Written by a professional clown for the nonprofessional, this book stresses the art of "acting" the part of a clown, not just dressing like one. Some good skits.

Behind the Scenes (David Ginn). My third video. I recorded it in a studio with my two assistants, Holly and Mary Thomas, who helped me teach 50 tricks and gags in one-hour. Great feedback on this from my clown friends, who found the comedy magic easily adaptable.

Big Laughs for Little People (Samuel Patrick Smith). Sammy Smith's first hardbound textbook on working comedy magic for children. You'll find some particularly good advice, plus 15 complete routines for preschoolers and elementary age children.

Birthday Fun (Greg McMahan). Greg's follow-up to *Balloons on the Mailbox,* teaching several sponge ball routines, a hat juggling act, ways of packing and setting up your show, and lots of fun with Rocky Raccoon.

Birthday Magician's Handbook (Dave Fiscus). The author's complete text on doing birthday parties as a sideline, from booking to performance.

The B. J. Hickman Magic Show (B. J. Hickman). New Hampshire magician B. J. Hickman put scenes from two shows on this 40 minute video, plus has his daughter helping teach a couple of simple tricks. Great to watch a professional work some standard magic for live audiences because you see what reaction a pro can get out of simple props by plugging in personality. Worth watching!

Bobo Magic Show (J. B. Bobo). A lifetime of magic direct from a veteran school show magician of over 50 performing years. Bobo loves children and knows how to entertain them, as you'll see in this big book.

Bonzo's Complete Book of Skits, Volume One (Barry DeChant). This book contains 38 skits for one to twelve clowns, plus a host of solid tips on performing them.

Booked Beyond Belief (Mick Palmer). An interesting audio tape with an emphasis on organization and goal-setting.

Booking Yourself (Samuel Patrick Smith). This is Sammy's first audio cassette tape package of advice on promoting your act or service and lining up engagements. Down-to-earth, practical advice and easy to listen to.

Bringing Home the Laughs (David Ginn). Thirty-five items to get kidshow audiences laughing at your show, my follow-up to *Comedy Warm-Ups.*

Bunny Book for Magicians (Frances Marshall). Dozens of ways to make live and fake rabbits appear and disappear, many of which you can construct in a home workshop, plus lots of advice for performers using rabbits.

Children Laugh Louder (David Ginn). My sequel to *Professional Magic for Children* includes my first "Bongo Hat" routine, plus the very versatile Charlie's "Invisible Message" and dozens of gags and lines for kidshows.

Children's Magic the Herbert Way (Terry Herbert). This video released by Supreme Magic in England features British magician Terry Herbert, who does a super job working with kids. He performs a 25 minute show for a live audience, then explains all, including tricks and philosophy. Excellent!

Clever . . . Like a Fox (Karrell Fox). Karrell's first Supreme book packed with simple, effective tricks for closeup, stage, and trade show work.

Clown Act Omnibus (Wes McVicar). A compilation of 168 clown skits. You're bound to find something of use here.

Clowning for Children (Richard Snowberg). Clown Camp director's first book on working with kids. Some good comedy magic and advice.

Clowning Wherever We Can (Richard Snowberg). In this book the author discusses places and seasons where clowns can get work.

The Clown in You (Richard Snowberg). After teaching clowning for four years at the University of Wisconsin in LaCrosse, Dr. Richard Snowberg put his basic course into print. A good, solid beginner's textbook which explains makeup, costume, shoes, wig, attitude, and more.

Comedy Is No Laughing Matter (Steve Varro). How to mix comedy and magic by a fine Christian entertainer. Some excellent advice.

Comedy Linking Rings (David Ginn). My five to eight minute routine developed over 20 years and used in over 2,000 live shows. Employs two audience helpers and a standard set of eight rings. It still entertains!

Comedy Magic Textbook (David Roper). I consider this book THE definitive textbook on comedy magic, for clowns, magicians, or any family-oriented entertainers. Roper dissects comedy logically and teaches you how to mix it with magic in a dozen ways, always offering solid routines as examples. A book you'll want to read over and over because you'll use it.

Comedy Techniques for Entertainers (Bruce "Charlie" Johnson). The best thing I can say about Charlie's book is that it makes you think, and that's very important. This is the text of a course Bruce has taught in a college in California. Edited and published by Richard Snowberg, the book is filled with good, solid examples.

Comedy Warm-Ups for Children's Shows (David Ginn). This book explains the basic "warm-up technique" taught to me by Harold Taylor 20 years ago, then shares 17 tricks, gags, and bits of business to get your kidshow audiences in the palm of your hand.

Comic Props Made Easy (Daren Dundee). A potpourri of sight gags by a man who dreams them up and makes them.

Contract Book (Jim Kleefeld). Written by the illustrator of this book, Jim's *Contract Book* explains the hows and whys of using contracts for your shows, with practical examples. He also includes blank contracts you can adapt for your own use.

Creative Clowning (Bruce Fife, et al.). A giant textbook by the publisher of this book, featuring experience and advice from eight different authors. The book touches on magic, clowning, juggling, music, balloons, props, mime, character and costume, physical comedy, advertising, and much, much more. A very valuable resource text.

Dewey's Clown Gags and Giggles (Ralph Dewey). Over 250 gags, one liners, skits, and stories for clowns or magicians who are family-oriented. One of them even developed into a skit in this book!

Dewey's Gospel Clown Skits (Ralph Dewey). Good, clean clown fun with a Christian message in each skit.

Dewey's Gospel Paper Tricks (Ralph Dewey). Over a dozen paper mysteries and paper tears which lend themselves to Christian messages.

Dewey's Other Books. Ralph Dewey has written about twenty books on balloon sculpture, gospel balloons, and Christian clowning. I cannot list every one of them, so I simply recommend them all.

Doing Magic for Youngsters (Bert Easley and Eric P. Wilson). When I got started in children's magic as a teenager, this was about the only book around. Some good routines and advice.

Dorny's Comedy Blackouts (Werner C. Dornfield). Dorny compiled this book straight out of vaudeville, but amazingly it has plenty of stuff adaptable to clowning. I even used it to teach a class at Clown Camp one year! Recommended.

Do the Stuff That's You, 2 volumes (Chris Carey). Practical experience and routines from an author who has played tons of schools and created numerous theme park shows over 20 years. Chris emphasizes developing routines that fit your personality and character.

Duane Laflin Gospel Magic Books. Each of Duane's books contains over a dozen routines with gospel messages and references. Some of the titles include *Practical Gospel Magic, Powerful Gospel Magic, Beautiful, Dynamic, Effective,* and so on. Highly recommended for church work as a magician or gospel clown.

Edwin's Magic, Volumes 1 & 2 (Edwin Hooper). The author of these books started Supreme Magic in England in the early 1950s and masterminded the company for 34 years until his retirement in 1988. In these two huge 300-page volumes, Edwin explains virtually all the great magic, much of it especially for children, that he invented and developed for sale. In most cases he offers the patter and presentation, plus the construction of the tricks, allowing you to make them for your own use. I consider these volumes monumental.

Edwin's Magic Finale (Edwin Hooper). The fourth volume of Edwin's retirement books and, in my opinion, the best. Lots of new children's magic here, plus insight into working with kids and creating magic they love.

Encyclopedia of Impromptu Magic (Martin Gardner). There is a school of thought among magicians which says you should always be able to do a trick when requested. This huge book gives you that kind of ammunition, with over a thousand entries.

Feather Flowers from Nowhere (David Ginn). One day I realized that there was no definitive textbook on using feather sleeve bouquets in magic. So I compiled material for five years and wrote it. This book teaches you how to care for, hide, produce, and steal these beautiful feather creations in a magic or clown show.

Find the Stuff That's You (Chris Carey). In this 200-page hardback, Chris Carey shares insights into performing, advertising, and creating your act and onstage character. A book that will cause you to think about who you are and what you wish to be.

For My Next Trick (Karrell Fox). More good, simple magic and comedy.

Gene Gordon's Magical Legacy (Gene Gordon). Some funny magic in this wonderful book by the founding father of the International Brotherhood of Magicians. Out of print at the time of this writing; I hope it will be reprinted in a few years.

Goodies (Karrell Fox). Karrell's 1991 Supreme book, filled with more simple and useful comedy magic than any of his preceeding books. A treasure trove!

Handbook for the Magical Party Clown (Don Sminkey). One of the most valuable books a clown can own, with advice, lists, and sources for everything you'll ever need. This should be in your top ten book list!

Happy Birthday Business (Frances Marshall). A compilation of advice from many performers, clowns, and magicians, on the business side of working birthday parties. Lots of useful information.

A Host of Surprises (Edwin Hooper). Edwin's third book, filled with good magic, much aimed at children's audiences.

How to Be a Goofy Juggler (Bruce Fife). A beginner's juggling book high on comedy and fun, showing easy methods to get started.

How to Be a Magic Clown, 2 volumes (Ernie Kerns). Plenty of good material for clowns in these books.

It's About Time (David Ginn). My second videotape is a complete live school show from start to finish, featuring an educational slant on watches, clocks, and calendars. You'll see 500 kids learn while having fun, and a 52-page book accompanying the video explains how it all works. This is the type of thing I've done over 300 times a year for 21 years, and I love it!

It's Not What You Do, But How You Do It (Don Sminkey). More good comedy material from a troupe of working clowns.

Just for Laughs (Richard Snowberg). Snowberg and friends share ten comedy clown routines for family audiences. The trained dog routine using a rubber pig is my favorite.

Kidbiz (David Ginn). I never realized how popular this book would be among clowns, but now it's in its third printing. In 300 pages hardbound, my friends and I share over 500 gags and comedy lines, plus full routines for children and family situations. Many clowns say this is my best book.

Kiddie Patter and Little Feats (Samuel Patrick Smith). In his second kidshow hardback, published in 1993, Sammy Smith shares many routines for preschool age children. Also, you'll find important information on how to keep the attention of the very young while entertaining them with magic and funny bits of business.

Kid Stuff Series (Frances Marshall). Five paperbacks and one huge hardbound book, compiled by a grand lady of magic, sharing children's magic from many performers—both clowns and magicians. *Kid Stuff Five,* the big hardback, features a school show theme with a ton of adaptable material.

Kornfidentially Yours (Karrell Fox). This little first book by the King of Korn still contains a lot of usable comedy magic material. Check it out.

Live Kidbiz (David Ginn). My first video is a composite of 12 scenes from different shows, featuring musical magic and talking magic, all shot live. A 144-page book explains everything on the tape from behind the scenes—not only the tricks but the philosophy of working with kids. Clowns will enjoy and adapt most of this.

Live Kidbiz II (David Ginn). My fourth video, going back to the format of my first: Various live-show cuts with a book of explanation, featuring my "Snake Basket," "Disbanded," "Instant Puzzle," and much more.

Lost City of Atlantaloon (Stan McGahey). A collection of nine oceanic balloon sculptures including King Neptaloon and his sword.

Magic and Monsters for Kids I Love (David Ginn). My 1984 book of spooky comedy magic with the likes of Dracula, King Kong, snakes, spiders, a guillotine, and some of the corniest monster jokes and riddles (thanks to Bill Rath!) you have ever heard.

Magic Digest (George B. Anderson). A wonderful book written by a magician who worked carnivals and sideshows. Good magic from an experience point of view.

Magic with a Christ-Centered Flair (Steve Varro). No tricks here, just good advice for performers who wish to share the gospel in their shows.

Magic with Everyday Objects (George Schindler). Practical magic with ordinary things found around the house or at the dinner table. Really good!

Make It Happen (Samuel Patrick Smith). Sammy's second set of three audio cassettes teaching booking and promoting techniques. Again, very good and thought provoking. Sammy will motivate you!

My Latest Book (Karrell Fox). Easy comedy magic by the Korniest Magician I know. Besides me.

Nearly Unpublished (David Ginn). My second "unpublished" book, which includes my "Magic Drawing Board" routine, "Which Movie?," some rabbit stuff, more banana magic and much more.

150 Comedy Props (Patrick Page). Some easy to make, some more difficult, but filled with gadgets that will stimulate your creative thinking.

Partly Unpublished (David Ginn). Third in the series, this one houses my "no-mess" cake baking routine and a lot of other surprises.

Party Pieces, More Party Pieces, Further Party Pieces, and *Still Further Party Pieces* (Trevor Lewis). Four books by the Welsh magician who started us on the blooming bouquet, filled with easy magic Trevor has developed working home parties in the United Kingdom.

Practical Magic for Kidshow and School Show Entertainers (Duane Laflin). The title is too long (and Duane knows it!), but this book is filled with good kidshow magic, including a lot of tricks with live rabbits. Much you can build if you have a home workshop.

Professional Magic for Children (David Ginn). It seems like a hundred years ago that I wrote this book, my main text on entertaining children with comedy magic, but it was only 1976! In 16 chapters I share ways of working with children, plus some of my best routines (that I *still* use!) and two complete birthday party shows. My first hardback.

Promoting Me and You II (David Ginn). Contains 500 pages of material from myself and 100 contributors, with their flyers, brochures, photos, news releases, letters, and more actually bound into the book. My wife Lynne and I wrote a commentary on each promotional item, along with comments from the contributors, making this book a very educational experience. Much better than the first PMY book (out of print).

Prop Yourself Up, 2 volumes (Blinky the Clown/Bruce Nelson). A good selection of walk-around props by a clown with over 30 years experience. Some are even designed for kid clowns and lady clowns in mind.

Reflections of a Clown (James "Tiny" Payne). Early in my magic lecturing days I met Tiny out in California, a real nice gentleman. This little book is full of interesting insight into his life and times as a clown.

Rice's Encyclopedia of Silk Magic, 3 volumes (Harold Rice). A must for the reference shelf, over 500 pages per volume, teaching thousands of ways to produce, vanish, color-change, transport, store, and care for silks.

Safety Magic for Children (Karl Wagner). After 10 years crisscrossing the United States doing school shows, Kaptain Karl Wagner finally put it all down on paper, and I edited and published this work of a lifetime. In 320 pages hardbound, with over 200 illustrations, Karl not only shares how to mix magic and messages, but how to work with crowds of children as well. I consider this an *absolute must* for kidshow workers, whether you do safety magic or not. In reality, if you absorb this text, you'll learn how to deliver any kind of message to any children's audience. And that's saying a lot!

School Show Presentation, Volumes 1, 2, and 3 (David Ginn). From 1983 to 1985 I put together this set of two 90-minute audio tapes and 300 pages of text, sharing nearly everything I knew about working in schools, from routines and publicity to logistics and show organization. Believe me, it all still works . . . because I'm still living it!

Sell Your Act with Posters (Samuel Patrick Smith). First in a series, Sammy Smith and friends (including me) share posters/flyers used in promoting and booking school, party, and theatre dates. There's more to it than meets the eye.

Sell Your Act with Letters (Samuel Patrick Smith). Here author Samuel Patrick Smith shares his own thoughts and thoughts of others about writing effective booking letters, with over 50 examples from magicians, clowns, and public speakers who book themselves. You'll learn a whole lot and you'll adapt a lot.

Sell Your Act with Brochures and Flyers (Samuel Patrick Smith). Packed with material from about 50 performers who use these materials to promote themselves. After an introduction on the layout and design of such materials, author Smith comments on each contributor's flyer or brochure (bound into the book) with keen insight. Well worth studying.

Selling with Magic (Michael Jeffreys). Aimed at salesmen, this book teaches easy tricks to break the ice in making sales. You can learn from it.

Speaking with Magic (Michael Jeffreys). Companion book to the one above, this book is aimed at public speakers. Again, lots of easy magic and good presentations.

Stein and Day Handbook of Magic (Marvin Kaye).

Actually, a pretty good text for the beginner in magic.

Straight Talk about Entertaining Children (David Ginn). A 90-minute audio cassette which presents six routines plus a 45-minute interview which discusses things children enjoy and ways to present comedy magic for kids.

Strutter's Complete Guide to Clown Makeup (Jim "Strutter" Roberts). Released in 1991, this is perhaps the best clown makeup book on the market, filled with color photos and step-by-step instructions.

The Success Book, 4 volumes (Jay and Frances Marshall). A ton of promotional ideas and material in four big volumes. Certainly you'll find something of value.

The Table Book, 2 volumes (Frances and Jay Marshall). These two books show a variety of magic tables and carrying cases with details on how to make them in a home workshop. Good ideas.

Tarbell Course in Magic, 7 volumes (Harlan Tarbell). A virtual encyclopedia of magic, both in tricks and performance, presented in seven hardbound volumes by a master teacher. Every serious magician and magical clown should have this on the bookshelf eventually. Read through it once, bit by bit, then keep it for reference throughout your performing life.

Trevor Lewis on Kids (Hank Lee/Magic City). A 60-minute video with this funny Welshman showing some of his best children's magic, explaining how it works and why.

Twelve Gospel Tricks You Can Make (Del Wilson). Twelve gospel tricks with patter. A great resource for church programs.

The Volunteer Book (Jim Kleefeld). My illustrator friend produced this book when I wasn't looking! In it he covers every aspect of using audience helpers on the stage, from courtesy to applause to giveaways. You'll learn lots.

Volunteer from the Audience (Walt Hudson). A nice compilation of material about using audience volunteers, plus some interesting ways of cuing helpers to do funny things.

INDEX